EXTREME LANDSCAPES OF LEISURE

To the newest lady in my life, V.C. Cosmo

Dedicated to the memory of my grandmother:
Lydia Bilodeau Langlois (1917–2009)

Extreme Landscapes of Leisure
Not a Hap-Hazardous Sport

PATRICK LAVIOLETTE
Tallinn University, Estonia

ASHGATE

Published by
Ashgate Publishing Limited
Wey Court East
Union Road
Farnham
Surrey, GU9 7PT
England

Ashgate Publishing Company
Suite 420
101 Cherry Street
Burlington
VT 05401-4405
USA

www.ashgate.com

British Library Cataloguing in Publication Data
Laviolette, Patrick.
   Extreme Landscapes of Leisure: Not a Hap-Hazardous Sport.
   1. Extreme sports--Social aspects. 2. Extreme sports – Environmental aspects.
   3. Adventure travel – Social aspects. 4. Adventure travel – Environmental aspects.
   5. Risk-taking (Psychology) 6. Dangerous Sports Club. I. Title
   306.4'83–dc22

Library of Congress Cataloging-in-Publication Data
Laviolette, Patrick.
   Extreme Landscapes of Leisure: Not a Hap-Hazardous Sport / by Patrick Laviolette.
     p.   cm.
   Includes bibliographical references and index.
   1. Extreme sports. 2. Sports – Anthropological aspects. 3. Sports – Environmental aspects. I. Title.
   GV749.7.L38 2010
   796.04'6–dc22
                                          2010034772

ISBN   9780754679585 (hbk)
ISBN   9780754698982 (ebk)

Printed and bound in Great Britain by the
MPG Books Group, UK

Contents

List of Box Inserts

List of Figures

Preamble

Nearly 25 years ago now, the famous British anthropologist Nigel Barley recounted how, in planning for a forthcoming research trip to Indonesia, an insurance company had classified ethnographic fieldwork into the indemnity category *Not a Hazardous Sport* (1988). He facetiously decided to choose this as the title for the book that he wrote from the data and material he collected from that trip. The insurance policy stipulated that what Barley planned to do as a European visitor would best fit into the category for those non-dangerous activities which are not akin to either business pursuits or sight-seeing tourism. In other words, Barley was to be covered for embarking on some ambiguous form of working holiday – a type of active vacation that was not purely rest and recreation but which clearly did not involve 'risk and recreation' either. Fortunately, as an ethnographer who engages in participant observation, he was not studying risk sports or adventure tourism, otherwise he would never have been able to sufficiently fund the project to insure himself. The present volume provides a somewhat overdue response to this phrase which Barley appropriated from his policy statement.

Anthropology, like many social sciences in recent times, has actively begun to engage with the study of hazardous practices and the places associated with them. Dangerous games and adventure tours have shifted from being marginal, exotic or even just plain crazy to being more than merely acceptable. They are now exemplary, mainstream even. They are being centre staged in a number of ways: there are a variety of new types of them, increasing numbers of people are doing them and they are being appropriated and have infiltrated more and more contexts.

The trope of play used here itself wears both the mask of engaging with activities that are deadly serious as well as creatively performing spontaneously semi-rehearsed actions which have the capacity to alter the physical, political and imaginative body. In this sense, hazardous sports and adventure tourism become rather paradoxical. As a set of activities where players or holidaymakers are closer to danger and death than they would otherwise be, they are the complete opposite of normal games, leisure pursuits or vacations. Until the end of the twentieth century, these were not only thought of but were also defined as escapes from seriousness – refuges from life and death issues, where adults could play to relive their youth and momentarily immortalise themselves whilst they retreated from everyday concerns and stresses.

Yet the truly adventurous event has the potential to reverse this definition so that in most scenarios, the shallow or superficial game is transgressed. As play gains depth, it accrues power. Playing games is therefore only flippant insofar as they are conceptually distanced from the realm of creativity – in this case, the sites of the embodied imagination. Such a serration fabricates situations where leisure and playscapes are not believed to have any significant transformative potential. Some might be more risky than others, but risk in itself is not the feature by which the depth of play can be graded or measured since risk is too general a category, encompassing everything from finances to morality, from the physical to the psychological. So in flattening the trope of play and in perceiving the associated actions as feeble, one disarms Johan Huizinga's (1938) idea of the play instinct. Now there was a time when such theories, when inflated to the point of determinisms, could do with some tempering. But in an era when we are ever more aware of the dangers of determinisms, surely we should be able to formulate new ideas and ways of thinking that can create cultural value for danger itself.

We enter the second decade of a new millennium when people around the world are already taking such principles for granted. The more cynical appreciate that there is mileage in such musings but also warn that perhaps such a thesis is an exaggeration? Surely it is, or can be, to a degree. Nevertheless, once we understand more about the hazards of life – historically, socio-psychologically, geo-politically, ethnographically, and so forth – the more chance we have of sustaining life as a principle and as a real tangible thing. In this sense, the material and the immaterial reflections on minute risks of the everyday as well as the epic legends of lore, when framed through bodyscapes and the embodied imagination respectively, have the potential to reveal back to us a vast amount about the human condition.

In picking up on these themes, my own angle in this volume is also to explore how adventurous practices have become activities which are germane to the dawning of new forms of individual and social imaginations where a different world becomes possible. Hence, this book addresses issues that deal with the intimate connections that exist between adventurous pleasure and certain moral responsibilities towards egalitarian social thought and the environment. Hence it is my contention that dangerous practices, as well as the agency of the places or landscapes in which these activities are performed, are existentially grounded within the socially somatic imagination. The focus of this book, if one single one is possible, is therefore on the embodied imagination.

Acknowledgements

I am eternally grateful to a number of friends, research participants and colleagues for assistance in producing this particular volume, as well as the articles and conference papers upon which it is based. At the risk of forgetting too many, I would nevertheless like to mention a few – by organisational association and/or individually:

First and foremost, Valerie Rose at Ashgate, who initiated the publication of the volume and who could not have provided a smoother pathway for these words to see print. I would also like to thank the rest of the editorial team at Ashgate, especially Carolyn Court, Jude Chillman, Katy Low, Kirsten Weissenberg and Katharine Bartlett. Thanks equally to Surfers Against Sewage UK; Surfbreak Protection Society NZ; TVNZ; and the School of Visual & Material Culture at Massey University, Wellington. SVMC has been particularly generous in providing leave support and conference funding. I also wish to acknowledge the assistance of the Heartlands Regeneration Project in Cornwall UK. Acting as an artist consultant on this project with one of my colleagues at Massey, Kingsley Baird has allowed me to have access to some research funds which have been invaluable in completing the manuscript. In this sense, I am grateful to James Oliver and Rodney Reynolds for their assistance with vetting the entire manuscript. Additionally, in no particular order except alphabetically, my warmest thanks to the following:

Robert Aiken and Jane Barr, Barbara Bender, Henry Broughton, Mark Burgoyne, Hélène Buzelin and Jean Sébastien Marcoux, Carl Cater, Ben Cook, Phil Crang, Michael Gunson, A.J. Hackett, Chris Hines (The Blue Gym), Abi and Dan Harding, Pat Hudson (Eden Project), Andy Hughes, Tim Ingold, Michael D. Jackson, Rohan Jackson, G. David Jones, Kerstin Kary, David and Mercedes Kemp, David Kirke, Phil Matthews, Regina Maria Möller, Nicholas Pavitt, Spencer Pawson, Nigel Rapport, Paul Shanks, Paul Syrett, Chris Tilley, Tom and Alex Wells, Peter Wilkinson.

Allen Abramson in the Anthropology Department at UCL was an intellectual collaborator on more than the joint papers and presentations cited herein. On top of our countless discussions, we bonded during some participatory fieldwork when he introduced me to two of London's climbing walls. I only wish I had brought my camera along at the time but it is my hope that we may collaborate again on this topic in the future.

Doug Munro (Adjunct Professor, VUW) has recently provided me with some valuable material on jumping suicides in New Zealand from 1926–1994. A brief consideration of some of this data, which he has also been collecting for a large 'History of Suicide' project (led by Professor John Weaver at McMaster

University), has found its way into this current volume. It is my intention to use this material more comprehensively in the future.

Thanks are also due to the following for providing images, all of which are reproduced by permission:

Dafydd Jones for the book cover;
Charles Baker and Alex Barrow of *Diplo Magazine* for the frontispiece;
Mark Burgoyne for Fig. 3.1;
Kerstin Kary for Figs 1.2, 3.5, 3.8, 4.5, 5.1;
Spencer Pawson for Fig. 3.6;
Michael Gunson for Fig. 5.2;
NZ Ministry for the Environment for Fig. 7.4

Thanks to the following for granting the right to reproduce the quotations that start off Chapters 3, 4 and 5 as epigraphs: The University of Queensland Press; The Society of Authors as the Literary Representative of the Estate of Virginia Woolf; and Dr Hugh Firth. I am also in recognition of Brill Publishers for allowing me to reproduce here as Chapter 4 a substantially modified version of my 2006 article 'Green and extreme: Free-flowing through seascape and sewer' from *Worldviews*, 10:2, 178–204 (© Koninklijke Brill NV, Leiden, 2006 *Worldviews* Also available online – www.brill.nl).

Various draft versions of the material that make up some of the chapters in the book have been presented at a number of conferences and seminars over the years. So last but far from least, I am grateful to the organisers and participants of the following events for their insightful comments and suggestions:

'Cliff jumping in Cornwall: An ethnographic exploration'. *Anthropological Association of Ireland Symposium: Engaging Imagination*. The Humanities Institute of Ireland, the Dublin Business School & University College Dublin, June 2003.

'A leap of faith into the Devil's Frying Pan'. *Social Anthropology & Material Culture Seminar*. University College London, Dec. 2003.

'Surfers and the materiality of waves'. *ASA Conference: Locating the Field, Metaphors of Space, Place and Context in Anthropology. Durham University*, March 2004.

'Free-flowing through embodied seascapes'. *Anthropology & Sport Seminar.* ICSHC, De Montfort University, Dec. 2004.

'Jumping off cliffs in Cornwall' (with A. Abramson). *Research Seminar*, Hull University, March 2005.

'Deep and dangerous play'. WAC & UNESCO Forum, *Cultural Landscapes in the 21st Century,* Newcastle University, April 2005.

'A hazardous sport: performing adventure tourism'. *CTCC Conference: Tourism and Performance – Scripts, Stages and Stories*. Sheffield Hallam University, July 2005.

'Risk and risqué'. *ASA of Aotearoa/New Zealand: Taboo Conference*, Waikato University, Nov. 2007.

'A design for long-life'. *Society for the History of Design Conference*, Falmouth College of Art, Sept. 2008.

'Board of pollution'. *ASA Conference: Ownership & Appropriation*, Auckland University, Dec. 2008.

'Ritualistic diddle'. *Metamorphoses of Rituals Conference.* Vilnius University Lithuania, April 2009.

'Redefining risk'. *12th International Cultural Studies Symposium,* Ege University, Izmir Turkey, May 2009.

'The ledge over the edge', *School of Social & Cultural Studies Seminar Series,* Victoria University of Wellington, Aug. 2009.

'Playing in the danger-zones'. *Contemporary Culture & Society Seminar Series,* Melbourne University, Aug. 2009.

'The accelerated flâneur'. *EASA Conference: The Crisis of the Imagination,* National University of Ireland, Maynooth, Aug. 2010.

PATRICK LAVIOLETTE
Wellington, 30 June 2010

Foreword
Déranger Les Sens

By David Kirke
Co-founder, Dangerous Sports Club, Oxford

The games invented by the Victorians and those who came before them have become distorted. Tennis courts were not measured out for people who could serve at 140 mph and inflict the grunts of a Roman amphitheatre on an overweight audience. Cricket gave up many claims to sportsmanship when fast bowlers began to be used against tail-end batsmen: at least spin bowlers against slow batsmen had a measure of elegance.

It was such considerations that made us think it was time to invent new sports. Sportsmanlike behaviour, with its trusty companion random craftiness, went out of the window when the money men turned sport into an industry. Not many people have read Maurice Kean's book on chivalry and understood the chivalrous aspect of sports, which was embodied in the original Olympic Games. Football now amounts to the unspeakable applauding the unthinkable. Wimbledon is a sweaty traffic jam served up as a trinket for rich sponsors.

I do not mean to be facile in making these points when so many people enjoy our sports as they are. One of the standard brakes on progress in under-educated middle England is sneering at innovators for being elitist. Of course, there is a certain melancholy and a need for self-deprecation in the English, the reverse side of which is a need to pick oneself up by putting other people down. So of course there are people who will put you down as a sociopathic risk-taker who is probably a threat to law and order. Innovation inevitably brings criticism. We had a Nobel Prize nominee working on the mathematics of bungy jumping, and part of the real pleasure of this game is working out everything that could go wrong beforehand. It's an intellectual challenge loaded with laughs in which there is always something you haven't thought of. On the first jump we had to get round the bureaucracy surrounding the Clifton Suspension Bridge which wouldn't even allow the BBC to film costume drama on it. Our penalty was a night in jail for breach of the peace and a small fine.

But we started something that spread around the world. We're considered the founders of extreme sports, particularly in Britain, but very few people know the history of these things. Since those days 80-year-olds have been bungy jumping. The DSC tie is black with a silver wheelchair and a blood-red seat. People in wheelchairs get the point. They love and encourage it – a suitable counterweight to all those who are crippled by caution. Blind people also really love bungy jumping because their senses are so finely tuned. But I had a vision, which no-one else in the Club had at the beginning, that what the DSC stood for could spread. In the early morning of the first jump, I literally had to bang two heads together to make it happen.

One of them is now running an investment company which puts tons of money into new ideas and the other is one of the world's best rocket scientists. In the same way, we helped pioneer hang-gliding and microlighting, and new forms of skiing and ballooning. So many advertising companies have copied our ideas, and as founder of an amateur club, I was proud of being the eternal student who never made any money out of it. We let others capitalise on the ideas because we were always interested in the next idea. Anything that came in we tended to spend, and we weren't very good at tidying up afterwards.

People have a love-hate relationship with fear, and applaud a degree of recklessness. The DSC was based on a recklessness of innocence nourished by a recklessness of contempt. There was an element of rebellion in risk taking. It was a time of innovation and excitement, when new equipment was coming in such as hang-gliders with stall-resistant Rogallo wings. Certain manufacturers even loaned us machines to fly off Mount Olympus and Kilimanjaro because they wanted to say their machines were the first.

Much of what happened at the DSC was based on improvisation and accident. Surrealism, which caught the imagination of the fast-changing and chaotic twentieth century, was also an influence. Putting bathtubs and grand pianos down a mountain on skis is part of a long tradition stretching back to the master Buster Keaton, who found extraordinary ways of moving himself through the air. And for him, as for many people who have been to the extremes of sensation, the withdrawal process is not easy. Some use intoxicants such as alcohol to try and keep up with the high – or at least to avoid descent into the low – whereas others find highs in poetry, writing beautifully, or just in pure risk-taking.

Producing a beautiful flight is the key for me – any beautiful movement, whether it is colour, or curve, or water, or air, or machine, or music, or religious vision. It's a heightening of the senses that makes you feel special rather than ordinary; there's a surplus of the ordinary well beyond its sell-by date in our mass culture.

So the intention behind the DSC has always been to dance a sideways shuffle with the French concept of *déranger les sens*, which has produced some of the best French poetry and a thousand deaths in the gutter. Looking back, it's curious how every member of the Club sees it differently. Everyone had their own impact and they all feel they were a big influence. Yet over the years it has been an entirely voluntary association, a network of friends, and that has really been the only way to run it.

Organising civilians to take quasi-military risks at some expense is not the easiest of jobs. You cannot play it by golf club rules. Like many artistic or surrealist activities it was a reversal of normal practices and expectations, wrong-footing people – exploiting the gap between expectation and reality – and we had a lot of laughs wrong-footing officious bureaucrats.

Charlie Chaplin said that comedy is not a man slipping on a banana skin: comedy is a man stepping absent-mindedly over a banana skin and then falling down a manhole. Having been down a few holes, I had more belief in the DSC concept than anyone else, and it slowly picked up. I always said it would take 15 years to get across and now I look at the whole phenomenon of extreme sports across the world. Many of our ideas have been copied, and that's a laugh because we started a lot of that by getting it on TV.

In the early days of microlighting in America they used to say the most dangerous thing was your local TV station and the manufacturer of our machines went out of business when a new extension to his flying machines resulted in the death of a reporter demonstrating it on ABC television. I pioneered BASE jumping with a military target drone catapult designed to shoot me against the wind over the steep cliffs of Moher in County Clare, Ireland and into the sea – a tricky job that no-one has repeated. Vital chemicals for solidifying foam to spread the pressure on my back were late in the post and there was only one day left. The job came off but the result was what a world-leading spinal surgeon has called one of his most difficult operations. I can still walk but the pain comes and goes. I would still do it again with the same consequences because it was a unique moment of some beauty but I remember a sense of foreboding. That decision came up time and again in those early days and I remember those who are no longer with us.

We used the fields of sport and aviation because most people can relate to those. Take the St Moritz ski race for instance. Someone once told me they had been in a little African village which had one television run off a generator. The villagers saw snow and a piano for the first time in their lives and they instinctively burst into laughter. I thought, 'that's not bad, we've got across'. The authorities of my old Oxford College regard me with caution. But the thing is, they might not realise or care that I've got across to more people in the world than most of them or their pupils. The ski races alone were seen by more than a billion people. I stand by my belief that they were works of art.

Yet in practice I have only done a small part of what I feel I should have done, which is to try to introduce new ideas. Nowadays there are combinations of books and film on CD which open up new possibilities. At the end of the day, though, it's the book that counts. There aren't many computers for people in most countries in the world. The DSC was trying to make art out of sport, and making literature out of those two is not easy. Very few books have ever been written with lasting humour about sport. There is Surtees on hunting, Jerome's *Three Men in a Boat* and, in the best sense of the word, *Don Quixote*.

It is a little disconcerting that at my age, having been flung into jail many times and having picked up a few wounds on the way, the great Miguel de Cervantes had already recounted a tale of adventure which many writers say is the greatest novel ever written. Time perhaps to put my finger in the air and write my own book.

The Dangerous Sports Club (DSC), co-founded in Oxford in the late 1970s by Chris Baker, Ed Hulton and David Kirke, is still a vibrant and active organisation dedicated to inventing challenging sports and performing spectacular events. It is perhaps best known for 'inventing' bungy jumping but amongst other activities, members have also performed feats such as hang-gliding from active volcanoes, zorbing, microlight flying, BASE jumping and human catapulting. For more info or to contact David Kirke, see: http://www.btinternet.com/~dafyddk/dsc.htm

Frontispiece, the participant observer, by Alex Barrow.

Introduction – Fearless Theorising

But to be able to fall down in such a way
As to appear in the same second as if one stood and walked,
To turn the leap of life into a walk,
Absolutely to express the sublime in the pedestrian –
This only a knight of faith can do – and this is the only miracle.

        (Kierkegaard [1843] 45–46, trans. I. Veloso).

Aptly enough, this passage by Søren Kierkegaard is from his book *Fear and Trembling*. It provides a rather fitting introduction to a volume on the myriad relationships between the body and the mind, between the social imagination, the environment and the adventurous spirit. It is especially riveting since such a poetic evocation is crucial in trying to capture in language the full force of meaning intrinsic to those types of substantial experiential sensations which largely exist outside the linguistic realm – out of descriptive reach, just beyond the logical progression of words.

Indeed for Kierkegaard, this is exactly what fear and trembling amounts to, that moment of being dumbfounded when one faces his or her own God, an all encompassing understanding from the body that exists outwith rhyme or reason. Pure viscerality, as it were. So when we are confronted with an intellectual impasse or a thwart of the imagination, when reason or poetics reach their logical extreme or creative end – a complete and all encompassing existential insecurity – we are forced into devising some form of ontological means of continuing. Or in Kierkegaardian terms, of making some type of 'leap of faith'.

Bodily understanding and the knowledge that it produces through action are therefore essential elements when studying those types of adventures where fear and danger are prominent. The phenomenological perspective is one of the best-suited for studying bodily sensations and throughout its history it has been linked with existential philosophy. Phenomenology was founded at the beginning of the twentieth century by the German philosopher Edmund Husserl. Its goal as far as he outlined it was to suspend, as far as possible, the presuppositions and method of traditional science so as to describe the world as an arena of intentionality and meaning. At its heart it is concerned with essences, to return to things themselves as the object of human experience. The phenomenological method generally consists of four stages. These are: the careful description of the observed phenomena's essences; the identification and examination of the relationships between these essences; the examination of the ways in which these phenomena, within their fields of meanings and relationships, can manifest themselves; and the exploration of our consciousness' constitution of the phenomena.

There are many justifications as to why an existentially informed phenomenological position is central to overcoming the language impasse when it comes to the description of all sensations, thrilling sensations included. To find one of them we must return to the Hegelian observations on the nature of truth and reality. Comprehending the mind phenomenologically had been the objective of most of Hegel's oeuvre. For him, phenomenology was simply the science of the experience of consciousness. Understanding consciousness occurs in the experience itself, where consciousness undergoes its experiences in and with itself. This means that experiences are experiences of consciousness, so the mind is the object of this experiencing.

An experience in this sense requires us to seek recourse to the intuition as the means of observational confirmation (Heidegger 1988). If we conceive of intuition as the manner of confirming an opinion on an immediate matter, then the notion of an 'intuition of essences' emerges. The intuition that delivers such essences is the phenomenological intuition which is confirmed in terms of the things as observed, in and of themselves. We can refer to this then as intuitive observation. One of the main intuitive observational distinctions that we make is between the human mind, the body and our surroundings. The interchangeable landscape–body–mind metaphor is important in representing an actual form of symbiosis between what we think, what we feel and the world we inhabit. In many regards this metaphor approaches Pierre Teilhard de Chardin's (1955) phenomenological concept of the noosphere or even James Lovelock's (1979) Gaia hypothesis, both of which also include consciousness into a synergistic symbiosis of the earth's eco-systemic functioning. Hence, the relationship of mind–body–landscape becomes analogous to a global system of innercosm–microcosm–macrocosm. Essentially, this is an extension of the existential phenomenology proposed by Porteous (1990), who placed home–away and insider–outsider as other important antinomies.

One of the critiques frequently targeted against phenomenology is the difficulty in verifying the metaphysical truth claims devised by applying the tenets of this mode of investigation to the letter. In an oft quoted passage, Hegel exclaimed that the true is the 'Bacchic delirium, in which there is not one of its components which is not drunk' (in Husserl [1913] 1973, 59). Put differently, the true relishes in the spirit of excessiveness. This resonates with de Sade's perspective where we find humans trying to existentially free themselves, not via remorse but via the complete indulgence in the sensual pleasures of the world, especially those that conventional society attempts to restrict or inhibit.

This view that existentialism is a philosophy that is dangerous, excessive and practised in the style of the thriller has persisted for a number of reasons. Initially it was because existentialism was a direct challenge, sometimes a relentless attack, on theology, the Church and most western forms of organised religion. Also, it has maintained a strong rapport with the literary medium that it grew up alongside (Karl and Hamalian 1973). Foremost though, it had been created and recreated in those fearful times of violent unrest and global warfare. More cynically, but appropriately reflexive for a philosophical form of iconoclasm based on irony, this sense of danger has equally resulted from the personal profiles of some of its main proponents, many of whom explicitly encouraged the public mythologising of their wild, flamboyant and radical airs. Always pushing the limits of conventional thinking, power structures and decadent behaviour, the art of ambiguity has been a favourite tactic of the surrealist and existentialist alike.

This is an interesting development since a level of anti-heroism has always been part of existential thought. In initially being concerned with individual action above all else, early existentialists provided a philosophy of ethics, not a code of social morals. On the whole, existentialism isn't a direct call to social action or revolution; instead of offering the rules, it outlines the ontological framework within which people can search for meaningful experience. This is not to say that existential thinking only applies to analyses of individual being, however. Far from it. Ethnographers and other writers have embraced its premises in order to better understand inter-subjectivity, social structures and coexistence. With his emphasis on the phenomenological approaches to social relations, Alfred Schutz refers to this empathic and mimetic inversion of experience as the 'reciprocity of perspectives' (1970, 183). For his part, the anthropologist Michael Jackson (2005) reminds us that an existentially grounded approach to anthropology is both humanistically motivated by empathetic sensitivity and politically charged with the vision and intent of overcoming complacency in the face of social contingency.

In this sense, Jackson could be said to have taken up Jean-Paul Sartre's challenge for making phenomenological existentialism compatible with Marxist imperatives to strive for change – of making better places, if not of making the world a better place. Hence with regard to the latter ambition, the scale is different, it is more micro-political:

> Yet hardly a day passes that one is not overwhelmed by the human capacity for love and joy, by what some people accomplish with limited means in a world of scarcity and inequality, and by the ingenuity with which people reimagine and surpass the situation in which they find themselves (2005, xv).

The existential imagination is therefore not grandiosely heroic. Instead it is about every person's ability to heroically overcome banality, hardship and loss. In appealing for the democratisation of experience, it fits the punk slogan of the 1970s 'no more heroes' – at least in the sense that everyone has the ability to have epic experience and to become heroic.

Another characteristic feature of existentialism which is pertinent for us here is that it is largely a philosophy of disorientation. This makes it applicable to Roger Caillois' (1958; 1963) concerns for both the vertigo and the surreal elements of thrill-seeking activities. These descriptions of physical movement and distortion equally correspond with what Mihaly Csikszentmihalyi (1975) has called 'flow experiences'. A person is in a state of flow when fully absorbed in an activity to the point where s/he loses their sense of time and everyday bearings. As Arland Ussher remarked at the height of the existential turn:

> Existentialism sees life as an adventure rather than a scheme – a play in which
> we pick up our parts as we go along; and it is therefore appropriate to an age in
> which the moulds of life and thought are broken. Or as we may put it in the more
> romantic terms of Jaspers, it is a 'philosophy of night' – a way of thought for a
> time in which men must walk alone, groping their way, and when all distances
> and proportions dissolve in relativity (1955, 10).

The effects of walking alone through what Camus thought of as the unreasonable silence of the world was unbearable. Absurdly unequivocal. Beyond what reason could expect a social being to be able to tolerate. When French existentialists such as Sartre, de Sade or even to an extent Merleau-Ponty speak of absurdity they are referring to the inadequacy of logical explanation. This runs somewhat against Kierkegaard for whom anguish, despair and dread were equated with the sheer impossibility of rationality. Drawing from the significant repercussion of utilitarianism at the end of the nineteenth century, and the view of not only acknowledging but also trying to regulate irrational behaviour, Merleau-Ponty was prompted to exclaim that it was the special task of the twentieth century to devise a comprehensive way of explaining the irrational (Ussher 1955).

This immediately begs the question as to what the special task of the twenty-first century might be. One possible answer lies with what the cultural historian Henning Eichberg (2001) calls a system of thinking contradictions. Not in the sense of oppositions, of course, since this was one of the methodological results of the structuralist project. Nor with the realisation that arguments harbour many contradictions which from being exposed can be smoothed over. This is the rationale behind dialectical reasoning. Rather, the framework for thinking in contradiction verges on what Edward Soja (1996) has referred to as trialectics. In short, this is a process of thought development which takes place in directions that sometimes converge, sometimes diverge and occasionally emerge but which are always open to radical otherness, to extreme alterity. This takes us beyond the conventional formulation of thesis, antithesis and synthesis to a perspective immediately concerned with a way of imagining 'other-than' alternatives. Similar, perhaps, to the popular adage 'thinking outside the box'.

With an Active Imagination

In his own active imagination Kierkegaard was compelled, in dualistic terms, to oppose faith and reason in a similar way to how William Blake had opposed imagination and reason. With their fascination with narrative and literature, the existentialists foregrounded the significance of the metaphorical imagination in human reason, Sartre (1940) in particular. The absurdist and ironic imaginations were thus described in terms of being 'as if' imaginations. By the turn of the twentieth century, a more widespread recognition that the way we perceive reality was to some extent an imaginative construct and that even rationality itself was beholden to imaginative insights or desires, made the indulgence into imaginative worlds more permissible, not only for children and the young but for adults as well. One could actively believe, albeit ironically, in marvels and wonders, without compromising one's standing as a rational or responsible citizen. It was during this *fin de siècle* that the productive realm of the imagination, designed for the habitation of adults and directly addressing the disenchanting facets of modern realism, appeared in full swing on the stages of literature, the arts, worldly travel and philosophy (Lengkeek 2001; Saler 2004).

This volume explores the conceptual links between a prospective anthropology of the imagination and a reflexively based existential phenomenology of our bodily senses, movements and emotions, as they experience danger, fear and euphoria in adventurous places. The imagination is a crucial factor for exploring and bridging these conceptual areas. Yet it is still usually understood as images and dreams engendered in the mind through cognitive and cerebral processes. The idea here is therefore to challenge such a conception, perhaps even turn it on its head in a way reminiscent of a growing body of anthropological work on experience and events (Turner and Bruner 1986; Jackson 2005).

My use of the imagination is different from that found in the anthropological studies which focus on the cultural construction of dreaming (Tedlock 1987; Stewart 2003). For the French sociologist Gilbert Durand (1960), the imagination was the source of symbolic mediations that are both therapeutic and transcendental. His theory is grounded in an esoteric Platonism supported largely by a philosophy of the rational imaginal. Indeed the first wave of the anthropology of the imagination culminated with Durand's lines of imaginative regimes whereby he had devised a tripartite symbolic classification consisting of myths and symbols of the diurnal realm, myths of nocturnal exploration, and lastly, mediational activity of the Freudian life-affirming Eros instinct.

One would fit the desire for adventure into this last category of the imagination. In seeing Eros as the instinct for life, creativity and procreativity, we could easily see another relevant connection to the deliberate performance of hazardous pursuits – the death drive, or Eros' counterpart in Greek mythology, Thanatos. According to Freud (1919), when daredevils are compelled to excessively pursue self-destructive behaviour, they are acting under the Thanatos impulse (although this terminology was not his). But sensation seekers who search for thrills through dangerous activities which marginally put their lives at risk were harder to classify in Freud's schema so he lumped them into the category of sublimation activity since such participants might be taking these risks to substitute for either of the two other opposing instincts.

In a second wave of theorising, George Rousseau's (1991) take on the anthropology of the imagination was essentially an attempt to demonstrate the ways in which this modality had been excessively medicalised during the early Enlightenment. The emerging anthropology of the imagination generally offers an alternative to psychological interpretations which tend to reduce the imaginative to cognitive and cerebro-physiological processes. Less overtly but increasingly so, it also strives to achieve a different outlook from those literary and artistic perspectives that essentially see imagination as a creative faculty, allocated to people in different doses, endowing some whilst depriving others.

Seeing the imagination in a dialectic model of metaphorical knowledge, Paul Ricoeur (1991; 1994) has argued that it is a creative mediator between cognition and language. Within his hermeneutic framework, the imagination functions at the limits of thought and expression, as a catalyst that can provoke new insights and ways of seeing/being. It is a theory that supports the rehabilitation of the imagination from formerly denigrated or suspect categorisations. It also offers a unifying, although non-empirical, perspective on the anthropology of the imagination which would permit a better understanding of specific local character and configurations of cultural identity. Here Ricoeur uncovers the basic social practices not in the entirely 'raw form' which thinkers such as Foucault (1977) saw as the only kinds of experiences and reality to exist outside power-imbued classifications. Rather he places such practices which include the imaginary into a certain class of immediate 'visionary' activities and observations. The imagination here is a socio-cultural tool. It provides markers and pathways in the political landscape of local groups who move through those historical thresholds of hegemonic crisis, permitting the collapse of old regimes and the reinstallation of a new social order. These are new spaces and moments of identity creation which anthropology is well suited to open up through imaginative ethnographic investigation (Fernandez and Huber 2001).

This connection to identity resonates with the ideas of Benedict Anderson, who was pivotal in the transformation of the way in which the imagined could be understood. Anderson argued that imagination/imagining was not fantasy or fantastic, nor was it something negative. Rather, it was a positive form of social identification that formulated the possibility for group self-creation. It doesn't really matter that Anderson could not prove his insight; many have jumped on the bandwagon and so he has shifted the academic momentum in a particular direction of the conception of what it might mean to imagine. Charles Taylor's (2002) work on social imaginaries has built on the argument about empty time present in Anderson's musing on imagined communities. Only the former has linked them to action and contextualises social imaginaries in terms of modernity and its demands. Taylor makes the point that secularity and modernity should be understood as articulating a place for religion in daily life. This has allowed a certain temporal transformation to occur thus permitting people to fill their time with meaning-seeking activities such as political activity and revolution.

Similarly, instead of equating the imagined with a realm that is concerned only with fantasy and the fictitious or the dreamscapes of the mind, I shall locate part of the imaginary occurrence in the body, in somatic experience. This I feel is one of the 'limits of expression' that Ricoeur speaks of, if we interpret this term as widely as possible. Such an approach provides a critique to both western psychoanalytic theory and the ocular-centric insistence on those definitions which purely equate imagination with visible mental images. In short, the intention is to breathe new life into the cliché 'an active imagination', hence intertwining activity and imaginary into an amorphous, ubiquitous amalgamation that involves the body's interaction with the landscape it moves through and its adaptations to contingencies.

For the cognitive linguist Mark Johnson (1987), the imagination does not just play a role in such things as creativity, innovation and discovery. Instead it is an essential ingredient in rational thinking. I have no problem with this opening up but perhaps it doesn't go far enough because it is still not focused on experiential being, only on how thinking and language relate to some static hypothetical form of the body. Yet Johnson's project is undoubtedly to suggest that there is a bodily basis for imagination. And it is there as well as in one of his later texts written with George Lakoff, *Philosophy in the Flesh* (1999), that I find considerable conceptual parallels. They undoubtedly make an important contribution to the ongoing debates about the roles of syntax, semantics and knowledge in linguistic understanding, as founded in human perception, interpretation and the mechanisms for interacting with the world. The problem still remains, however, that their approach over-emphasises the unconscious and excludes other non-cognitive or philosophical approaches such as Aristotle's view of the psyche, Bachelard's take on symbolism or Jung's idea of archetypes, for instance.

In Johnson's (1987) earlier work he ultimately sides with Kant on the general premise that the imaginary is there to mediate between the contents of our sensations and abstract conceptualisations, thus making it possible for us to organise and understand what we receive through the perception of the senses. Where he critiques Kant, however, is the limitation of not providing a coherent theory because of having established a first principle that dichotomises rationality and the body, conceiving of them via an unbridgeable division. Johnson's aim is to challenge that dichotomy and he goes on to provide the five minimum requirements necessary for building a comprehensive theory of the imagination. These are: categorisation; schemata; metaphorical projections; metonymy; and narrative structure. What is unclear from this is how his perspective ultimately differs from Sartre's phenomenological position, except for the fact that he has clearly bypassed the corpus of research on the imagination which does not fit into his cognitive paradigm:

> Without imagination, nothing in the world could be meaningful. Without imagination, we could never make sense of our experience. Without imagination, we could never reason toward knowledge of reality … It is a shocking fact that none of the theories of meaning and rationality dominant today offer any serious treatment of imagination (Johnson 1987, ix).

What's shocking is that he has failed to notice or cite at least a dozen prominent scholars working in this area. Indeed, except for Gadamer, Hobbes, Kant and beginning as far back as Plato, Johnson hardly pays any attention to the vast literature on the topic that has developed over the past 150 years. In terms of one who he has conveniently left out, the rationale could hardly be more similar to his own, if for the French philosopher Jean-Paul Sartre: 'There could be no developing consciousness without imagination and vice versa. So imagination, far from appearing as an actual characteristic of consciousness turns out to be an essential and transcendental condition of consciousness' (1940, 273). The imaginary for Sartre is a structurally unique phenomenon distinct from both the structures of perception and conceptual thought. It is based largely on a Husserlian distinction between the matter of an experience and its form.

Crucial for establishing my own position, this perspective of bringing matter into the equation is critical and it complements the position put forward by Gaston Bachelard. An obvious point of reference for any concern with the anthropology of the imagination is the large corpus of writings penned by Bachelard. Given the basis of the present research, as well as the phenomenological caveat that I have just outlined, we particularly need to consider his groundbreaking exploration of the material imagination through his reflections on the elemental substances of fire, water, air, and earth ([1938] 1987; [1942] 1983; [1943] 1988; [1947] 1988). Indeed, Bachelard bears witness to the imaginative human freedom whereby we are asked to lay aside or suspend preconceptions. Instead we are encouraged to cultivate a capacity for awe and wonder. But he nonetheless falls into a Husserlian phenomenological perspective which prefaces the transcendence of our cognitive faculties (Husserl 1931). That is, Bachelard still views the originality of the poetic imagination as an opening up of ourselves to the revelations of the image, as opposed to an opening up to experience. Or even more radically, where the image or experience would open up the potential for the imagination itself to be possible.

To an extent then, Bachelard's phenomenologically informed approach to psychoanalysing dreams undermines lived experience. It suggests that our encounters with the world do not guide our imagination but rather are guided by it. In existential terms this is tantamount to reversing the very maxim of that perspective. In other words, if we distil this idea down to the bare elements, push it to its logical end, it is pretty much equivalent to saying that essence precedes existence. Significant though his contributions are, and indeed heavily relied upon in this volume, I nevertheless want to open up some of these normative perspectives concerning the cognitive imagination.

Conversely, I propose that the interaction of body, landscape and danger is an experiential and existential arena from which the imagination can both arise and derive. The practice of stretching the mind and body to the limits – of playing with danger and death – establishes an ontological basis for an embodied creativity, for a creativity of the body. So the basis for my arguments in what follows is that the imagination exists in the ways in which the body encounters the physical world. Now here imagination is a central theme for the study of adventure since both are inherently bound with existential concerns as well as with the notion of discovery. From an existentially informed phenomenological position, this book considers the inter-relationship between the embodied imagination and the euphoric adventure that occur in a diversity of thrillscapes.

Bodyscapes and Bodyscrapes

As an anthropologist who, amongst other things, studies epic places and extreme practices, I too have had my fair share of tumbles and near misses. Indeed, on occasion I have one of those haunting visions of someone having to scrape up my tangled water-swollen body from some pool at the bottom of a cliff, sea cave or craggy hill face which I'd been exploring alone. Stupid – the act, yes, but maybe not the vision.

Yet I am not the only one who equally admits to enjoying precarious moments of solitude along the shore and in wild landscapes. We are a specific creature. Not with a death wish as some would have it. Not particularly brave either, it must be said. Interestingly, my own research isn't really concerned with asking why people do these things, at least not at an individual level. This is largely the terrain of the psychologist. No, I'm interested in certain social whys; the contexts and networks of relations that are created as well as the issues to do with how, when and where such activities take place. So in providing a precursory anecdote about myself, the idea in this section is to use it as a prism for reflecting the larger issues of how certain people explore some of the risks, thrills and leisure opportunities that adventurous landscapes have to offer.

This particular story starts on a visit to Cornwall, UK, in 2006. I had returned to my place of original ethnographic fieldwork, having spent several interrupted years doing multi-sited research there since 1998, to give a paper in Penryn at the new Tremough campus of the Combined Universities in Cornwall. It was the last weekend of the summer, so the hour was about to go back on Sunday morning. To mark the occasion I decided to undertake a night-time trek over the six miles between my B&B in Penzance and Lamorna Cove. I left at midnight sharp on Saturday 29 October. But it was of course still 11 pm. I was walking back in time. Cornwall has often felt to me as much a time apart as a land apart. Perhaps the two are indistinguishable.

I was wearing my wetsuit and was resolved to go swimming in the sea during this limbo period when time repeats itself. The obscurity and incessant rain made my voyage – nay, pilgrimage – all the more significant, if rather miserable. I nearly turned back after reaching the outskirts of Mousehole, the halfway point, discouraged by the remaining distance. Somehow I persevered and began jogging. I finally reached Lamorna which I had chosen as a destination from the shame of never having been there before. Setting the timer on my camera I took a couple of photos of myself to testify to this bizarre experience. I then proceeded to take off the drenched clothes over my wetsuit and went swimming in the cove.

At first I thought of staying out for half an hour or so, to make the long trek worthwhile. But after a few minutes a thought entered my head. It had been planted there sometime before by a friend who once pointed out, after I had told him about going swimming alone off some steep cliffs near St Agnes, that this solo wanderlust of mine was rather selfish. Even though he was confident that I was prepared to deal with the consequences of something going wrong, an onlooker might take it upon themselves to call the coastguard even if I was not in distress. This, he added, would not only cause embarrassment to me but also all sorts of inconvenience to others, perhaps at the expense of someone else's safety. The argument was persuasive. Hearing it increased my awareness for how certain personal quests might implicate others negatively.

So as I swam alone at midnight in Lamorna Cove, I gave some thought to what might occur if someone nearby happened across the sounds of some splashing around in the harbour. The surroundings were deserted so this seemed unlikely. But of course the night of my chosen adventure meant that there would be an extra hour of drinking time. And even though it had now officially well gone midnight, it was obvious from experience that the bonus drinking hour would increase the likelihood of pub lock-ins, meaning that people could be returning home at all sorts of hours. I therefore decided to spend only a few more moments in the water.

Recounting this story is not the most archetypal way of saying something about the culture of adventurous practices. After all, it was a personal event not a social activity as such. Yet this night swimming was enmeshed in a series of relations in which I am implicated. And as an individualist expression, existentially grounded, it does open up a few questions about the body, the senses and the social influences upon these. Indeed, my rationale for this escapade was inspired by the social significance of time, place, leisure and how these relate to the search for some meaning of freedom in a world that seems to be increasing its distance from nature and the specificities of culture.

Furthermore, one hopefully understands from this story and as the remainder of this volume unravels that I was not alone. Memory, friendship networks and social responsibilities meant that I was very much tangled up in a cultural narrative informed by being a researcher in this region with a particular professional position which allows for, as well as restricts, certain sets of experiences and relationships. Let us therefore examine some of these in more detail to see what emerges regarding the social construction of epic landscapes and adventurous practices.

The advent of extreme activities and adventurous leisure exists at the edge of modernity. As Norbert Elias (1982) and Richard Sennett (1994) point out, the civilised body, with its repugnance for violence, emotionality and cruelty, underpins important shifts both in social practice and people's experience of their corporeal self. Adventurous practices within the space of leisure and protest offer participants the chance to cast off the normative body by pushing that body beyond its everyday social, emotional and sensual parameters. They are part of the civilising process that articulate a particularly sensual dialectic (Macnaghten and Urry 2001). Simultaneously, they allow for the development of consensual social frameworks that support the existence of such sensually creative practices, without challenging the overall incarnated dynamic of bodily control upon which the civilising process is built. The words of the Turkish scholar Nilüfer Göle remind of this normativisation:

For the modern individual the body liberates itself progressively from the hold of natural and transcendental definitions and enters into the spiral of secularisation; it penetrates that realm in which human rationality exercises its will to tame and master the human body through science and knowledge (Göle 1996, 18).

So in terms of adventurous practices, applying such a sensual dialectic illustrates more than people simply letting off steam in order to escape the confines of the sedentary, controlled body that structures western experience. Instead, it offers access to an alternate socio-sensual perspective upon the everyday world, as well as the symbolic and ideological frameworks that reside within. This sensual edge of extreme activities can exist as an embodied critique of contemporary experience that is played out in the realm of feeling rather than via language, symbol or ideology. Yet these socio-sensual states also generate altered emotional, physical and social frameworks. As Derek Gregory notes: '"adventure" surely requires the emotional investment and the affective response' (1994, 20).

Such a position challenges the embodied relationship between culture and the body, as articulated in Pierre Bourdieu's notion of *habitus* for instance, where *habitus* is akin to routine (1977). Instead they generate novel 'embodied metaphors' (Lakoff and Johnson 1980) that precipitate fresh articulations of self and other, new perspectives upon modernity and networks of social relations. Hence, whilst most writing on phenomenology or praxis treats the pre-eminence of the corporeal as equally a pre-eminence of the routine of everyday life, the pre-existent physicality of sociality in the domain of the extreme potentially subverts the praxis of routine. Such haptic metaphors are in keeping with Leonard Cohen's definition of a marked body in his classic *The Favourite Game*: 'a scar is what happens when the word is made flesh' (1963, 7).

These sensual shifts have often been overlooked by social scientists because they are not grounded in language, nor do they create obvious ideologies or symbols. Rather, they operate at the level of the flesh, the importance of which is only recently coming to the fore. Numerous scholars are now suggesting that social and cultural worlds are intimately related to the bodies which inhabit them. From this perspective, human consciousness is grounded within the body rather than being a specifically mental phenomenon. For instance, Lakoff and Johnson (1999) have concluded that language is built upon embodied frameworks of feeling. We can elaborate on these assertions, taken from a wide range of disciplines, to explore how non-linguistic and other material cultural practices are equally built upon experience.

Like Husserl, Maurice Merleau-Ponty (1962) disregarded the notion that the phenomena of consciousness and behaviour were identical to the universals upon which mathematics or physics were based. For him, the Cartesian division between subject and object evoked the epistemological perspective that the mind is the only forum for subjectivity; where the body and its experiential potential is an object that the mind moves, manipulates and bestows meaning upon. For Merleau-Ponty then, the world and our bodies as perceived through the senses are both creative shape-shifting entities. We can thus perceive water, rock and air through their metaphorical potential. Consequently, in the context of much of the research that I shall describe, it might be relevant to add a couple of layers to Merleau-Ponty's analogous connection that links the flesh of the body with the 'flesh' of the world. Analogies where our body as fluids connects with the fluids and the fluidity of the world are also apt, as are those that connect the visceral to air, wind and flight.

In this metaphorical embodiment, extreme water activities like surfing, cave diving and cliff jumping or air-based practices such as sky diving, hang-gliding and kite surfing therefore become bodily tropes for existence and identity. They provide fleeting resolutions of a struggle between locality and the global, modernity and nature, freedom and constraint. The body is rarely more unregulated than during these few moments of gliding, free-fall or submersion. They are both the most natural and unnatural sensations, since being truly free is unnatural.

In addition to the obvious connection of Merleau-Ponty's work on the phenomenology of the body, the practices of extreme adventure also tie in nicely with what Marcel Mauss calls 'techniques of the body' (1934) – corporeal ways of Being that become 'natural' but are also contingent, malleable and allow for a creative physicality. These practices are thus expressive of symbolic actions: they are means of liberation and freedom, a way of searching for the unknown. Such techniques of the body can therefore be seen as therapeutic, emancipatory and of cathartic value – vehicles for individual and social healing (Csordas 1995; Lewis 2001).

Deep and Dangerous Play

Inspired by Jeremy Bentham's (1748–1832) political economy of 'deep play', Clifford Geertz used this notion to his own ends when he famously described how the Balinese cockfight theatrically staged a scenario that transformed the central values of Balinese propriety into the symbolic immediacy of experiential bloodiness which validated a social game of life and death. In his words: 'Bentham's concept of "deep play" is found in his The Theory of Legislation. By it he means play in which the stakes are so high that it is, from his utilitarian standpoint, irrational for men to engage in it at all' (Geertz 1973, 440). The ethnographic analogy was such that two types of severe penalties could result. The status associated with this type of gambling meant a bettor could lose most of their fortune on a single fight if the ante was high enough, or deep enough as the case may be. And collectively, participants faced the threat of being arrested because these events were strictly banned by the Javanese authorities. So even though the fights were usually public affairs, they were always fraught with an air of illicitness, excitement and a depth of experience not present in most communal village activities.

Since Geertz's popularisation of the term, misappropriations of deep play abound. For instance, according to MacAloon and Csikszentmihalyi (1983), dangerous games like rock climbing are also perfect examples of deep play because of the irrational nature of taking such a life-threatening risk with no obvious reward except the one that exists in the act itself. Yet Geertz was more on the money in linking deep play to Balinese cockfights since Bentham's (1840, 440) original utilitarian formulation was made clearly in terms of economics, that is, of gambling with currency or personal possessions: 'it is irrational for anyone to engage in it at all, since the marginal utility of what you stand to win is grossly outweighed by the disutility of what you stand to lose.' A term referring to the notorious high stakes gambling of Georgian London, Bentham would have himself borrowed it from the everyday parlance of the time, in an attempt to rectify the flaws in the dynamics of the new capitalist order. Indeed, deep play's explicit connection with decadence and illicit behaviour marks it out as a concept to be reckoned with, feared and in the case of succumbing to the influence of the Protestant work ethic, to be stamped out. The highwayman Macheath from John Gay's *The Beggar's Opera* (1728) rallies his gang with the temptation of looting: 'There will be deep play tonight at Mary[le]bone, and consequently money may be picked up upon the road. Meet me there, and I'll give the hint who is worth setting' (quoted in Dugaw 2001, 19).

Geertz's emphasis on the irrationality of accepting incomparable odds has therefore misled many people into thinking that the deep play concept is synonymous with any kind of high stake risk. But unless we are talking about competitive climbing for instance, the fact that there is nothing to win from participating does not automatically mean that the only reward exists in the activity itself, or in its irrationality. This is a tautology which leaves out a fundamental scenario, the possibility that danger has any intrinsic value.

It is surely more appropriate to qualify the deep play concept then, which has now had lots of mileage, into that of deep and dangerous play for the purposes of physical gambling where the stakes so highly involve the danger of serious accident or death. In this sense, the only semantically valid analogy that can be made between deep play and risking one's life would be in considering Russian Roulette. Since this is such a fundamentally different kind of scenario from that which Bentham had in mind, the ongoing usage of 'deep play' when applied to voluntary risk pursuits is inappropriately weak (cf. Pritchard 1997; Ackerman 1999). Besides, there are few anthropologists who would be willing to undertake a study of Russian Roulette from the perspective of participant observation.

As a result, this book shall provide interactive responses to the rapidly growing domain of deep and dangerous play. Alternative sport and adventurous leisure activities have shifted from being marginal, exotic and even elitist, to being more than merely acceptable. They are now exemplary, mainstream as it were. Growing numbers of people are doing them and they are being appropriated, applied and are infiltrating an increasingly wide array of contexts – academic research being one and anthropology increasingly so in recent times (Sands 2002; Rinehart and Sydnor 2003; Wheaton 2004).

The research on the cultural practices in question incorporates the phenomenon of adventure or alternative sport into a framework of risk positive. I hope the reader will share a feeling that it is significant to investigate the proliferation of the alternative sports movement at the end of the twentieth and beginning of the twenty-first centuries. They demonstrate how such sports make for a contested series of memorable adventures, adrenaline experiences and social narratives. Many of these practices find themselves rapidly evolving as activities that are sometimes carried out purposefully for their own sake. But most are often performed as optional elements in a package or assemblage of activities that are highly embodied and often 'techno-rebellious'. In this format, such recreation is frequently negotiated in a non-competitive, free-style and often rather spontaneous manner. Admittedly, these practices do exist as commodities and competition sports to a certain extent. Nevertheless, they make up a distinctive sub-cultural style united by a certain hedonism, anarchism and moral concern. That is, they occupy a zone that seamlessly takes in the centre of society as well as the liminal fringe of both nature and culture. Frequently therefore, they are played out on the social margins.

Hazardous sports are not necessarily defined by their danger, although some potential risk of harm must be evident. Rather, they are part of a largely subversive, counter cultural lifestyle. Here the legal, civic or moral risk can be just as important, if not more. Paradoxically, this subversiveness is infiltrating the cultural norm. One significant reason for this is because this counter cultural ethos has become germane to the dawning of green social thought. An intimate connection with the moral responsibility towards the environment seems to be developing in an ethos of green and extreme. The environment here is played out on an eco-political plane concerned with the sustainability of the leisure industry, while seeking danger at the same time strives for the survival of feeling alive by courting the unexpected. It is for this reason that the activities that I consider here are non-motorised, even though countless risk sports are highly dependent on energy intensive, mechanistic technologies.

There are three basic ways in which to categorise voluntary risk taking when it comes to seeking thrills and peak experiences: on the one hand we have those who place their lives in the hands of the suppliers of adventurous recreation. These are the activities for which a thrill is sought but under the overall assumption by all concerned that this is under a highly safe and controlled setting whereby risks are perceptual but not real and only a fluke accident can result in any calamity. Bungy jumping, roller coaster riding, climbing wall practice and so forth are the most typical activities. In such scenarios we are dealing with an industry of service providers, where insurance and compensation issues become something to deal with in terms of verifying whether negligence was involved in an unfortunate incident. On the other hand, at the other extreme in other words, are those completely unregulated and sometimes even illegitimate practices which are undertaken solely on the basis of individual choice. Here the participant, who might of course be naively coerced by friends, nevertheless assumes the sole responsibility for their actions and safety, often fully aware of the potential consequences. Examples include cave diving, urban exploration, BASE and cliff jumping, climbing up buildings as a protest or a feat of conquest, and so on.

Mid-way between these opposites is a grey area for those practices which are semi-regulated and for which a third party may potentially be held responsible for an accident but where disclaimer forms and similar contracts are often drawn up to ensure that the participant is aware and willing to succumb to any possible mishaps. Deep sea diving, climbing competitions or mountaineering expeditions, hang-gliding and microlight flying can fall into this more ambiguous category, for which the limits are often set depending on the type of group or party that is set up to oversee the activity.

Reflexivity, Multi-Sitedness and Autobiographical Ethnography

Methodologically the research in this book grounds itself in various ethnographic case studies with autobiographical undertones (Radin 1963; Okely and Callaway 1992; Okely 1996; Reed-Danahay 1997). Edmund Leach who defended the autobiographical approach towards the end of his life certainly advocated that this was necessary for the future prosperity of social anthropology: 'Unless we pay much closer attention than has been customary to the personal background of the authors of anthropological works, we shall miss out on most of what these texts are capable of telling us about the history of anthropology' (1984, 22). A few years later he was even more explicit: 'Ethnographers must admit the reflexivity of their activities; they must become autobiographical' (1987, 12).

I would justify the use of the autobiographical angle in the following chapters simply as a necessary part of examining one's own preconceptions to overcome the generation of anthropology that Judith Okely had identified as problematised by fear, the 'fear of subjectivity' and its oppressive associations, as they were (1986, viii). For Okely, personal anthropology provides a certain bastion of reflexivity for the social sciences and humanities, a way to reinvigorate theories of human behaviour and keep them fresh. Despite the heightened discourse over reflexive issues in the social sciences, it is nevertheless remarkable that more than 20 years later so few anthropologists have risen to the challenge of overtly writing autobiographical descriptions of ethnographic scenarios that are of empirical and political significance to their own societies (Holman-Jones 2005).

Indeed, the concentrated and coherent interest in the study of academic research is a relatively new phenomenon. An overall dearth of verifiable material concerning such findings exists. Until recently, most studies consisted of reflections and exhortations, seldom based on empirical data. Early pioneers such as Max Weber (1949) nevertheless highlighted the idea that researchers were no more exempt from interesting behaviour than were the people they studied. He made this the basis of his methodological discussions and was thus amongst the first significant thinkers to emphasise an outlook which scrutinises the career of sociologists in tandem with the academic spheres in which they circulate. His work integrated the study of professional careers insofar as the choice of professions was influenced by academic training.

The intellectual impact of Weber's work has been vast. By the end of the 1940s sociologists had established the sociology of science (including their own) as a distinct sub-discipline of the humanities and social sciences. Education became a focus of rigorous sociological research after World War II. It was then that sociologists turned to questions of social integration, group consensus and the role of education in promoting intra- and inter-generational mobility. It was also at this point that they tried to establish correlations between social origins, education and occupational mobility. The sociologists of this epoch, however, paid little attention to the social processes that produced the effects they were measuring.

The basic theoretical assumption in the heyday of Lévi-Strauss was that the major paradigms of the social sciences fell under the structuralist heading. This outlook prevailed for so long because it was a simple and economical framework to work with; it remained compatible with dominant politico-economic interests; it elicited data that confirmed the analytical framework which had generated the research design; and it was supportive of power structures in the scientific community, thus helping to establish rigid systems where the status quo could survive (Shanks and Tilley 1987). Hence, structuralism was practical. It appealed to those who had obtained eminence in the academic community. Their whole theoretical orientation was behind the conviction that the system was morally right and that change must be slowed if not resisted outright.

The anthropologist Jeremy Boissevain (1974) has argued that certain correlations exist between an historically specific nexus of political elites and the propagation of theories that are convenient for maintaining social segregation. He suggested that processes operating outside and within the scientific community eventually forced the turnover of dominant paradigms. Scientific theory is thus no different from any other social process. He identified three procedures working towards change within the scientific community: biological processes; epistemological considerations; and sociological factors. Increasingly, Boissevain saw that researchers were beginning to examine the birth of social forms. Their focus was not on the forms *per se* but on the social processes that created them. As such, they were not asking what the social order consisted of or how it was maintained. Instead, they were curious as to how and why the forms that existed came to be as they were.

Some of the conclusions of this research revealed that power relations within the scientific community were asymmetric. This meant that those in superior positions intentionally used their access to resources to protect their theories against rival ones. These rival theories could not spring up at random. They would come from specific groups within the academic community, namely young newcomers – who would advance cutting edge theories because they sought recognition and because they had not been fully socialised into the rules of the dominant paradigm. Consequently, they were trying to gain status in a competitive community. One of the ways that members of the new generation would establish themselves was by 'synthesising the established and variant concepts and procedures of their discipline into original patterns of their own' (Boissevain 1974, 223).

As structural functionalism's power started to crumble in the social sciences, the speed of disciplinary paradigm shifts increased. This was both the cause and consequence of a public demand for more accessible entry into higher education. Such an increase in the power of the grass roots did not result, as some had anticipated it would, in the end of the university as a community of scientists. Conversely, it was a sign of the more rapid development of theories and concepts, something that many scholars were beginning to fully embrace (Bourdieu 1988).

More recently, the study of research has gained interest through the development of Science & Technology Studies and the work of such intellectuals as Bruno Latour. But again the theoretical formulations that deal with the study of research have been largely concerned with the study of laboratory based scientists.

This takes us to the contemporary investigations of education and research. Reflexivity is certainly a significant trend of prominence in the social sciences. It has taught us that our depictions of the world communicate as much about ourselves as about our representations of it. Such innovations have allowed insightful and far reaching observations into the nature of academia and the processes involved in the production of knowledge. Notably, recent approaches in the sociology of science and technology studies have generated a number of case studies in the vein of understanding how scientific analyses are vulnerable to the researcher's interests and values (Burawoy 1991; Latour 1999; Livingstone 2003).

With such examples in mind, let us now consider a parallel development within social and culture studies: the decentring of ethnographic research so that it can maintain a fascination with other societies but whereby it does not need to fall victim to the idea of only existing in its most valid form when it is practised in a single site, in a context unfamiliar to the ethnographer. To an extent, this could be seen as quite a fundamental challenge to the anthropological enterprise. The objective here is not so bold as to scrutinise anthropology as a whole, however. Rather, I hope to contribute to a growing conceptual dialogue about the reflexivity of fieldwork by providing a glimpse into the processes by which anthropologists gather some of their materials of analysis, particularly in this case when they play with adventurous methods, techniques and ideas.

Questions about the effects of cultural decentring have inspired anthropologists such as George Marcus (1995) to situate writing culture in the context of a global ethnography based on a changing world system. He has argued that the struggle between the dominant self and the other is not a struggle over whether there is to be global integration but over the terms of such integration, and in particular, over who or what defines the identity of social groups. For him, the relations between core and periphery are not just relations of struggle but are negotiations as well. Increasing globalisation brings with itself a rise in the level in which these spatial categories will share and negotiate boundaries or resources.

Marcus proposes a methodological praxis to deal with changing culture and ethnography. He defines multi-sited research as a project involving chains, conjunctions, juxtapositions, paths and threads of locations among sites that define ethnography's argument, its *raison d'être*. In it, the ethnographer sets up some form of literal, physical presence that ties and connects ethnographer, subject and milieu. Hence, ethnographers move from their traditional single-site location to '... multiple sites of observation and participation that cross-cut dichotomies such as the "local" and the "global", the "lifeworld" and the "system"' (1995, 95). This kind of ethnography maps a new object of study, one where prior situated narratives, like that of resistance and appropriation, become more ethnographically accessible and that also problematises the relation between subject and object, ethnographer and informant, environment and material culture. Anthropologists engaged in multi-sited space move across various sites/sights of activity. The emerging sense of activism that develops between them and their affiliations with the producers of cultural knowledge preserves an essential link with the customary practice of participant observation and traditional single-sited ethnography.

From Marcus's article we begin to appreciate how the changing world system has substantially altered the experiences of informants and ethnographers. Sequentially, the relationship of ethnographer and subject to their terrain has meandered. By default, spatial relativism has crept in where it might not have existed before. Space and place acquire existential, if not surreal, attributes. For locales and milieus to become existential they must assert themselves in a spatial praxis. To do so, they inevitably receive certain marginal and peripheral attributes. Fringe space becomes a more open-ended space. It re-contextualises spatiality and engages us in a phenomenological re-mapping of our numerous real and imagined worlds.

Like many social sciences in recent times, anthropology has shown an increasing interest in the study of games, play and recreation (Harris and Park 1983). Regarding ethics and methodology, this is rather unproblematic. Considering games which are rather more unorthodox than traditional team sports can become more complicated, especially when such studies begin to involve imaginary and genuine risks for informants and researchers alike. This involves a fundamental challenge to the notion of responsibility, the nature of the imagination and even the character of participant research.

It also raises considerable concern for insurance companies, ethical committees and funding bodies alike. Methodologically, the discipline itself should certainly not be considered as a haphazard activity when exploring the proliferating arena of alternative sport and adventurous activities through the ethnographic bastion of participant observation. The reasons for this are not only epistemological. Indeed, the activities in question are themselves far from 'hap-hazardous'.

Despite involving some degree of risk as well as accepting that certain elements are of course left to chance, the anthropology of sport has convincingly taught us that alternative sporting practices are as paradoxical as any other social phenomenon. They are simultaneously structured and fluid, guided and spontaneous. We thus come to understand the creative role of risk's extremity in adding value to the personal experience and collective products of adventure tourism and dangerous play performed in wild, natural and urban areas.

Overall this volume presents an interdisciplinary framework for the study of adventurous landscapes and hazardous leisure. In doing so it reviews the relevant literature for such research, drawing together the work of a number of scholars in a variety of disciplines such as anthropology, geography, media and cultural studies, sociology and environmental psychology. Phenomenologically and reflexively influenced, this study investigates an experiential conception of the imagination through an exploration of the extreme body. Foremost, it sets the scene for a conceptual consideration of adventurous practices. This potentially pushes the level in which we can reflect upon such a thing as an existential or embodied imagination. Here modernity's levelling of the docile body is challenged. Hence, in focusing on these sub-cultural practices that involve the hazardous use of landscape, I propose an alternative scenario in which to consider the creativity of the body. One in which extreme acts can be interpreted beyond most notions within contemporary thinking in the anthropology of sport or the sociology of risk, to a more far-reaching – perhaps 'extremist' position – where they can be understood as existentially poignant, performative acts of the social imagination.

The book attempts to cover and acknowledge the work of as many authorities in the field of risk sport studies as possible, bearing in mind it is not strictly speaking just about these activities. So some effort has been made to include an interdisciplinary representation of approaches. But in trying to provide a set of cross-disciplinary discussion, the book nonetheless emphasises an anthropological perspective and I hope to have kept ethnographic methods and interpretations as the core of the discussion. One reason for this is controversial but worth questioning – isn't anthropology still rather conservative, at least when it comes to defending itself in the sea of multi-disciplinary sport research? Shouldn't we perhaps be taking more risks in our analyses, theorising and methodological approaches, especially with regard to the less than accurately chartered terrain of alternative sports. This means truly accepting that ethnographic practices are themselves inherently grounded in reflexivity, educated guesses and calculated risks that allow us and our discipline to survive, both in the perilously haphazard arenas of academia and the world outside it.

So in dealing with the interviewing, participation and observation of such fleeting moments of euphoria that deep and dangerous play provides, the social anthropologist has necessarily reached a new methodological frontier. The most established way we have of exploring this horizon is by the practices of detailed description and participant observation. This involves a domain whereby environment and the body, identity, experience and imagination come together through a curiosity for understanding thrillscapes, whether urban or in the countryside. It is therefore encouraging to take note that recent research nevertheless engages in the process of questioning whether corporeal regimentation is the only result of modernity, the only framework in which to consider risk taking (Le Breton 2004; Zaloom 2004). Something else is surely at work here, an alternative scenario that ethnography, perhaps inspired by more open-ended, post-modern or phenomenological approaches, has begun to pursue. This volume is therefore an invitation for anthropologists and other social researchers to persevere with the non-haphazard study of risk, danger and adventure.

Chapter 1
Poetic Experience, Literary Encounters

It was at the close of an early spring day, when nature, in a cold province of Scotland, was reviving from her winter's sleep, and the air at least, though not the vegetation, gave promise of an abatement of the rigour of the season, that two travellers, whose appearance at that early period sufficiently announced their wandering character, which, in general, secured a free passage even through a dangerous country ...

(Sir Walter Scott, 1831 [1903], 3).

Quoting out of context can be amusing. Lest we forget, however, the matter for consideration in this volume can also be – without question – deadly serious. The lines above open Walter Scott's last novel *Castle Dangerous* (1831). They invoke a painful anecdote which not only situates some of my own infatuation with adventure but also hints at the real risks that lurk beneath the surface of wanderlust and the 'wonderlustrous'. In this case, I'm thinking of how such a passage, safe or not, can equally be indicative of the many tragedies that result from sheer bad luck, neglect or overzealousness. All of these elements and more are present in the following recollection.

At the close of an early spring day in 1996, returning from the funeral of a friend in the northernmost tip of Scotland, I exclaimed to my companions that I wished to finish the rest of the journey to Edinburgh alone. The young man to whose funeral I refer was in his early twenties and had been my flatmate for well over a year. A brilliant mind, he had just finished a bachelor's degree in conservation ecology and was set to continue his career as a marine biologist in the autumn by taking up further postgraduate study. Through an incredibly unfortunate accident that left his diving buddy injured, he had drowned in a loch practising his passion of exploring underwater environments. We were told by the police that his scuba cylinder had malfunctioned at a depth of around 60 feet (20 metres). He and his partner had then begun to share the breathing apparatus of the other tank and proceeded with the standard resurfacing method whereby his partner started inflating his safety jacket to give enough buoyancy to bring them both up gradually. They progressed with this technique for not much more than ten feet when they suddenly lost grip of each other, precipitating the positively buoyant diver up to the surface. Due to the lack of decompression time he suffered a punctured lung. This impairment also meant it took him considerably longer than it would normally to alert the members of the shore team who sent a rescue diver and called for an ambulance. The body was recovered about 20 minutes after the incident which in cold-water diving conditions can sometimes result in successfully reviving the victim.

It goes without saying that the loss to his family was enormous. He was such a charismatic and proactive person that a huge circle of friends was also left grief stricken, many of whom travelled up in convoys to his hometown for the service. In the car on the way back, after a couple of days of communal mourning and quite unsure about my own future career path, being in that limbo phase of having just finished a formal qualification, I was desperate for some reflection time. We were all emotionally distraught but in a sense I was fortunate enough to be free of any pressing commitments. So despite my hazy mind, I somehow reassured everyone in the car that I had enough gear, provisions and stamina to hitch back in my own time. It was a beautiful sunny April afternoon. They must have dropped me off somewhere either side of the Moray Firth since I had a vague plan to walk away my confusion in the Cairngorms.

Passing a couple of hours along a quiet roadside with no real desire to catch a ride or speak with anyone, I eventually kipped down in a little pine plantation. I recall spending most of the next morning doing the same thing in similarly glorious conditions. After a lift or two in the afternoon, I reached Aviemore in time for a pint. Being early in the week, there weren't many people out. But there were some friendly locals sitting around the bar so eventually we got talking. We drank until closing. Given their queries about an itinerary, it must have been obvious that something wasn't quite right. Yet with the drink flowing and the bravado of anonymity, I kept my story close to my chest, explaining instead that I was doing some trekking and would check out the ski resort which had been part of the topic of an increasingly inebriated conversation.

I stumbled away from the town for a couple of miles in the direction of Loch Morlich and crashed out at a roadside lay-by. It was an early hung-over rising but the next day started out fine. The weather greyed over as I slowly walked along a hilly road where there were so few cars that lifts were not really an option. By the time I reached the base of the ski trails just before midday, it was overcast. The snow at this altitude (1,800 ft) had long vanished but the ground was nevertheless boggy from melt water and rain. It was hard to make out the conditions beyond a few hundred feet because mists and low-lying cloud had now crept in, concealing the hills and ravines. Determined, I started ascending on the eastern side of the ski trails, beneath the line of a chair lift, near what is referred to as Gully 2.

As I rose in elevation, the weather got decidedly worse and the drizzle turned to a downpour. A lack of proper waterproofs meant it was time for a break. Finding an overhanging rock with enough shelter to crawl under, I curled up and rested for a couple of hours. I was quite exhausted and pretty much out of food at this point. My drinking bottle was nearly drained and all that remained of my depleted rations was a few biscuits and a can of baked beans. Moreover, my kit bag hadn't been packed with the intention of doing any serious climbing or wilderness excursions. In fact, it only consisted of some spare clothes, a very basic map and my deceased friend's rain resistant sleeping bag. With its separate arms and hoodie, this bit of equipment resembled some form of army surplus hunting attire which hybridised the functions of an anorak, a primitive dry-suit and a bivvy sack.

As Laurence Gonzalas (2003) explains in his populist account *Deep Survival* this was a classic example of a potentially disastrous scenario. The type where people make split second decisions that can result in perishing or not. The type that Jon Krakauer describes in his biographical account of the tragic story of Christopher Johnson McCandless, *Into the Wild* (1996), when the young man got caught out trekking in the Alaskan bush for 16 weeks before starving to death. Doubtless it was time for me to turn back. Or at least to stay put. Any rational person would have known that. Funnily enough, despite my troubled state, even I knew it. Somehow though, the agency of the landscape, the challenge of ascent and the ritualistic adventure of mourning, which was initially shared collectively, coalesced into an individualistically driven force to experience something life-affirming in the face of loss.

Instinctively, intuitively, and yes, incredibly naively, I believed in this promise of an abatement of the season referred to in the quotation above by Walter Scott. It was April after all. The days were decidedly longer and the temperature was relatively warm. The rain returned to a drizzle so I changed my sodden socks and, considering that it was approximately 4 pm, decided it should be possible to easily return to the same rock outcrop for one more night of roughing it. One could say that I was seduced by the setting as well as the journey which now seemed to take on a life of its own. An impulse to reach the snow line, if nothing else, was overbearing. After that, turning back would be an option.

Within a short time the drizzle turned to gentle flurries. Another 45 minutes of slow ascent, being mindful not to get unnecessarily wet, allowed me to come within reach of a plateau. Just as the hill began to level I crossed the threshold of snow. Suddenly everything was still and quiet. In hindsight, it might have proved wise to be more attuned and wary of clichés. Sighting some grouse walking on the soft white carpet kept me going instead of retreating back downhill. Some structures began poking out of the smooth ground, indicating the terminus of the chair lifts, power generators, perhaps also a toilet block. Misguidedly interpreting these as signs of safety, I pressed on. From the map I estimated myself to be near the Ptarmigan summit (3,600 ft).

I wandered round ever higher, initially with the destination of Cairn Gorm (4,084 ft) in mind, a mere 484 ft further up. The adrenaline kicked in from realising it was getting late and would be dark fairly soon. Yet the visibility had improved and at that point things seemed good. Captivated by a spectacular view to the east of a deep crevice and neighbouring summits, the instant camera in my rucksack came to mind. After a few moments' pause for contemplation, I turned in the opposite direction, enthralled at being able to make out the glow of a distant sunset through a haze of windswept flakes. It was behind a high rising white wall to the south-west. Beyond this must rest the Cairn Gorm summit. I searched for a way around the powdery wall which was unclimbable except to an equipped and experienced mountaineer. To the east was a precipice, so venturing west was the only option.

This is when things began to go very wrong indeed. Without sensing it coming, the wind began to gust up and a blizzard hit fast. I tried to retreat to the photo spot but was beginning to lose my bearings. Afraid of going too quickly, moving too far and plummeting down the eastern ridge crevices triggered a most horrible sensation of entrapment. Going slowly uphill in the north-western direction would allow me to steer clear of any danger. As I crept along with trepidation, I experienced what was undoubtedly the most frightening experience of my life up to that point and perhaps still. The storm's intensity left me completely snowblind. Panicked, I froze and waited for some moments. After a few minutes the whiteout cleared enough so that I could at least see my hands at arm's length. Still awfully anxious, I got down on all fours and started crawling. The snow was getting deeper so I risked moving down slope. To top it off, it was clear that the light levels were dropping quickly as the obscured western glow disappeared below the crest of the hills.

Somehow I rejoined the spot where I'd taken a photograph. Famished and frightened, I cracked open the can of baked beans on a rock. Eating them frantically with my last biscuits, I then panicked again. The weather conditions were still severe and it was too dark to risk moving very far. Running for it could work or could result in falling off an edge. So I scampered cautiously down a little gully and found two big stones emerging from the snow. In haste, I dug out a shelter and prepared to camp down.

Foolishly, but it was enough to keep me optimistic, I felt secure that the sleeping bivvy thing, which I had previously borrowed on a number of occasions from my mate, would do the trick. Layering up and snuggling in, with not much comfort, I began to realise that it was warm enough in this makeshift burrow. It wasn't so much of an igloo-bunker, since it was a pure survival cave, but rather an excavated trench wedged between some large boulders. Struggling initially with whether staying awake was the best option, I began to relax after some time, realising that the night was clearing. Hopeful at not getting completely buried alive, I took heart in still being fairly warm and so allowed myself to drift off. I must have slept for several hours because I awoke just after dawn, relieved to notice a cloudless sky. The morning conditions were clear and crisp, with the threat of severe weather remaining abated. Momentarily reliving the panic of hours gone by, which was joined by taking stock of my increasing fatigue, hastened me to action. Mindful of getting caught in another storm, I quickly found my bearings and decided on both getting down below the snow line while equally heading towards any sign of help, life and civilisation.

At times I ran, desperate to physically warm up and to reach safer ground. My canvas trainer booties and blue jeans were frozen stiff around relatively dry long-underwear and woolly socks. As I moved on towards the south-west, I was both pleased and shocked to see that it had been the right decision to remain in place during the evening. Faced with steep drops hundreds of feet down, I again had to proceed with caution, not wanting to slip through a small avalanche on a ridge, or twist an ankle on some concealed stones. Luckily the weather was holding.

Nothing but blue sky meant I was warming up quickly and seemed to be covering some ground. The main focus was on roughly trying to keep in the same direction, confident at that point of being able to rejoin the main road which runs south-west from Aviemore.

Of course, the lower I descended and the more I sweated from the anticipation and progress, the warmer everything got. My frozen trousers began to soak my leggings and socks. I took a break, had a drink of melting snow and rummaged round for the only dry things left to wear – fresh socks and a large tweed blanket. Removing the damp layers against my skin, I wrapped my lower half and carried on, revived from the water, warmth and surreal humour of what all this must look like from the perspective of anyone who might happen to be watching from a distance. I could only laugh at that point. It was slowly sinking in that I was more than fortunate to still be alive. By then I was low enough that some larger stones were exposed. Ice and snow became softer, slippery. Tiny streams formed through some gravelly bits. Heather tops and vegetation began poking out. With some consternation at the possibility of breaking a leg only a few miles from the road, I increased the pace, hopping and slaloming down over troughs and scree.

Eventually I did indeed get off the range via the south-west, passing Ben Macdhui (4,296 ft) and Braeriach (4,252 ft) and rejoining the A9. It was around midday by then. So with no time to waste, it was back to hitching. Being realistic though, the tramp-like sight I must have been, with drenched trainers, wrapped in a blanket with a sodden jumper and rucksack, in addition to there not being many passing cars, meant that the decision to keep going was an obvious one. If I was correct in reading the map, the next town, Kingussie, was only a couple of miles down the road. After everything I'd been through, I would certainly walk to the next town if necessary. It wasn't. Within 15 minutes or so, after stopping and trying to look respectable for the few vehicles that did pass, a car pulled over whilst I was walking with my back turned, my thumb in the air and my hope of getting a lift exhausted.

The story should end here really, because this autobiographical tangent might seem too longwinded for some readers. With some self-indulgence, however, I'll continue for those who have a taste for such things but also for reasons that should be immediately clear.

My 'rescuer' was not only an agreeable and tolerant person, he was a real character as well. He came out with some dreadfully funny stuff like: 'What with that kilt thingy, I thought you were a bird, that's why I stopped to pick you up'. He was a great storyteller and within minutes of conversation my own concerns and sorrows were at least temporarily absolved. It turned out that he was also a journalist and an avid abseiler, who was out on a scouting tour of the area to find suitable shoot locations.

Seeing that this was before my formal academic interest in such matters, much of the ethnographic learning opportunity was lost on me at the time. More so perhaps, because I intuitively understood much of the appeal of what he was describing, despite having never abseiled myself. Consequently, one could say that his ideas appeared somewhat contrary to my recent experience even though they were directly allied. In other words, I guess the difficulty I had in fully grasping the significance of this episode was the result of a more or less egotistical feeling of having just survived 'the real McCoy'. Having said this, one thing did emerge in terms of personal development: I was certainly drawn further out of my own chasm and seduced into this unfolding narrative which was being led by a spontaneous encounter. There seemed to be a lot more than charm to this knowledgeable chap, with his many intricately woven intentions for adventure.

The journey southwards took quite a while. It was intermittently broken up by some site visits. My guide's snapshots, he explained, would hopefully serve as some preliminary material for the promotion and production of a short film he was researching. The locations were therefore paramount. They mattered to him not only because they would be aesthetically interesting 'backdrops' but also because he wanted them to tell something of the region's historic significance. Indeed, the places on his itinerary were genuine heritage locations, some formally, others in a more taken-for-granted way.

Our journey included three notable stops. First, the town of Pitlochry as an emergency break for some quick visits to the post-office, newsagents, loo and general road trip provisions. Some coffee and a warm bakery snack were certainly on my breakfast agenda. Second was a bridge above the River Tay, somewhere near Aberfeldy. The water landing was not very deep at all, only a few feet. So starting with the simple premise that hitting shallow water at an angle while travelling at speed (especially with wires and some bulky equipment) could get nasty, we pondered over a few solutions for some time. He had in mind various rope angles, support 'guylines' and similar swing harness ideas to absorb the rapidity of downward descent. Our third main stop was a luxurious hotel, refurbished from an ancient castle settlement within the general vicinity of Perth. After we ordered some take-away tea, my journalist companion inquired as to whom he should contact about the possibility of using the roof and one of the high reinforced walls as an abseil platform.

We travelled, talked, ate and scouted together from early to late afternoon. During these many hours we stopped at several other significant places with features not dissimilar to the ones just described. Since at this stage I can provide but the sketchiest of recollections of our route, the clues to uncovering our further conversations, not to mention my tour guide's complex scheme, are lost, save in the material gist of what might be left behind. For instance, whatever might have resulted from his scoping exercise, or some of the basic details of the sites that spring back to memory – two more bridge structures, a freestanding archway of some height above a railway line (or small B road) and a short pathway cutting across a deep narrow gorge. From this humid, sheltered spot and the misty spray that rose from below, we could decipher a river section emerging from the hills. The water was running fast and must have been icy cold.

Figure 1.1   Cairngorms, Scotland (photo by the author)

It was time to part at around 5 or 6 pm as he dropped me off at a junction just south of Stirling. I caught one more short lift to the outskirts of Edinburgh, where this excursion ended after a short hop on a local bus to the city centre and a walk home to Marchmont. Drained and exhausted, at least I was in my own boxroom bed (such as it was), by nightfall. After some much needed sleep, the process of striving to repress the shock could begin. We do not need a trained psychoanalyst to suggest that there is likely a quite clear connection that transpires here between this period of mourning the loss of a friend and 'inadvertently' risking my own life. Perhaps obviously, however, the point is that it is essential to reflect on such experiences beyond the individual level. Indeed, such adventure stories abound in the biographical literature of explorers and frequently, if there is any to speak of, the level of analysis largely remains within two realms: the psychological, or that of the epic exploit which has benefited humanity by the utter magnitude of the heroic act (Marshall 1954; Stark 2001; McDonald 2002; Hewitt 2007). Undoubtedly both spheres are important but on the whole they are of little concern to us here. Rather, the main objective is to explore the incremental extensions of the human imaginary; to unpack such experiences in terms of the more everyday implications of their wider socio-cultural dimensions.

At the surface this raises a conundrum if we uncritically accept Simmel's (1911 [1997]) basic premise that adventurous activities are, in their very classification, opposed to the mundane features of everyday life. How then could one study that which is not of our daily life-world from the perspective of everyday life? This immediate disjuncture between adventure on the one hand and the everyday on the other is not irreconcilable, however. Our phenomenological notion of comparative inter-subjective experience is what bridges or links what is mundane from ordinary occurrences to what is special from those happenings which break up the routine. So to grasp the various levels of that which is irregular for some people but not for others means we must document the experiences of the body through a comprehensive and cross-cultural examination of the different ways in which the somatic is embedded in mundane as well as extreme socio-cultural worlds.

This approach also provides the caveat of being mindful not to fall victim to over-glamorisation when studying adventure. Hence as one anthropologist has pointed out:

> we cannot allow ourselves to enter into an unexamined agreement with the thrill seekers and the hedonists that we will be interested in the manifestation of the human spirit only in aroused states; we must manifest our interest in the quotidian experiences as well, and perhaps even in the depressed states of boredom, lassitude, even dispiritedness (Abrahams 1986, 48).

Such a starting point has had significant sway in the humanities and social sciences precisely because of a simplicity which reflects an implicit epistemological truth. My intention is therefore not so much to undermine it at the core, as it is to appropriate, revisit and to a degree deconstruct such a tenet in its ideologically informed structural grounding. The idea behind using a more nuanced approach to the topic of adventure and to the ways of breaching it results from a number of ethnographic situations which reveal the limitations of conceptual definitions that become stagnant, taken for granted and separated from ever shifting social realities.

Wanderlustrous Landscapes

Now since I would surely describe the personal vignette above as a near-death experience, it felt about as close to true wilderness as one could get for a number of reasons. In this case, it must have been the moment in my life of being the furthest physically from another human being. Looking at a map some time afterwards made it possible to work out that, with the exception of the airline planes above, which would not have found anybody in a hurry, the nearest person could have been up to five miles away, at least in the middle of the night. Thinking back now I might challenge the possibility of such a statement but no matter, there were certainly not many people sleeping out in those conditions. And if I had not woken up, it is conceivable that the windswept snow would have concealed me for days, perhaps many.

Finding the following lines, which were the closing words of Sir Frank Fraser Darling's (1903–1979) Reith Lectures in 1969, prompted me to think through the experience in terms of wilderness and 'being-wildered':

> Most people will never know true wilderness although its existence will not be a matter of indifference to them. The near landscape is valuable and loveable because of its nearness, not something to be disregarded and shrugged off; it is where children are reared and what they take away in their minds to their long future. What ground could be more hallowed? (Darling 1970, 110).

Informally, I began asking friends about this idea of wilderness and how far they had ever been from the next human being. Some years later, better able to come to terms with some of the reasons for ending up in such a situation in the first place, this type of question factored itself into my fieldwork interviews in Cornwall. Sensing as I did that there might be isolated settings in this much smaller region (like Bodmin Moor), which in their own distinct way could be as remote as parts of the highlands of Scotland, a certain curiosity to explore the not-so-near landscape was ever present.

This is not particularly the right place to go into an analysis of those findings. Except perhaps to say that, when placed in the context of risk, there were some fascinating answers, not to mention lots of interest in the question. For instance, one woman challenged the very nature of the interrogation by choosing to interpret distance not spatially but psychologically. She said the closest she felt to being alienated from people was in a moment of being trapped by an 'assailant'. The specifics of this incident remained undisclosed but it led us to talk about how many people, even or especially in the most crowded cities, could feel very far indeed from the next human being if they were so disempowered by a situation as to end up frozen; paralysed, unable to ask or scream for help.

So we can easily agree with Darling that the 'safeish' ground needs to exist for most people and it needs to be hallowed since it is the ground of the next generation. Changing the tone slightly, it is a different way of articulating the well known adage 'we borrow the earth from our grandchildren'. Yet the unmentioned in these wise words from the 1970s are important. Who are the exceptions? Most if not all societies have often sought 'heroes' who have ventured into the non-safe, non-hallowed territories; the 'wild', untamed, unexplored areas at the edges, margins and peripheries of the known world. Such places, the distant landscapes as it were, are at the very heart of where the unexplored and thus the potentially dangerous might lie. Admittedly in a different context, this is still part of the profundity in Victor Turner's (1974) postulate of the 'centre out there' phenomenon, whereby through some form of socio-spatial inversion, the margins or an area situated outside the home environment becomes the core feature of a cultural expression – centralising the peripheral landscape as it were.

As the focus for several journals and countless books, conferences and research projects, an overall concern with landscape has been burgeoning amongst social theorists for the past two decades. Even though this interest originates in human geography, art history and archaeology, there is hardly an area of scholarly inquiry in the humanities or social sciences that has not lent its disciplinary expertise to the advancement of the landscape studies field. Additionally, this interest is not restricted to academics. Since it is a heartfelt, vocational and political topic as well, the regard for landscape has become appropriated by a wide range of people or groups in a multitude of socio-cultural spheres.

The geographer Carl Sauer's (1925) work on the morphology of landscapes was one of the founding approaches to an experiential understanding of space. It was conceptual in its ability to capture structural units as well as methodological in its formulation of a temporal framework which embraced the human impact on landscape change and evolution: Sauer's focus on cultural landscapes is as influential on anthropology as it is grounded within it. In terms of spatial phenomenology, such a perspective echoes the idea that space mirrors humanity. In this sense, the landscape is analogous to the interior of our mindscapes in that it completely reveals the ends that have directed human energy. The means to the ends are either rational or irrational but the ends themselves are neither. Instead, they rest on a different discursive plane.

Somewhat contrarily, Merleau-Ponty's view was that our human 'being in the world' equates a bodily being. Subjectivity is a bodily experience. Our behaviour, then, does not mirror the willingness of the mind in which the body mechanically executes the mind's commands. Instead, consciousness is 'a being-towards-the-thing through the intermediary of the body' (1962, 137). Mobility is therefore not the transporting of the body to a point in space where we have created an *a priori* representation. Rather, the meaning of mobility is in the action of movement itself not given to the action by an external agent. In sum, bodily subjectivity implies that meaning does not invariably originate from explicit verbal formulations or from the conscious mind. Meaning should not be reduced to these mediums since it may exist in the doing of an action or in the manifested accomplishment of that action.

Though these views contrast, they equally complement each other in revealing that phenomenology's anthropocentric basis leads to the potential of understanding humans and space as a single system. Human relationships with space are understood not simply as cognitive relationships but as something that permeates our whole being. Similarly, humanity permeates space. The human-environment system is therefore flexible and in flux. It is composed of a multitude of world views that are unified into a synergism or *Gestalt* via common experiences and intentions.

In steering away from Sauer's Berkeley School view that culture is a totality which imprints its message mechanically upon the residents of a cultural area, geography's initial enthusiasm for landscape has shifted towards seeing society as constituted by a plurality of cultures – some dominant, others marginal. This outlook has further shifted away from the search for the meta-significances of locations of power towards considerations of mundane everyday spaces (Lefebvre 1991). David Lowenthal's (1985) considerations of past places, J.B. Jackson's (1984) work on vernacular landscapes as well as the approaches of Donald Meinig (1979) and his colleagues on ordinary landscapes are exemplary in this respect. Such authors have introduced the existential importance of the localised life-world by turning our attention to the spatial detail of habitual geographies.

Along parallel but slightly different lines the contributions by those geographers have been primarily concerned with the state of landscape as a visually symbolic medium. For instance, Denis Cosgrove and Stephen Daniels' (1998) *The Iconography of Landscape* was timely in integrating the strands of visual analysis that had long been implicit in human geography. By examining a variety of methods in the social sciences and humanities, their book foretold an imminent shift in the study of landscape that originated from the inherent instability in the structures of signs and symbolic imagery. Consequently, traditional practices, descriptions and conceptualisations no longer apply, especially since the pace and scale of societal changes are so unlike anything previously encountered.

Trevor Barnes and James Duncan's (1992) *Writing Worlds* and Duncan and Ley's (1993) *Place/Culture/Representation* were also indicative of this spatial turn. The essays in the former volume form a tripartite model for understanding the world that considers cultural environments as texts, discourses or metaphors. By examining the relationship between landscape and metaphor, many of the articles here are pursuing the idea that metaphors are implicated in the geographic fabric of our lives, societies and social processes. The thrust of both contributions is that writing itself is constitutive, reflexive and based on rhetorical processes that are central to conveying spatial meaning. These works challenge human geographers and social theorists to consider the discursive issues of landscape studies by focusing less on visual representations and more on written ones. Inspired by the problematisation of cultural representation in anthropology and sociology, they argue for a deconstructivist landscape project – one that can take into consideration recent advances in post-modern theory and can depict the world in a diversity of fragmented ways.

In combination with certain major philosophical realisations about the ontological importance of space and place, ethnographic accounts have allowed social theorists to explore the existential nature of environments that are culturally lived in, shaped and construed. One of the first significant steps in this direction was an edited volume by Miles Richardson (1984) entitled *Place: Experience and Symbol*. By allowing both social anthropologists and human geographers to examine together the formation of spatial identities, this book proposed some novel evidence for describing the ways in which people form affinities with locations and nurture rooted empathies with places.

Picking up the baton, James Fernandez (1991) undertook a study that made the performative character of spatial metaphor explicit. He proposed that the mission of tropes as signs and symbols is to fill inchoate frames with genuine models of experience so as to radically alter the subject that the trope syntactically extends. While scholars have traditionally seen metaphor as corresponding with the feelings of experience, expressing a sensational similarity to something lived in the inner world of emotion (textual tropes), he suggested that metaphor corresponded more accurately with the shape of actual performance (cultural tropes). This expresses the similarity to something directly encountered in the physical world. Consequently, it is through metaphor that the essential meaning of the experiential endeavour is achieved. Metaphoric knowledges are not owned, always remaining a step beyond our present understanding; maintaining reserves of wisdom *in lieu* of our intellectual advancements.

Subsequent anthropological studies have advanced the realm of landscape research by theorising place in relation to its disputed characteristics as well as its ties with local and global power relations. Consequently, the anthropological concern with place increasingly revolves around issues of topographical contestation, the abuse of social justice and the chronicle of cultural struggle. Human environments are rarely passively internalised. They are negotiated, resisted and appropriated. For example, Barbara Bender has demonstrated on several occasions that landscapes are best recognised as major political sites of contention (Bender 1993; Bender and Winer 2001).

In the compilation *The Anthropology of Landscape*, Eric Hirsch and Michael O'Hanlon (1995) set out to critically acknowledge the traditional conceptualisation of landscape. Their volume serves as a catalyst in understanding analogous cross-cultural perceptions and ideas concerning the human environment by taking as its point of departure the premise that the notion of landscape should be conceived as a cultural process existing between a fore grounded actuality of 'placial' imagery and a back grounded potentiality of spatial representation. In this context, they suggest that the possibilities of anthropology are particularly appropriate in deconstructing Euro-American preconceptions of landscape. This is so because ethnography has resided at the heart of artistic depictions of other places and people. Further, the ethnographic enterprise has been crucial in placing the geographical imagination. It has indeed been formative in generating a social fetishism with the rural, the exotic and the changeless nature of colonial elsewheres. And yet, as opposed to prevailing inert visual methods, this collection demonstrates that anthropology is able to theorise landscape as a cultural process in the understanding of social identities.

Equally concerned with the engendering of the cultural senses of place, Steven Feld and Keith Basso (1996) have considered the concept of place to be either pre- or post-modern since the notions of space and time have overshadowed it so effectively. The various authors in this collection attempt to subvert the exclusive monopoly that these latter notions have held at the expense of place in the rise of modern thought. In his philosophical introduction to their ethnographic anthology, Edward Casey asks if a relational universal of experience can be found in place since it neither exists in space or in time. He concludes that the properties of perceptual experience require cross-cultural and multi-sensorial conceptualisations of place and landscape. Unfortunately, visualism has dominated most of the work on senses of place since it is so deeply rooted in the Euro-American understanding of landscape. Hence, Casey's (1996) treatise follows Chris Tilley (1994) in noting that conceptual concerns with the ways in which embodied agents constitute their landscape and take themselves as connected to place have been sparse. As Setha Low and Denise Lawrence-Zuniga (2003) remind us, place becomes an agent, an embodied surrogate for values, desires, and dreams. Theories that fathom the diverse perspectives from which people embrace and are embraced by their surroundings are now starting to surface with more regularity (Thompson 2008), as are comparative studies of the ways in which people dwell – an interest that we therefore need to broaden so that it captures phenomenological questions of play and adventure seeking.

Kate Flint and Howard Morphy (2000) address the ways in which scholars are beginning to tackle the shortage of detailed descriptions of landscape experiences. In *Culture, Landscape and the Environment,* they point out that recent writings by cultural geographers, historians, ecologists, landscape theorists, political scientists, sociologists and social anthropologists have reinvigorated the fascination with the intricacies of place and landscape. Their broad-ranging perspective reveals the ease with which the problems of culture and environment trespass on conventional disciplinary boundaries. This inter-disciplinarity is evident in the essays of their volume which itself provides a comparative angle on the conception of the environment as a cultural process. Such collaborations inform us that the relationships between culture and the environment centre on the considerations of perception and positionality.

Tim Ingold (2000; 2004) has also recently focused on acts of environmental perception, experience and movement. He argues that perception is not merely a mental process but is instead achieved by the perceiver's whole body in its surroundings. Ingold has thus reintroduced the importance of our tangible surroundings in shaping the ways in which we make our worlds. In an attempt to overcome extreme forms of cultural constructivism, he contests the view that the human organisation of landscape is a process where pre-established cultural blueprints impose a social order on the environment.

Whereas certain forms of cultural determinism imply that the structured world into which we are born predetermines the shape and content of our actions, Ingold is suggesting instead that the environment is continuously being remade according to the tools of perception that we use to examine it. This middle ground in the cultural constructivist debate reveals that the values which environments have are objectifications of values gained through the spatial engagements in social processes. These alter according to one's relationships with place and are therefore not absolutely fixed. Instead they exist in a flux of relationships and movements. It is human beings, through a process of changing experiences and in the context of changing conditions of existence, that reproduce the conditions necessary for livelihood, dwelling and skill.

Skill is of course a central theme in terms of negotiating hazardous landscapes so the present study attempts to integrate some of the insights provided by these various and multi-disciplinary perspectives. I intend to explore the many ways in which both everyday places and epic cultural landscape icons are experienced, appropriated and transformed as well as how they increasingly help formulate adventurous identities, sub-cultures and the social imagination.

A Short Anthropological History of the Hazardous

Anthropologists, especially but not solely in the past, have frequently been seen as a type of adventurer and the history of the discipline has occasionally been characterised in such terms. The 'rescue anthropology' of the turn of the twentieth century, especially via Alfred Haddon's expeditions to the Torres Straits Islands, was to change the discipline through the global export of ethnological field researchers. Alfred Cort Haddon [1855–1940] masterminded the first comprehensive ethnological team research in the English speaking world – the famous Cambridge expedition to Torres Straits and New Guinea (1898–99). His contribution to international research expeditions, in terms of anthropology, consisted in attempting to establish a rigorous how-to process for collecting knowledge about human behaviour. The objective was one of the orders of the day: to be able to salvage cultural information that was been unprecedentedly changed due to the increasing pace and scale of global cultural contact, amongst other factors, the result of colonialism and imperialism.

Given the disciplinary signatures of the era, the tyranny of distance as well as the theoretical pedigree of the arm-chair theorising necessary for making cross-cultural comparison, these field expeditions were undoubtedly adventurous orchestrations.

In a time before the established ethnographic method of immersive participant observation, such initiating phases of rapid-fire fieldwork techniques, developing towards longer-term and repeat field visits, did indeed verge on adventure 'sport'. Perhaps this analogy is being stretched too thinly. Yet in looking back at those early days of anthropological 'mission work', there were undoubtedly elements of the gentry's sporting adventure attached. If nothing else, then at least one could argue that this was so in terms of the institutional backing necessary for the 'collection' of ethnological material.

Bronislaw Malinowski's later contributions to the anthropological oeuvre, pioneering in systematising the collection and analysis of field data, would bring in another dimension still. In slowing the whole process down, it potentially weakens the comparison by making ethnological fieldwork more 'controlled'. Notwithstanding, he had to endure many real hardships and health risks during his extended field research (Young 2004). In anthropology therefore, the process of doing ethnography has institutionalised the practice of adventurous travel to discover something new, for the self and for the discipline. And there still exist elements of valorising field research on the basis of the harshness of experience that one needs to overcome.

It is this historical enigma that is itself cleverly captured in Nigel Barley's (1988) humorously serious book title *Not a Hazardous Sport*. In bringing together issues of travel insurance, trans-globalisation and the nature of field research in 'distant' lands, he has certainly played on some of these aforementioned features in the legacy of the ethnographic method. For his part, A.C. Haddon was equally an unfathomable product of his time. Influenced significantly by many of the other types of adventures in the post-industrial age of revolutionary ideals about progress and science, as well as attempting to come to terms with the engineering feats of people such as Isambard Kingdom Brunel, Haddon also strove to leave a mark. Or rather, to secure the unique marks of culture that, according to the doomsday prophets of the time, were being lost forever. The task that he and his followers set themselves was thus to provide a rapid response for helping to preserve whatever 'pristine' cultural information might still exist in the more remote and foreign parts of the British Empire.

Today, the globalisation of sporting spectacles benefits from a different type of empire, massive financial sponsorship. The huge economic associations that they entail and the grandiose scales at which they operate are difficult to take in. The World Cups of football or rugby, the Ashes, Masters, Opens and Olympic Games are indeed as internationally known, standardised and systematically broadcast as the attention given to major world religions, especially in the increasingly secular societies of the most economically prosperous nations.

When the major national and international sporting competitions get underway, entire populations are glued to the television in support of their home sides. Sport enthusiasts travel for miles, at great expense across borders and continents, to personally witness their sporting heroes in their favourite games. The competitive edge that results from the odds calculated by the bookies dominates discussions in the media while myths are propagated about the moral and physical prowess of the players and their coaches. The popularisation of competitive, mostly team sports such as football, rugby, cricket, hockey, rowing and tennis is historically linked to their adoption in institutional contexts – in educational establishments, in business corporations and for civil defence. Learning institutions forged alliances with sports in Britain through the public school system, so that by the late nineteenth century competitive team sports were included into the ideal of educating for a 'muscular Christianity'. This represented ideal physical and spiritual attributes of manhood for moral and military leadership, part of the training for the leaders of an expansive empire. The spread of sport has therefore had a long relationship with the processes of colonialism.

Because of this association anthropologists have long shown an interest in games, play and sport. Indeed one of the earliest armchair theorists, Edward B. Tylor (1879), provided a brief cross-cultural history of games long before fieldwork was part of the discipline. We then inherited a small but rich body of ethnographic knowledge on sportive activities as embedded in particular social settings. Examples include: Alfred Howitt's (1904) tribal ball games in Australia, Raymond Firth's (1930) work on hallowed types of dart/spear matches in Tikopia, and the representation of Trobriand cricket through ethnographic film portrayed by Gary Kildea and Jerry Leach (1976). In America, Edward Norbeck (1974) was certainly amongst the most celebrated ethnographers to further the significance of studying the gamut of sport practices in their full cultural contexts. In 1974 he led an interdisciplinary group of researchers in the formation of The Anthropological Association for the Study of Play, known as TAASP (Blanchard 1995).

A handful of scholars such as Mauss (1934), Huizinga (1956), Bourdieu (1984; 1990) and Deleuze (1992) additionally produced influential theoretical analyses of sport, games and gambling. Johan Huizinga's reaction to the Marxist ideology that humans were principally defined through their labour as *Homo Faber* was amongst the most exhaustive. It resulted in a theoretical depiction of humanity not as a maker but as a player, defined symbolically and instinctively under the rubric of *Homo Ludens*. There also exists a small anthropological legacy in studying certain types of extreme behaviour, Napoleon Chagnon's (1968) research on Yanomamo feuds and Rodney Needham's work on headhunting (1976), for instance. But the idea of bringing the two together, however, of ethnographically studying the extreme as well as the sporting world, is a fairly new phenomenon (Vivanco and Gordon 2006).

As a co-edited collection mostly aimed at tourism studies scholars, Hudson's (2003) volume *Sport and Adventure Tourism* has been one fairly recent attempt, although it is rather general and the use of the ethnographic method in any of the chapters is minimal. The compilations by Rinehart and Sydnor (2003), Wheaton (2004) and McNamee (2007) are more interesting conceptually but they still present many of the disjointed elements common in edited collections from disparate authors. Their focus on philosophy, media, consumption and identity also means that they differ radically from my ethnographic emphasis on social and physical landscapes. Somewhat more coherent and equally challenging is Ford and Brown's (2005) book *Surfing and Social Theory*. Their case study material focusing solely on one activity, however, does limit the overall contribution that the volume makes to social theory and the cultural construction of landscape perception. It is this wider niche encompassing the physical environment with culture, leisure tourism and risky recreation which the present volume attempts to fill.

One of the most comprehensive anthropological accounts in this regard stems from the work of Sherry Ortner (1999) who has published some fascinating research around the topic of climbing culture in the Himalayas. Hers is not an ethnographic or biographical account of the European expedition members as such. Rather, she has mainly focused on understanding the Sherpa people of the area who have a long history of assisting foreign mountaineers. Yet through the lens of working with this 'ethnic group', the numerous and complex patters of cultural contact in the region – where East and West have existed in an interesting tension for centuries – becomes glaringly significant to her compelling anthropological descriptions. From her detailed and prolonged ethnographic knowledge, a vivid glance into a diversity of climbing identities emerges, which other anthropologists have since been drawn to and elaborated upon with an explicit focus on the climbing cultures of the western world (for example, Abramson and Fletcher 2007; Adams 1996; Frohlick 2003, 2004; Palmer 2004; MacFarlane 2003, 2007).

Given his significant and extended dealings with the Sherpas for over five decades, Sir Edmund Hillary is of course centrally marginal as well as marginally central to her accounts. Born in 1919, Hillary grew up in Auckland, New Zealand. Although initially taking up the family beekeeping business, he became interested in mountain climbing, mostly as the result of abstaining from joining the air force for several years until he eventually succumbed in 1943.

> I was very restless and unhappy and the first few years of the war were the most uncertain and miserable of my life. I was working very hard and had little time to spare for entertainments but I tried to get some small outlet for adventure in the hills and mountains (Hillary 1975, 28).

He trained as a mountaineer in the Southern Alps of New Zealand's South Island, then in the European Alps before finally travelling to the Himalayas, where he climbed 11 of the peaks over 20,000 ft. By that time Hillary felt ready to take on the world's highest mountain. Over a dozen major international expeditions had failed to reach the summit of Mount Everest between 1920 and 1952. In 1924, the famous British mountaineer George Leigh Mallory and a 22-year-old Oxford engineering student Andrew Irvine had perished in their attempt under mysterious circumstances which left their bodies officially lost for 75 years (Firstbrook 1999). Hillary signed up for an Everest reconnaissance survey in 1951 and again in 1952. These exploits brought him to the attention of the leader of an expedition sponsored by the Royal Geographic Society and the Joint Himalayan Committee of the Alpine Club of Great Britain which would make an attempt on Everest in 1953.

Shy of the summit by about 300 feet, Charles Evans and Tom Bourdillon, two members of the team led by John Hunt, reached the South Peak on 26 May. After that, everyone except Hillary and Tenzing Norgay, a Sherpa climber who had been part of five previous Everest missions, were forced to turn back because of exhaustion, high altitude sickness and problems with the closed-circuit oxygen equipment used by some climbers. On 29 May 1953, four days before the coronation of HRH Queen Elizabeth II, Hillary and Norgay were finally successful on this, the ninth British expedition, after 31 years of trying to summit the highest point on earth. The news reached London the day before the coronation, turning the already high-profile accomplishment into a celebration of national identity which reaffirmed the Commonwealth's domination in the realm of adventurous exploits, in a time of post-war struggle for the Dominion.

Hillary then dedicated several years to further adventurous conquests, namely by forming an expedition in 1958 to undertake the first overland crossing of Antarctica to the South Pole since Robert Scott's famous journey in 1912. Combined with his Himalayan conquest, this feat of endurance, bravery, skill and determination amidst the planet's harshest environments, placed him in the company of the most renowned explorers in history, alongside Columbus and Cook, Livingstone and Lindsbergh, Shackleton and Scott (Herzog 2009). He returned to Nepal to help establish the Himalayan Trust in 1960. This Trust is best known for providing hospitals, medical clinics and schools in the region but it has also been involved with many reforestation and environmental protection programmes as well as developing an airstrip. To reach Lukla airport one has to take a short half-hour flight from Kathmandu or a five-day walk from Jiri. At 9,380 ft in elevation (2,860 metres) it is far from the highest in the world but Lukla has the reputation of always being present on the lists of the most dangerous due to its exceptionally short and narrow runway of 1,729 ft in length (527 metres) by 66 ft in width (20 metres). It also has a 12 per cent slope gradient. Since 1973, 38 people have lost their lives in accidents at this airfield which is the last before the base camp for Everest, still a ten-day trek away (Heydon 2005).

Thereafter, Hillary's persona was characterised by its associations with adventure and exploration. Since its inception in 1989, Edmund Hillary has been the life-long Patron of *New Zealand Geographic* magazine (published by Kowhai Publishing Ltd., part of the Rural News Group). Along with this role he was initially listed as being the Chairman of the Scientific Research and Expeditions Advisory Board. This was during the time of the magazine's founding years when it also had an Editorial Advisory Board. This has since been replaced by the current format which comprises an overall editorial services team.

I purchased *Nothing Venture, Nothing Win* (1975), Edmund Hillary's autobiography, the day the world was told he had died of a heart attack on the morning of 11 January 2008. Given this recent passing of such a 'larger than life' figure, nearly a decade after the publication of Ortner's Sherpa monograph, it is worth mentioning a few things about the global mourning of Sir Edmund Percival Hillary, if for no other reason than to position the current volume. Responses to the news from many international figureheads and political leaders have focused on the imaginative and physical exploits that Hillary achieved which in turn encouraged the strivings of others. Unusually, yet unsurprisingly for New Zealand's most famous person, he was honoured with a State funeral in Auckland on Tuesday 22 January. Later in the year, on 8 April, a special 'Knights of the Garter services of thanksgiving' was held at St George's Chapel Windsor, hosted by HRH Queen Elizabeth II and other members of the royal family. The service was attended by many distinguished guests such as fellow discoverer Sir David Attenborough and the New Zealand Prime Minister, Helen Clark. On the date of this ceremony, British PM Gordon Brown praised 'a truly great hero that captured the imagination of the world, a towering figure who will always be remembered as a pioneer explorer and leader'. Similarly, Australia's acting PM Julia Gillard said of Hillary that he was 'one of New Zealand's giants. [His] name is synonymous with adventure, with achievement, with dreaming and then making those dreams come true'.

The national New Zealand psyche was certainly affected considerably. Hillary was on the cover of all the newspapers in the country with a special eight-page pullout section of the *Weekend Herald*. The aforementioned magazine *New Zealand Geographic* put out a 'Hillary commemorative issue' in March/April 2008 which contains two pieces by Vaughan Yarwood as well as a photo requiem by Arno Gasteiger. Initially there was considerable talk in the media that he would be removed from the five dollar note because historically he had been the only living person to appear on a banknote (except the Queen). Such speculation also suggested that he would be placed onto a different banknote. These turned out to be unfounded rumours which were eventually dismissed officially by the New Zealand treasury.

In 2010, one of the world's most experienced high altitude mountaineers, Apa Sherpa (aged 50), was scheduled to make his twentieth ascent of Everest to scatter some of Hillary's ashes on the summit. The act was meant to be in honour of his immense contribution to Nepal's eastern Himalayan communities. But Ang Tenzing Sherpa, chief of the Sherpa citizens' group 'Khumbu Civil Society' said that scattering the ashes on the mountain, considered as a deity by the Sherpa people, would go against their culture and tradition. The ashes will thus remain in a monastery in the area and shall be kept at a memorial during the 2011 golden jubilee of the first school Hillary opened in Khumjung.

Conclusions

Contemporary adventurous practices, as we currently understand them, can claim an identifiable origin as a by-product of the earliest instigations of modernity, that is, with the onset of colonialism and imperial exploration. These processes implied going beyond the limits of the empirically known, mapping the spatial co-ordinates of human existence on all planes. Exploration implied the encompassment of the larger cosmic envelope in which the much smaller empires of peoples and territories would be politically and religiously contained. Through its connection with the pride of national conquest and the celebration of the individual hero, mountaineering lays claim to being most comprehensively the first and foremost of adventurous pursuits even though the off-shore navigational expeditions of two centuries previous were just as perilous. The historical subjects of certain anthropological studies have become ever more mythologised and de-mythologised in terms of discovery, adventurous spirit, and so forth.

During those early origins, dangerous activities and hazardous games were rather marginal in western society. But they have spread noticeably in the past few decades and much of the ethos of present-day extreme practices is to act as a resistance to, and even subversion of, this class-based historical pedigree (McNamee 2007). Rather than being eccentric, activities like cave diving, kite boarding, big wave surfing and *parkour* free-running have become significant contributors to popular culture in a relatively short period of time. They have also become appropriated by many psychological, moral and political discourses so that the extreme is increasingly taken up by all sorts of social institutions – many of which are antithetical. Herein lies one facet of the paradoxical nature that dangerous places and hazardous event activities cannot truly escape.

The adventure therefore offers a particular kind of freedom. Its recklessness and abandon produces an internal feeling of enjoyment, achievement, conquest even. It is often justified as a means of retaining control over one's life, or put differently, of being in charge of one's destiny. In Simmel's terms the adventure has significance precisely as a form of experiencing. But there is certainly a downside to his discourse which he articulates in terms of the external factors that exist between morality, risk and society. That is, since the adventurer functions with a disregard for the ordinary apprehension of causes and effects, he or she must do so unselfishly, otherwise his or her actions are unethical: 'Only a romantic excitation' ([1911] 1997, 221).

The question then arises as to how and why increasing fractions of the population are tending to become intimately connected to the environment by way of potentially lethal games rather than ideologically or not at all. To tackle this question means turning to the recreational facets of extreme games and to the contemporary capability of risk-laden activities to recreate transcendent agency within microcosms of direct control.

Now even though it is clear that landscape and recreation have always mutually attracted and tended to merge, what is less obvious is why, at the beginning of the twentieth century, their transforming trajectories should converge to promote potentially lethal play amongst much larger swathes of the global population than was previously the case. So what has to be explained is not extreme human practice or behaviour *per se* but the tendency for what was once an eccentric and marginal sub-culture to grow outwards, permeate institutions, and ethically suffuse society. Thus newly emergent sub-cultures incorporate new extreme games that supply more life to style and more capital to symbolically invest. Consequently, more individuals jump, dive, climb, fall, and hurtle to meaningfully sub-cultural effect. As the plethora of magazines, companies, websites, competitions, extreme TV channels and advertising become increasing noticeable, dangerous games assert their distinction from other sports even more overtly (Rinehart and Sydnor 2003).

Yet contemporary approaches to modern risk are still in the habit of presenting hazardous activity as a major barrier to the realisation of human potential. Some anthropologists such as Williams et al. (1992) have looked at the safety of ethnographers and informants in dangerous places or aggressive fieldwork situations. Unfortunately, however, they have only considered risk mitigation strategies, especially in potentially violent scenarios. It is as if violence was the only companion to risk taking. At no point do they address the issue that ethnographers might intentionally enter the study of physical or emotional risk in itself – that their research setting might deliberately involve a participation in hazardous situations – as opposed to it resulting as a by-product of studying street crime for example. Against this background, the positive exploration of risk has itself expanded and intensified, notably in the area of dangerous games and alternative sports but also in the fiscal areas of venture capitalism or investment banking. Thus, in extreme games, survival programmes and charity events, the practice of stretching the mind and body to the limits, of flirting with danger, have established the basis for a sort of vernacular, ordinary person's mundane heroism. Indeed, much research on such cultural practices now incorporates the phenomenon of adventure sport into a framework of 'risk positive'.

Risk perception research is indeed a vast field. It is not my intention to review that literature or provide any comprehensive summations of it here. The range of anthropological and sociological perspectives on the topic has reached far and wide, particularly since the 1970s, when the repercussions of certain international crises were being examined and theorised at large macro-scales (Douglas and Wildavsky 1982; Beck 1992; Furedi 1997; Caplan 2000). Rather, the idea is to deal instead with the issue of perception from a particular stance, one which posits that the phenomenon of perception encompasses not only a material dimension, but its own material imagination as it exists in an interaction of body, environment and the world of experience.

The proliferation of extreme games now in existence, compared to the late eighteenth century when mountaineering came into being with the ascent of Mont Blanc, is a notable historical oddity. As adventurous play has socially democratised to incorporate ordinary persons, so it has culturally moralised and become institutionally generalised. This process has occurred in outdoor training courses, charity practices, reality TV, motivational talk, green political protest, adverts and sponsorship, social rehabilitation, community health, education and personal development, adventure holidays and the efforts of the disabled or terminally ill to alter the perception of biological human limits. In these domains, hazardous

**Figure 1.2   Sand dune surfing, 90 mile beach, Northland New Zealand
(photo by K. Kary)**

play is taken up and symbolically elaborated in the shape of moral example, an exemplary heroism of a vernacular kind for a new age.

Indeed, social life in the contemporary western world is increasingly adumbrated as an adventurous arena. This is because, as Beck (1992) and Furedi (1997) have astutely pointed out, given the enormous scale and unpredictability of both global technology and political intervention, and given the post-modern seepage of epistemological authority out of the sphere of discourse, uncertainty about the world and its political changeability have significantly intensified. In response, the masses and fractions of the elite have disengaged from the historical mechanism of the State, ensuring that history once made by populations to control the future has now been replaced by history that mainly happens to them within the confines of the present and its immediate aftermath. Consequently, in the modern West, the figure of the transcendental and unified 'subject of history' is dead. The goal of transcendence has passed from a politically representative society to individuals acting directly.

Crucially, however, even though contemporary western populations have lost faith in the State's power to free, redeem or progress them forward, the idea of exerting historical agency *per se* in the world remains critical to their modern western mind set. Consequently, two strategic re-orientations to the demise of this total historicity have gradually formed. One of these strategies breaks away from the illusory self-containment of the totality, broadening the causal nexus of human destiny by embracing the riskier macrocosm. This shifts the centre of gravity of existence from the political field of the State to the wider governance and complex determinacy of the ecosystem. By contrast, a second, exactly opposite strategy shrinks rather than broadens the causal nexus of human destiny, recomposing an ideally totalised nexus at the level of personal lives. To this end, and across the vast decentralised political expanse of the personal, agency re-materialises in the ideal control of microcosmic spaces and temporalities, a domain in which, in the contemporary west at least, the civil subject is undoubtedly hegemonic.

In which case too, this analysis is left with the obvious paradox of how deep and dangerous play can simultaneously belong to the broadening of human destiny quested through the ecosystem and to the very shrinking of existence surrounding the body. For, it is precisely at the intersection of these two strategic trajectories that adventurous games begin to mutate from eccentric practice to social ethic – from mere pastimes to playful embodiments of a changing life-world.

Chapter 2
An Auto-Ethnography of Adventurous Innovation

We want, as much as this fire burns our minds,
to plunge into the depths of the abyss, Hell or Heaven,
what does it matter? into the depths
of the Unknown to find something novel!

(Charles Baudelaire, 1857, 160).

Innovation, a notion highly associated with the imagination, is also a theme that connects well with such things as adventure, discovery and a certain degree of risk taking. For John Stuart Mill, 'The father of English innovation, both in doctrine and institution, is Bentham: he is the great *subversive*, or, in the language of continental philosophers, the great *critical* thinker of his age and country' [emphasis in original] (1950, 4).

It is to a continental philosopher that innovation theorists often turn in terms of outlining an historical purview on the themes of originality and creativity. In grouping together memory, invention and imagination, the Napolitano philosopher Giambattista Vico wanted to reveal how reason and the development of logical arguments were inherently humanistic and poetic acts. Vico's position was radically different to Descartes' Cartesian method of arriving at truth through observation. Deduction and verification were fine for physics but Vico did not trust that they applied much to the world of politics or civic discourse. Instead he felt that truth was arrived at through making, the physical acts of fabrication and creation. He defined *ingenium*, the gift of invention, a type of wit, as 'the faculty that connects disparate and diverse things' ([1708] 1988, 96). Bringing something into being which had not previously existed was to enact a kind of myth-making, either through the lyricism of rhetorical linguistic expression or in the creative moulding of material form. From the Vichian perspective then, this type of practical wisdom is the reification or materialisation of abstract ideas *par excellence*.

Interpreted more recently by Paul Carter (2004), these ideas take hold in what he has evocatively called 'material thinking', a process that exists through teasing out a new form from matter. So after the rationally minded Cartesian subject we have the creatively minded making subject, a form which closely approximates Michael Polanyi's (1966) concerns with tacit knowledge. All three perspectives share the basic premise that the body and the unconscious working together are fundamental to exploratory acts and discovery because the tacit is the seat of informed guesses, intuition and imaginings. Implicit to these dimensions of evocation is the desire for change and cultural evolution through the incessant search for novelty:

> Apparently the encounter with the new has been tied up in our imaginations with the prospect of social, culture, and personal renewal. Indeed, one of the important meanings of the word [experience] refers, in shorthand, to conversion, to being saved. This obsession with novelty, accompanied by a fear of boredom, is deeply implicated in the almost compulsive need to move on (Abrahams 1986, 50–51).

Through the narrative style of thick description now characteristic of social anthropology, the reader should note that I have remained deliberately un-analytical in the tone of my writing in this chapter. As mentioned previously, this is in order to facilitate a slant of ethnographic writing which is heavily autobiographical in examining a few incidents which surround two principal innovators of the post-modern era in the realm of sport and adventure. Despite their respective success in turning bungy jumping into an internationally recognised phenomenon, it is interesting to juxtapose these two main protagonists with each other because they appear so fundamentally different in terms of background, attitude and personality. Indeed, we could almost see them as epitomising the Freudian polarisation of totem and taboo.

Taking the Bungy by the Gorge

One of Britain's most famous artistic emblems of industrial innovation, *Rain, Steam and Speed – the Great Western Railway* (1844), exalts the domination of British imperial power, with J.M.W. Turner envisaging London as the hub of a powerful international communications network. Hurtling towards the spectator, the Great Western train symbolises the splendour of Britain's technological achievements. This new line, easily the longest and most ambitious in the world at the time, stretched across southern England from London to Exeter and had been continued on from Bristol. It was designed by the industrial revolution's iconic architect and engineer, Isambard Kingdom Brunel [1806–1859], whose revolutionary steamboat *Great Western* further extended the reach of the route that began with the railway and spanned across the Atlantic to New York. Gliding along an indistinct streamlined track suspended over the River Thames, Turner's train seems almost to be furrowing through water as if directly linking the eastern and western seaboards of Great Britain. The railway was of course only possible because of a series of sophisticated tunnels and bridges with which he was also involved.

One such structure, the Clifton Suspension Bridge, has a complex past. It was the first major commission for Brunel, at the young age of 24. The foundations were laid in 1831 and it was characteristic of the period as well as his personality that Brunel sought to match the grandeur of the setting with an extravagantly noble design. The principal spanning towers were originally to have had sphinxes and hieroglyphic decorations, inspired by the gateways of an Egyptian temple. A more simplified version of the support pylons was finished in 1843. Like many of his projects, there were financial and material restrictions to the initial designs. Had he not secured other commissions to prove himself, the project might never have been realised at all under his instructions and would have tarnished the promising career that lay ahead. Even then it took until 1864 for the much anticipated passway over the River Avon to be finally complete and posthumously opened (Brindle 2006). But it was the audacity of those early ambitions which turned what was effectively a failure into an English landmark. It has been a Grade I listed structure for over 150 years. The span is 214 m (702 ft) and it appears even more daring as it hovers 75 m (245 ft) above the Avon gorge.

These oddities have been imbued into the memory of the West Country, the identity of the cultural landscape and the psyche of the nation. One remarkable example is that historically, the Clifton Suspension Bridge (CSB) leads directly to the western origins of 'modern' bungy jumping through the Dangerous Sports Club (DSC). On April Fool's Day 1979, without any preliminary trials except for a ten-foot crash from a fire escape, Brunel's bridge became the first test site for a novel innovation. Commenting on the earth dive rituals in Pentecost Island which became known in Britain in the 1950s through one of David Attenborough's BBC documentaries, David Kirke has said the following: 'It was they who gave us the inspiration for what you might call urban vine jumping. Just adapting other people's ideas for one's own situation' (Kirke quoted in Morgan 1981).

Allegedly by happenstance, the bridge was selected since it was near Bristol where Chris Baker, an aficionado of fast bikes, cars and skiing, was staying. Chris was one of the three original founding members of the DSC. The other two key players at the foreground of the DSC's establishment were David Kirke and Edward Hulton. Previously mates as practical jokers in their student years at Oxford, they were involved in devising new and safer developments in hang-gliding with Chris Baker in Switzerland, after crashing machines based on nineteenth-century prototypes. In the accelerated process of getting to know each other in the Alps, this trio of adventurous characters came up with the ingenious plan of reifying the essence of their mutual interests into a more coherent organisation. They did so by the means of formalising their vision into a set of guiding principles – an ethos which would manifest itself as an informal institution. In David Kirke's words:

> I don't know how to translate this but we just did what we thought was natural as amateur sportsmen with a sense of curiosity. This was in deep dislike of the formality of the type typified by training certificates such as doing lengths of swimming baths underwater for a diploma in diving when resorts in the Virgin Islands let you dive after a morning's instruction – the whole ethos was fast informality and bypassing 'officiality' in any form. There was a direct reaction to the traditional discipline of schools like Eton and Wellington College.

The quasi-permeable material and social setting that resulted could put some tangible form around a humorous, subversive philosophy. Martin Lyster, one of the club members throughout the 1980s, has since described this union at length. As he states:

> Recognising the importance of imagination in adventure, they decided to start a Dangerous Sports Club. The Club would be dedicated to creating new sports – or at least, taking a new approach to existing ones. They had no idea, at that time, whether they would succeed in being innovators, but they had at least made the vital commitment to try (Lyster 1997, 17).

DSC had had an inaugural party some nine months earlier. In keeping with the spirit of initial intent – risk, exclusivity and dogged dedication – a cocktail party on an isolated and uninhabited granite outcrop some 200 miles from UK shores was deemed as the best place to hold a gathering as far away from London as possible while still in the UK. This 'christening' event took place in the North Atlantic, on a stony protrusion of Helen's Reef known as Rockall. This islet of 'disputed' ownership claims is 187 miles (162 nautical miles) or 301 km due west of the isles of St Kilda, Outer Hebrides. Again, as with the CSB, this site and its associated 'dangers' were a significant part of the rationale for the choice. It lent itself well to the Club's needs.

Within a decade of the 'summer of love' and within sonar distance of the off-shore pirate radio of that era, the year of 1978 would help lay the groundwork for the beginnings of another counter-cultural movement, this time in the early guises of a certain type of adventure sport which would eventually become branded in many ways. Between this inauguration and the growing 'fame' that resulted from the Clifton bungy event and their Golden Gate Bridge jump in San Francisco the following year in 1980, the Club tested the waters of their experimental 'follies' with hang-gliders and microlights. In an attempt to mock the colonial legacy of their own culture, they chose to 'appropriate' such internationally recognised landmarks as Mt Olympus and later Mt Kilimanjaro as the platforms for test flights into the unknown. During their first three years, DSC held 14 expeditions in 13 countries.

The aim here is not to provide an exhaustive survey of the DSC's past accomplishments since many others have and will continue to do so. Lyster's book and the documentary directed by Vivian Morgan are good starting points for those interested in pursuing this line of investigation. But what is interesting to the outsider is how these two sources in particular are somewhat contrary with each other in their tone and recollection of certain events.

For example, Lyster cynically refers to the organisation that David Kirke put into having Julian Grant film the Clifton jumps. Much footage had been taken at a famous Kilimanjaro hang-gliding expedition that took place in January 1979 and he argues that the planned Clifton event was a ruse to solidify the backbone for a proper documentary with possible commercial viability (1997, 32). Kirke could only obtain the many permits needed from the Tanzanian Government to film the Kilimanjaro hang-glider flights by having a film crew which he finally arranged with the financial support of the BBC. Failure by the initial film maker who was disliked by the Club (who did not enjoy being filmed) resulted in much debt and no independent documentary. This led them to try out the long-standing idea of bungy jumping to add material for a proper documentary. This led to a long struggle to obtain film rights and market the DSC film.

Lyster's historical account is unquestionably an informative and interesting read for those who are into that sort of thing. It is for these very reasons that it is worth engaging with it critically, both because of the flaws (and occasional factual errors) as well as because of the personal inside honesty that he has had the privilege, courage and occasional audacity to at least try to cover and report. In that sense, it is commendably good as untrained auto-ethnography and 'biography'. Whether he is correct in any complicit comparison with Churchill, however, by insinuating that history will be kind to him because he has written it, is open to debate. In many capacities, his BASE jumping actions speak volumes, whereas his book is in a lower key. Many of the comments about human 'universals' are rather easy, arguably banal and would at least need some form of substantiation to make it historically or academically credible. Yet paradoxically such tangents would then break up the type of story he is attempting to tell. My point, however, is simply that despite some interesting observations, context and comparisons, Lyster's book is far from being a social history of the DSC.

For a start, his text is caught in a dualistic trap of mostly considering the acts of jump or flight innovation as if they were opposites of each other and as if they existed in some form of cultural vacuum. In its sensationalistic tone, his narrative avoids mentioning similar exploits, except the non-western vine jumping of the Pentecost Islands which in a sense he is right in attempting to demystify by claiming that it is probably not as ancient as one might think (pp. 31,40). But besides (or leaving aside for the moment) the critique of being naive about the secrecy surrounding ritual knowledge, no reference is made to Philippe Petit who used a different series of 'rope' innovations to walk between the towers of the World Trade Center in 1974, only five years previous to the Clifton jumps. Furthermore, not that there needs to be in his type of book, but hardly any analysis (except for economic) is given for the reasons why the media and public imagination picked up so much on this type of event.

As one would expect from someone so much on the inside for so long, there are of course some internally referenced arguments put forth about the Club's contributions as well as those of certain individuals, which have unquestionably been vast. But despite the witty nonchalance about the distorted memories of Club members, Lyster's text has its own rather narrow-minded tunnel-vision approach to the limited historical events that he has chosen to recount. To be critically minded as a participant on the inside is certainly difficult. But to the student of cultural behaviour at least, it should not be difficult to sympathise with the idea that, if nothing else, critical analysis also requires an ability to be critical of those dismissive tones which downplay the significance of the non-internal or peripheral social structures that supported the DSC through the years.

Lyster does note the trademark features of class comically, even flippantly, when commenting on the stockbroker suicide parody attire of the four first Clifton bungy jumpers. 'No doubt Isambard Kingdom Brunel, himself a top-hat wearer, would have approved' (p. 35). Upon reflexion though, the less funny sides of the Clifton's uses shall be covered in my discussion of the politics of jumping section, in the last chapter of this volume.

Yet despite some inter-textual contradiction, it would be from much of Lyster's own evidence that one could argue just how few of the Club's decisions were haphazard in the early days. Their flirtations with danger and the selection of sites as well as the theatrical means for gaining notoriety were often quite explicitly calculated. Not everything was a chaos left to chance which the members heroically conquered individually. Not that much anyway. Instead, a lot of planning, experimentation and thought went into their daring feats. From his account we do get many examples which insinuate that a tension for invention had always existed beyond individual personalities and the internal rivalries within the Club. So regardless of the particular agenda that he might have had in writing down his observations and experiences, the book is valuable as a primary source of material, if an interpretative one at that. For instance, he points out that after the CSB jumps had caught the public eye, even the supportive architecture started to solicit jumping attention. 'The success of the world's first bungee jumps proved the concept of using elastic ropes in this way, and it became obvious that structures all over the world were just begging to be jumped' (1997, 35).

For me, these are the real ethnographic gems. As well, of course, as what remains unsaid, unwritten or what is simply hinted at. All this deserves unpacking here. For example, in making such comments he goes beyond the Cartesian dualism at the root of a logical argument. Effectively, these are interesting references to the agency of the sites for the events. Sure we can revert to many of the other biological explanations put forward, or to the economic determinism implied in talking about the Club's 'ultimate' commercial failure. But the contradiction is glaring since he admits early on that commercial success was never the intent for the founding members, even though it always was a necessity sought through more furtive means. In David Kirke's words:

> It was hard enough for me to find money for our first events as it was and to live without a job that would never have allowed the time in the day to organise and the time off to travel. In this respect my major achievement was probably keeping body and soul together.

Nevertheless, in returning to Lyster's overall chaos theory, that outsiders perceived the Club to be in disarray and largely opportunistic in its choices, one can easily draw some connections together. The fact that CSB has had such a significant legacy in an area near the DSC's Oxford/London home patch, while also being the highest in England, certainly justifies why there could have been few other choices. They equally chose the bridge because it was run by a Trust which had refused them permission. The bridge's accessible locality also meant that once the preparations were set, the exploit could be captured, recorded and thus magnified in the public eye, whether it was successful or not. Moreover, we must not forget the Club's rationale for engineering innovation which was mirrored in Brunel's own historical circumstances, as an internationally renowned creator with a certain class-privileged background. All this fits the DSC's profile, its overall habitus, if you will, to a T.

And so, as with the Clifton Suspension Bridge, there was a process of exchange between topography, cultural artefact and the organisation's collective consciousness. Rockall, Mt Olympus, Mt Kilimanjaro, the Golden Gate Bridge, the Royal Gorge Bridge in Colorado and so on – all these sites in and of themselves could naturally as well as culturally fit into a dialectical process for the elimination of other options which were less appropriate for the task at hand. One could thus argue that it was the legacy, the heritage factor of the material essences of each structure in their own surroundings, which helped spark innovative minds. Much of this must have been intuitive, and has largely been chronicled as if it was. But the argument here is to suggest that intuition does not just exist in the mind. Rather, as this case demonstrates quite nicely, social and material structures come into play so that the Club's intuitive decisions resonated with a series of highly educated guesses that shared a collective premise, an underbidding ethos for providing something on a par with the levels of past innovation. In other words, imaginative feats which would be made noteworthy to the world in a tangibly memorable way.

Bridge to the Final Outpost (Meeting DK for the first time in Oxford)

In his book, Lyster (1997) goes on to chronicle his version of the DSC's history via interviews and personal accounts from his own later membership, participation and significant contributions to the Club. To an extent the publication was facilitated by certain other members who gave interviews but it is not one which has been sanctioned by David Kirke (DK hereafter) who says:

> It was my painful introduction to what has been called 'the Judas syndrome', whereby the right-hand man betrays because he thinks he can do better. The classic case of a falling out in this field is between Messner and Habeler [the first to climb Everest without oxygen].

Although good friends for many years, the two of them no longer seem to see eye to eye on a number of matters. At least that has been my understanding. I approached DK by email in 2004 as part of my increasing interest in turning my Cornish surfing and cliff jumping material into a larger research project. We had a few exchanges but most of my fieldwork time in those days was divided between London and Cornwall. Besides, I did not want to bother him with half-baked ideas having little ethnographic understanding of the types of activities he was himself an expert on. One of these early emails indicated that I had just bought Lyster's book and would like to contact him too if possible. Did he have a contact number or email? DK replied with some reluctance, saying that Lyster was often difficult to get hold of because of living on a barge with the family. He would sometimes move along the canals when the weather was good. Besides, DK added, one shouldn't base too much of their impressions of the Club on that book since 'it's littered with errors ... over 421 at last count'.

The tension between these two characters, also sometimes apparent from (or should one say coded into) Lyster's text, was intriguing. Finally, a chance to meet presented itself in the autumn of 2005 during the Centenary Conference of Anthropology at Oxford and the 9th RAI International Festival of Ethnographic Film. I had planned to travel back and forth on the Oxford Tube between the Institute of Cultural Anthropology and West London for a few days. Using this university event as a pretext, I mentioned that I'd be in his patch on several occasions so asked when and where would suit for a talk. He arranged to meet at the Far from the Madding Crowd. The literary reference was most apt in drawing together the themes of philosophy, humour and the need to escape from madness by addressing it straight on. Fortunately, the pub lived up to its name. For one, I was able to escape the intricate power plays that take place at such conferences but more importantly, at midday during the week, there weren't too many people for lunch so we could talk without distraction.

DK had brought a bag with some DSC paraphernalia to show me. We spoke and drank for at least a couple of hours. Since the kitchen was about to close until dinner, we decided to order some lunch. During our conversation he indicated that he'd spoken to someone I might like to meet, a chap from St Antony's College who was doing a doctorate in sociology and was trying to include some of DK's archives and contacts into his thesis on social networks. He then called this person up and asked him to join us. This friend had even interviewed DK in the past and they eventually provided me with the rough draft of the transcript which they were editing. They also spoke of an idea of setting up an eBay bidding auction for old bits of kit and various DSC accoutrements to raise money for future club events and ideas.

DK had a small camera so we took a few photographs of this meeting, as he often did, 'for the DSC scrapbook'. On that occasion I chose not to take any myself although I had brought my camera, just in case it seemed appropriate. Happily disarmed by their initiative to get a visual record, it felt best not to overindulge this first face to face encounter, especially since my chosen point of entry had been under the 'pretences' of participating in a visual anthropology forum. We had discussed the significance of Attenborough's BBC footage of vine jumping in the 1950s so my ethnographic sixth sense had clocked on that they knew a good deal about the vitality of visual history, not to mention the many moral/ethical issues surrounding the evidence trail of image archives. At this meeting, DK stressed the artistic side of the Club, saying he often wished he had gone to art school. Many have placed him in the forefront of conceptual art.

We then met again for dinner at DK's place two days later. He cooked the food and despite my hangover from our previous meeting (as well as the conference socialising), I brought the wine. He mentioned that his friend might show up later but he never did. After hosting me, he showed me some interesting reference books and some photos as well as the other DSC paraphernalia that they had mentioned might be destined for eBay.

Our contact increased from then on. During 2005, the chance to go caving in the Bath area with another DSC connection presented itself. Possessing most of the required gear (helmet, gloves, wetsuit) I would borrow an attachable head torch from Allen Abramson. Wellies were a problem but I'd resigned to making do with some old trainers. The person organising the day out suggested he could collect me from Bath, Castle Cary or Warminster. After a day's preparations, only hours before it was time to leave, I texted him to cancel. With too many other things to do and not having a car, the travel time to this fairly isolated area in the Mendips was more complicated than I had bargained for.

It seemed I was destined to navigate around many other DSC members. Indeed, another more obvious test of my commitment, which again I failed, was to cycle over to East London to attend a little reunion with DK and a few other DSC members in an Italian restaurant. The invitation was spontaneous, my other work obligations pressing, and the invasion into a jovial gathering of what seemed like a well underway party was at a level of camaraderie which didn't seem to warrant an unprepared ethnographic presence. In hindsight, this would have been an opportune moment for better inclusion. Yet regardless, I was still gradually allowed by more virtual means to infiltrate this community. For instance, DK and some of his other contacts were occasionally copying me in on certain lists of private and 'open' email conversations. DK explains it thus: 'it is important to realise that the DSC, unlike other clubs, does not have a waiting list and expensive subscriptions but reverses standard procedure by welcoming everybody then seeing how they do. People leave of their own accord'.

Another noteworthy meeting with him took place in the autumn of 2006. This one was much closer to the madding crowd, in a busy Soho pub on a Friday evening just after work. He had a small travel bag by his side, one of the ones which go most everywhere he does, being a man who is rarely without an assortment of publications, photos, spare spectacles, a hip flask and so forth. From it he removed a German magazine with Justin Timberlake on the cover. Inside was a recent publication about him and the Club in *Galore: Das Interview – Magazin*. I texted someone to order a copy, suggesting as I did that I knew the perfect person to translate it for us. He seemed pleased.

It appears in English below, courtesy of the translator, with DK's permission. (The German publisher no longer exists.) It is not a direct 'translation', however. Rather, it has been slightly abridged and edited to smooth over the chronology of certain contested events as well as to remove repetition from previous material in this book (for example, the preface, for a start, but also other similar instances when I have included his own voice and directly quoted him).

Box Insert 2.1 Interview with David Kirke

GALORE / (2006)
(Translated by Kerstin Kary)
True sportsmanship wears morning dress and top hat
By Oliver Uschmann
If one sees young men in the fashion of trendy American clothes jumping cliffs or arduous slopes accompanied by hip-hop or rock music on MTV, one forgets quickly that today's craze for extreme sports came from style-conscious Britons with top hats and tailcoats. For David Kirke, Chris Baker and Ed Hulton, it was about cooperation, about conscious frontier-crossing and the true spirit of sport when they launched their club in the 70s.

'Sportsmanship in the world at large… ', as one can still read on their website homepage (www.btinternet.com/~dafyddk/dsc.htm) '…with its close community and inordinate shrewdness went down the drain as money transformed sport into industry.'

The club pulls this modern and alienated theatre, which came from the classic Victorian sports, to pieces. 'Tennis courts', it says, 'were not invented for people who serve at 140 km/h while inflicting the grunts of a Roman amphitheatre on an overweight audience'.

Today the loose network of Dangerous Sports Club members, operating worldwide, regard their own model of sport not only as events free of competition but also as humorous art. Thus their spectacular ski runs with home-made vehicles were screened around the world and even sweetened the day of the inhabitants of an African village with only one TV. 'For the first time in their lives those people saw snow and a piano and instinctively burst out laughing', remembers David Kirke. The Club, which combines extravagant sport with the spirit of happenings, even came to know an homage in the US series *Gilmore Girls*: here, Logan Huntzberger, the son of a millionaire belongs to a secret student association which meets regularly to indulge in dangerous and illegal pleasures while dressed in top hats and tailcoats.

The David Kirke Interview: Francesca D'Amicis / photos: Martin Steffen
David Anthony Christopher Kirke was born on 26 September 1945 on an airbase in Shropshire. Being the son of a schoolmaster and alpinist (father) and a concert pianist (mother), he spent his British upper-class boyhood with many winters and summers in France and Switzerland. While studying at Corpus Christi College, Oxford (Psychology and Philosophy, then English Literature), he got to know a like-minded student with whom he established the Dangerous Sports Club at the end of the 1970s. The group dedicated themselves to making extreme sports, as leisure activities, socially acceptable. The 60-year-old head of the DSC lives (alone) in Oxford where he thinks, writes and works on creating new bizarre sports events.

13/05/2006, Oxford. 'Welcome to the house of the eternal student!' The founder of the Dangerous Sports Club welcomes us into his flat on the outskirts of Oxford. Books, photos, letters and technical drawings scupper any seating possibilities. For this reason the real interview is held in Mr Kirke's favourite pub – with screaming peacocks and Chilean red wine.

Mr Kirke. The Dangerous Sports Club is committed to sport events of a special kind: the members ride down ski slopes on a concert piano or in complete eight rowboat formations, skate race with bulls in Pamplona or try to jump over in a car the span of the Tower Bridge as it opens. How did this scurrilous club come to life?

David Kirke: [laughing] Actually, the club was perhaps a formalisation of behaviour which existed for Oxford students for quite some time.

How can one imagine that?

Edward Hulton, for example, who was a co-founder of the Dangerous Sports Club, is an eccentric human. At that time he was a promising student in Oxford. He arrived at Christchurch College with a better portrait of Henry the Eighth, the founder of the College, than the one they had. But he was already bored to death in the second term. He was looking for a new distraction – and didn't come back until halfway through the next term, after leaving the picture in his room. A panic search and no threat of expulsion found him playing football against a few French policemen in the Sahara. My sort of chap. Another friend tried with me to pinch the statue of Mercury, a god of travel, in the central pond in the main quadrangle at Christchurch College. This idea was not exceptionally original; we later discovered Oxford students had tried the same for over a hundred years – with the result that the statue was welded down at some point. Then we tried a flying machine based on 1903 plans in the Bodleian Library, which unfortunately crashed from 70ft. One day when feeling bored we went to St Moritz, to see what attracted people to fast sports like the Cresta and Bobsleigh courses. It was OK but they had all been invented and developed by the British in the nineteenth century. There was room for new approaches that would be interesting. With the Cresta skeleton bob runs, there seemed to be too many rich people just trying to impress their mistresses with something that had become formalised.

So you created a new sport again?

You must know in the end most sports were invented by the English – and if a sport is accomplished for a start and is taken seriously, every amateur Englishman has a moral duty to think of a new one. In 1976 we set off to Klosters near Davos to visit our friend Chris Baker. Chris was sent down from Eton College because in his own words he stole everything that was not nailed down and experimented with hang-gliders at that time. Besides, he had set up one of the first shops for skateboards which was not as popular then as today. After our first expedition together he did a handstand on the board while dashing down the main road in Klosters and the writer Irwin Shaw gave us a party.

How did you come up with the quite unspecific but spectacular name *Dangerous Sports Club*?

As you would expect, it was partly meant ironically, or tongue in cheek, as the saying goes. Within the best of English tradition, we designed a necktie for our members: It depicted a silver wheelchair with a blood red seat on a black background. An Irish witch told us it would bring us good luck and every disabled person we've talked to tell us they like it.

The so-called surreal skiing developed to a speciality in the upcoming years.

We started this in 1983. It was about whizzing down a ski slope with the last sort of vehicle you would expect to see on a ski slope. Surreal juxtapositions. Everybody had a different idea. We tried it with an ironing board, a bathtub, four-poster-bed and a whole lot of other machines including a London double-decker bus and a Venetian gondola. Trouble was that some members behaved like rock stars but we never sold anything so bills came in for swinging on chandeliers and so forth. We never had a manager or proper financial back-up so after three years' worth of riots we called it a day.

The Dangerous Sports Club members are mainly former students of English private schools – nowadays artists, representatives, governors' children and quite a few Lords. Even Graham Chapman of the Monty Python troupe belonged to it.

Yes, but there were also lots of students from the supposed 'publicly owned' schools amongst the members too. Within 'private' school, one got a fair indoctrination in terms of discipline – which many of us felt was silly – but also a good introduction to genuine friendship. In Oxford one gets to know perhaps four, five people that become friends for a lifetime. But nobody amongst the Dangerous Sports Club members ever really asks where the others have been to school – that can remind one too much of snobbery and corporal punishment.

Are there actually women in the DSC?

Yes, though the Club in actual fact is not women's natural domain. That is a psychological problem, because with us it is like this: If one of the members breaks his leg, we can laugh about it, send a bottle of red wine and the case is done. If a female member breaks her leg, one automatically starts to worry about her: Shall I send flowers and chocolates and take the blame for what has happened?

This does not really suit someone who is regarded as the father of the beloved extreme sports in the present day. Your most known innovation is bungy jumping, right?

Indeed, whereas it was created by chance if anything. My friends Ed and Chris, whom I mentioned already, and myself had this fascination with flying, which was expensive. Although my parents were better off than most people, they were also wise enough not to give me a penny after my studies. Of course, I could not afford it, thus I made a virtue of necessity: The idea for bungy jumping came to us one afternoon after taking out an experimental hang-glider. Chris Baker had a flat, which was next to the Clifton Suspension Bridge, the biggest bridge in Britain. We developed a simple technology – I have been familiar with ropes and knots since my childhood, because my father was an enthusiastic climber. I only learnt a year or so ago that the others waited to see what would happen so I was the first, as it never occurred to me to doubt the calculations. Something perhaps they regret.

I jumped holding a bottle of champagne in my hand, for my breakfast, and wearing a top hat on my head. At the end the police arrested us for 'breach of the peace' and we spent the night in jail. Our success was that the police were so taken with the sporting spirit that they brought me a bottle of wine left over from the party in a brown paper bag which no other police force in the world would have done. And we were later fined £50.

And then?

After that we did not jump for four years. You know, all important English innovations need some time to develop. We waited a few years and killed time while flying kites, microlights and balloons.

Doesn't it annoy you that someone else makes money with it?

Too preoccupied to worry about making more than enough to survive. Aristotle Onassis said the only reason to earn money, is that it makes one's wife happy. Unfortunately my longest relationship lasted eight years. I was always thinking of the next project rather than making money from an existing one. We left that to others. Some of our ideas have already been used in James Bond movies. We never went after it and hadn't asked for any money. That could be said of many pioneers.

Money is one thing – But you did more than once risk your life with those audacious actions.

You know, fear is the biggest problem for human kind. On the one hand it is protective, on the other hand it is inhibiting. One is afraid that one's daughter could get raped in the park. Afraid, that one cannot afford a new car or even a cup of coffee. Afraid the husband might run off with a twenty-year-old. For me, I try and work out how to displace this fear. If you hang-glide off Mt Olympus with a kite, you get to know the difference between feeling fearful and feeling like a god. Thenceforward from time to time one will pay grateful homage to the Lord on Sundays.

Do you regret that you did not live at times of great discovery – that you, for example, were not the first white man to explore the Congo?

Oh no, I know my own borders. I am made for small explorations. The world has shrunk as explorers will tell you and that was often just a matter of crude endurance and native hospitality.

But not for a quiet life.

One cannot have an exciting life and spend a lot of time in a built-in kitchen. I see the members of the Dangerous Sports Club as peppercorns on a quiche, whereby the quiche represents society. The peppercorns give it a buzz, but without the quiche they are hard to digest and not much use. Unless, they are washed down with a bottle of vodka. I'm one of seven children divided into businessmen and teachers and they are entitled to the odd man out and have been extremely forbearing with me.

What gives you, while in your early 60s, the drive to come up with stuff, which more than a few people dispose of as crazy brainwaves?

I simply like the idea that people open up for new experiences and share them; that father and son can go skating together and bungy jumping. We gave a lot of people the possibility to express themselves individually with the Club. The essence of extreme sports has been allowing the individual to find his own route. What pleased me hugely was the way London took the lead in bringing in the Paralympics after English doctors discovered how the disabled like the opportunity to participate in sporting events. That is what I call a result. Blind people love bungy jumping because all their other senses are so finely developed.

I myself grew up in a family where team sport was important. But everybody has their perimeters and parameters. Perhaps my cricketing brothers could tell me which behaviour disorder people enjoy who stand in a circle waiting for the last drive of a cricket player? Maybe its suspense if it's a close result. Two of my brothers were downright obsessed with golf at one time but in my opinion, golf is the heroin among sports: absolute egoism without much team spirit but a great social life afterwards. Everyday life can be more relaxed at 60 but you are haunted by what you have failed to do.

And you've got a different point yourself?

In the Dangerous Sports Club we have always used our fantasy, our imagination. And to our surprise this imagination got appreciated amongst other people. After the first jump we never thought that Bungy Jumping would become so popular but that was true of the motor car. But obviously there was a certain imagination of the heart that was coming through. A certain *élan, joie de vivre* and contempt for bureaucracy was adding to this: so when we drove down to an Olympic white-water course with hired canoes and no experience, our battered Land Rover had what we called a Royal Straight Flush – no road licence, insurance, or MOT.

How many times did you hurt yourself?

You don't always get a straight answer from inventors with that question as it's an admission of failure. Not that often; broken leg and arm. My most ridiculous accident happened after a successful jump with a bungy rope. I was clapping my hands to celebrate my first jump after breaking my leg and the rope twisted my arm as it took up on the descent. So I got a spiral fracture of the arm (compound fracture). What did I learn from it? Metaphorically, walk slowly at night and speak softly by day.

In 2002, one of the Dangerous Sports Club members lost his life through a jump from a catapult. Where are the margins between passion for risk and social responsibility?

No. I was not there at the time and he was not a member of the Dangerous Sports Club but a member of an accident-ridden imitative outfit run by Ding Boston who was rejected by me as a member of the DSC after shady dealings with members' motor cars and what we believed was a primary interest in making money rather than pioneering intent. He imitated us with the Oxford Stunt Factory. The margin comes from lacking attention to detail. The chap was made completely aware of the danger of that action and signed a disclaimer but also some blame should be attached to the people running the trebuchet, though it was an awkward one and they did try their best to be safe. They were swiftly acquitted of wrongdoing in court and I was reminded of how many people I knew died in hang-gliders and microlights in the pioneering days.

Anyway, we can ask ourselves where the emphasis with the Dangerous Sports Club lies: is it dangerous, sports or Club?

The emphasis is different for each member. Actually the Dangerous Sports Club is a telephone network which expands from Hawaii to Shanghai: We are friends with different ambitions and responsibilities but we have one thing in common – the wish to enhance our lives. Of course we get confronted with the comment 'Are you crazy? Do you want to kill yourself?' all the time. The answer is no. We just love doing it; it is great fun for us [pause for thinking]. When you succeed in this field it is life-enhancing.

Where is the pleasure on crossing the English Channel with a hot-air balloon?

It was a sunny day and the view was wonderful. To sit in a little chair in silence floating over the shops and farms was unique. Well the balloon had the shape of a kangaroo and, as it were, I was sitting in the pouch. When French villagers stare at you as if you are an alien from Mars – that is already funny. If then the mayor gets around to inviting you for a pint of beer in his home – grandiose. And then you take off the neoprene suit within which you have spent the last five hours over the English Channel and leave litres of sweat and urine outside the door of the mayor's house and he doesn't mind [laughs]. I like the French. Their priorities are easy to understand.

Are there rules in the Dangerous Sports Club?

Just one, and this one is quite important: never make comments about who sleeps with whom, whatever your private thoughts. That goes back to the code of knights in the eleventh century, to act with discretion. If one does not follow this rule, you are looking for trouble. At the beginning we were worried about Graham Chapman, after all, he is gay and famous, which none of us were. But he always behaved like a gentlemen and it was a great pleasure to be in his company.

Are the Dangerous Sports Clubbers a dying breed?

No. I am the spider within the centre of the web, or a benevolent uncle to a large family, whichever way you look at it. But the web of 70 members still exists worldwide. One sits in the Congo, another in Mauritania, another in Shanghai. There is no membership fee and no member's card and some have succumbed to wife and children. If one is interested, one simply shows up at any one of our events. Whoever sits in for three events is taken more seriously. It's not one of those clubs where one waits for a place at the dining table.

Have you ever thought about the possibly of suffering from Peter Pan syndrome?

Suffering! Peter Pan was a great inspiration! Picasso said he spent his whole life learning how to paint like a child and every great artist and writer aspires to retain the wonder of childhood. Unfortunately he was always superficially portrayed, especially by Steven Spielberg. The point of Peter Pan is that he is able to fly and get away: God created humans with an appropriate defect, he didn't give them wings. It is rather unfair but quite right that we have no chance against the angels.

Actually I was thinking of Peter Pan as a symbol for someone who did not want to grow up!

Apparently so, that is a question which bothers mainly women. They think: If my man does not grow up, then he will not give me a nice car and children and a safe home. Therefore a man has to waste large portions of his life at his desk in a 58-hour working week [laughs]. Seriously, we have around 70 years to live on this planet. This is not a long time compared with trees. In the end, one really would welcome saying, I had a good time for my money! Or someone else's who could afford it but would have spent it on something less worthwhile.

If you could wish it, how should humankind remember your club?

For me it would be enough when long after I have passed away, a female Oxford student in search of an unconventional subject matter for her thesis comes up against a side-splitting group which sometimes – through all its mistakes – accomplished something really great. Almost needless to say everyone will inherit different interpretations flavoured with embroidery and inaccuracy.

Over the course of about eighteen months between 2005 and 2007, DK and I met up several times for a social or to talk shop. I noticed that I was (though informally) becoming more and more involved with the Club. Sometimes this was in subtle ways that I could pick up on. At others, the process was obscure and I was an unwitting participant. The idea of actually becoming initiated into the 'unofficial' side of the DSC member crowd certainly sprang to mind at times, especially whilst pondering over the nebulous and ambiguous nature of the boundaries that surround 'secret society' membership (Barth 2000). As the Club's official photographer stipulates on the DSC website:

> The Dangerous Sports Club is a circle of friends from Los Angeles to Shanghai linking through David Kirke … Many people claim to be members when they are not but that only amuses him. There are members of the DSC who do not know each other and prefer it to remain that way (Dafydd Jones, btinternet. thedsc.co.uk)

If one extended this line of reasoning further they might be led to wondering whether there were members who were so and didn't quite know it, in the metaphorical and literal sense.

In the last weeks before leaving for New Zealand in 2007, we met one more time in March so that we could share a drink and conversation. He gave me the names of a few antipodean contacts, including both friends and family. After that there were a couple of email exchanges but overall, this ethnographic line of research had to be put on hold for me. Until one morning, six months later in September, sitting at my desk in Wellington, I answered the telephone. It was a call from Oxford. Summarising it, the gist of it from the caller's end was this:

DK – 'Alright, how are you keeping? Listen, I'll be in Auckland next week. This is all supposed to be secret stuff until after the event but TV NZ's doing a show on bungy for AJ Hackett and they're flying us over … Yes, do keep it quiet but it's one of those *This is Your Life* things. Maybe we can hook up? Only there for two weeks mind, and will obviously be spending some time with the migrant side of the family. You remember, my sister and nieces who we spoke about? But anyhow, let's arrange to meet up somehow. I'll send you flight details and that sort of thing over the email shortly … Arrive on November 3rd then we're rushed into this TV thing on the 5th and 6th … yes, that's right. Then we'll be in the Auckland outskirts for a few days. So can we look at a few days the week of the 9th? Perhaps in Wellington or meet in the middle, or something like that? That would be grand … Listen, afraid I've gotta run but do keep some time free around then and let's be in touch online, alright? Cheerio…'

With a hectic schedule on, it was time to do quite a bit of thinking and planning about the significance of this event, after he'd sent me his flight details of course. Over email, I mustered up the courage to ask if it was ok to meet him in Auckland during the time of the show.

PL – ' … we might still be able to catch up the week of the 9th somewhere but I've got lots on at work that week. So, just in case things get really manic for me, the 5th and 6th are free at the moment. Now I realise you'll have lots of people to catch up with and it's not that I know Auckland especially well… but I have been a couple of times. We could always explore a little?' [send].

DK – ' … sure, great idea, here are the hotel and rehearsal details. We can work around this schedule. Turn up any time on Monday 5th in the afternoon, should have had a chance to get rid of the jetlag by then.'

So on the Monday, I took a midday flight from Wellington to Auckland to meet DK. Catching the airport shuttle straight to Hopson St was most fitting since the TV studios, his hotel and Sky Tower were all within spitting distance of each other (they'd put him up in the conveniently located and exclusive five-star Heritage Hotel). He was already wearing a beret and black tie outfit along with a pair of his old school spectacles. Assuming this was part of the attire for the 'performative' aspects of the DSC's eccentric and surreal legacy, I had packed my own version in anticipation. We made a quick plan for the next couple of days: 'Hey, I'll see with the producer what you can come along to'. We then taxied it to a restaurant in Newtown. Under the circumstances we had a substantially long lunch, with a bottle of wine, which he kindly paid for under the understanding that he'd be claiming it on expenses. He gave me more contact details for his NZ connections (more old friends, school mates, family relations and some contacts who'd had dealings with the DSC). Now pressed for time, we taxied it straight back to Channel One's offices.

The production assistant, who must have collected him from the airport, was already waiting for him at reception. We carried on our conversation through the doors since I was helping out with the infamous DK travel bag. He introduced us in that nonchalant 'this is one of my drinking buddies from London' way. As she got him to sign in, she gave me one of those knowing looks that said 'you're probably around for the duration then, aren't you'.

DK – 'So, my lady, how long is this whole shebang now? Couple of hours?'

PA – 'Oh, it's not a dress rehearsal or anything, Mr Kirke, that's tomorrow, remember? Although I see you've come prepared. It's just a briefing session where we can do some planning and quickly go through some paperwork … something like an hour and a half, tops.'

DK – 'Papers, perfect! We can start with this lunch receipt right here … right then, Patrick, does that suit? We'll carry on this discussion then? So guess the best thing is to see you here and, hmm, shall we wander over to the hotel lobby and take it from there?'

This was my chance to sort out somewhere to stay which hadn't been a priority until then. Even though it was only for two nights, the five-star option a few hundred metres away would not have fitted comfortably with my finances. Since I didn't know the city especially well at the time, the row of backpackers just off Queen's Street seemed to be the best solution. This wasn't very far so after a couple of tries, I found somewhere, dumped my bag and had returned with minutes to spare.

After the briefing, DK was escorted back to the reception. They passed the security desk and he signed out. He was with the production assistant (PA) and another woman who turned out to be the producer. I kept my distance as they were still finishing their talk. DK caught my eye and drew me over with a subtle gesture.

' … so you ok with all that, Mr Kirke?' said the PA, pointing to a newly printed schedule. 'Good, see you here for 11 am tomorrow morning then, for the mock up. No need for the fancy garb until the dress rehearsal at three, then it's the real thing at eight.'

As I tried to inch over without barging in, the PA had sensed the unspoken communication between us and leant over toward the direction I approached from with the schedule outstretched.

' …and of course if you're a bit jet-lagged you've always got your mate here to look after you.'

Happy to be assigned a role, I attempted to act the part of the good chaperone immediately by acknowledging both schedule and the comment with an understanding nod.

DK instantly seized the moment to introduce me: 'This is that chap I was telling you about, up from Wellington today to catch up. We can put him on the guest list for tomorrow's "big thing", right?'

There was obviously still a strict silence code about the event so that nobody would leak the guest of honour's name to the media, or anyone else who might spoil the national surprise.

'Sure, yes, and you've got another couple of possible guests, right? Let me take these names down…' She began by asking for mine while re-emphasising the sensitive and confidential nature of the recording.

Next day I met him at his hotel in the afternoon after his morning rehearsal. He told me about it over coffee in the lounge. We had a quick wander round the area to get some 'provisions' (that is, mixer for later). Stopping then for a quick glass of wine in the lobby, we carried on by testing the mixer for another cheeky drink with some of his mini-bar miniatures. Suddenly it was time to go to the full rehearsal. After sneaking a couple of drinks into the studio, we realised there was already a spread of food and beverages waiting in the green room. Most of the drink was at the softer end of the scale, with juice, beer and some white wine. There seemed to be a general managerial sense of having to control the nerves and excitement with a little booze whilst not wanting any of the key guests to get so pissed that they would peak too soon, thus failing to perform in the evening.

This is Your Life

It was during this time in the green room that I got to meet several other fascinating characters involved with the development of adventurous pursuits. They were obviously curious about my AJ Hackett connection. As one would expect, this was rather awkward since I tried to be as honest as the circumstances allowed. However, discretion and trying to keep as low key as possible was also implicitly expected. As the room filled up, it became clear that some of the people who were arriving had known Hackett since he was a child. This was his and their moment, not to be disrespected.

Early on, DK and I got talking with Chris Allum, one of Hackett's good friends who was an early partner in the development of the Hackett 'bungy brand'. He was relaxed, convivial and easy to speak with, particularly since he seemed to be waiting for his mates. The majority of the early arrivals seemed to be in small groups and had travelled in from a range of places in New Zealand.

Suddenly 'Sori', AJ's Parisian buddy who helped with the Eiffel Tower jump, arrived in the studio having been immediately brought via the airport from France. Presumably on the same flight was Hackett's Kiwi partner Amanda, now living with him in Normandy. They had met at the pub during the previous year at his Queenstown autobiography book launch. Chinese whispers and similar distorted gossip began to circulate that only moments later the man himself had just landed. The false pretext used to lure him was of having to deal with a fairly urgent part of his Queenstown bungy affairs. Tensions rose and it seemed he was showing signs of being reluctant to go through with the show.

Everyone became ecstatic as the presenter and host Paul Henry arrived and relayed to the production assistant and the producer, in such a way that we could all overhear, that somewhat reluctantly Hackett had eventually agreed to participate in the programme. Apparently, a letter or message from the Prime Minister had to be used as a 'coercive' incentive. Perhaps it was the pre-recorded message that was read out by Helen Clark during the episode.

I also spoke at length with Julian Bruff, who had Hackett's autobiography with him. It was a signed copy since Julian had been at the book launch. It circulated around the room and solicited stories from various people. By the time it reached DK, one of the ladies from the production team leaned over to show him the mention in the book of the DSC. This was how they had come to invite him in the first place. In replying that he had not yet been made aware of it, she promised that they would get him a copy. I read a few passages and noted it down as a reference to chase up. Later in the show, during the PM's pre-recorded message, Helen Clark made a special point of mentioning her launching of the book earlier in the year.

A fairly large group of childhood friends who were to appear as guests on the show for 'Hackett the early career years' section began arriving. There was then a section of people for the part dealing with 'Hackett the bungy/extreme innovator' which included many of Chris' mates and other AJ co-conspirators from Northland, Hamilton and Auckland. Things at that point were quite busy. There must have been over 25 people crammed into the small studio room.

As I listened in on all sorts of talk about Hackett, DK mingled with new people from all over. He was in his element, telling stories and socialising. Eventually his group of four or five guests got called in for the dress rehearsal. It seemed that these people were scheduled for an early spot on the show, testifying to the transition moment in Hackett's life when there was a shift from his national icon status to truly achieving international recognition through the Eiffel Tower escapade. DK fitted in at that point in the show's structure, as an earlier pioneer from overseas. Hackett has himself acknowledged in his book that 'Captain Kirke' was one of the living ancestors in the world of extreme sports:

> All they wanted to do was defy death – to have a go and see what would happen. The Oxford lads were the links that sparked up bungy, connecting the new, adventure-based Western activity with the original vine jumpers on the Pentecost Islands. I've thanked David Kirke for his role in gifting this inspirational thing to the world (2006, 101).

This was brilliant ethnographic research time which I had anticipated in the sense that I had done what I could to invite myself along to it. Having made at least certain conditions for research possible, it was nevertheless strange being ill-prepared for such a fast-paced field setting. Until then I had come to learn that the world of adventure sport was hard to study because of the speed at which everything occurs. Here in a studio, however, it was the professional institutional setting, with so many unknown protocols, which made it difficult to keep up. The producers had of course been primed to my background to a degree, yet the process was far from 'pre-ordained' research. I was there as a guest of a guest and needed to respect those confines. So this was one of those opportunistic, backdoor situations of covert fly-on-the-wall participant observation – where one can react but when it is near impossible to plan. I did muster the courage to take a couple of photos of DK and Chris in the green room which they seemed to 'invite', or at least tolerate. But on the whole, in a similar way as to when any type of researcher is in a delicate situation where there are risks – either to the participants, an institution or to their informant friends, as well as to themselves – the boundaries for the proper code of behaviour were very fuzzy. Admittedly though, they were blurred somewhat by the increasing alcohol intake.

Another group of guests began to arrive including Hackett's relations and childhood neighbours. Many of them were then herded into the studio. The whole onset crew also started swarming with activity as they circulated into action for the dress rehearsal. The seats in the green room cleared up quickly and eventually there was no longer anyone left but me. Having been stood in the corner of the room for some time, I tried to inconspicuously plonk myself onto the sofa nearby. The assistant producer finished ushering the last group of rehearsal guests through the door and down the corridor. In doing so, she glanced round the nearly empty room. At that point, there only seemed to be TV crew personnel drifting through. In that moment she caught sight of me. She must have seen my discomfort and sensed my indecision as to what to do next. Within seconds she poked her head back through the door and said it was ok for me to take a seat in the viewing gallery. A few other 'support' people and members of the production team were there to watch but not many.

Hackett was obviously not at the dress rehearsal since the guests were still a secret. But the crew nonetheless worked through what they could from the script. The host and the producer asked mock questions to the guests, all the while keeping track of time and what worked. DK's comments and responses formed into a short routine about the eccentricity of the DSC as innovators, not having ever made any money out of anything to do with their stunts. This fits his own character role which he acted up during some moments more than others. In order for Hackett to guess his identity, they got a funny sound bite of him talking about how he never really thought that the whole bungy thing would ever catch on – it being too expensive, too short a thrill and of course legally problematic.

This proved to be a clear enough clue for even a jet-lagged *This is Your Life* 'participant' to guess. The routine for the show was that after the sound bite, DK would appear on set, greet Hackett and talk to Paul Henry for a couple of minutes, before footage of the Clifton jump from *The History of the DSC* documentary was shown.

Once the rehearsals had finished, I accompanied DK back to his hotel for about five o'clock. We agreed to meet down in the lobby in a bit more than an hour. He'd have a kip, I'd rush back to shower and change. Returning back to the studio reception, I met his sister, a transcendental meditator, and other guests of the VIPs at a small champagne reception in the foyer. There was much excitement amongst the small gathering of gallery goers, some apparently did not know who the secret *This is Your Life* guest would be. Some were there, it seemed, purely by chance or under alleged false pretexts. Those who did know seemed to be acting along. A game of identity guessing quickly ensued.

I sat at the back of the viewing gallery with DK's sister. He got a big laugh from the audience when he answered the question of whether he regretted not commercialising the sport with, 'No, not at all. It was our job to waste money, not make it.' After the show, I asked one of the stage hands if he thought it was ok for me to take some photos. He said sure, so I got a few snaps of the inside of the studio. There was a brief post-show gathering in the green room for people to catch up and have a quick drink. But the real wrap party took place in town at the harbour front. We were in a crowded bar that was screening the episode. It had gone out 'live' and was now being repeated, presumably at the request of the station crew. I spoke to DK, Chris and Sori quite a bit. Hackett arrived some time later, having gone back to a hotel after the shooting to recover a little from the jet lag and the long stressful day. I got a chance to meet him on his way in. Not knowing what to say, I congratulated him on the honour of being selected for the show, adding that it seemed to go really well. Someone from the entourage, who'd remembered enough about me, then interjected to introduce me as a friend of DK's from the UK. Wanting to make the most of this fortunate opportunity, I instinctively tried to elaborate on our connection by making sure to get across two main points, if nothing else: that I had met DK in Oxford a few years before, largely because of my research interests in dangerous sport innovation, and that I had since moved to Wellington. We talked for a moment and he gave me his card for future contact (which I have yet to take him up on).

This after-show party continued in that bar for a while longer. It was so crowded and some people from the *This is Your Life* group started mentioning food and somewhere quieter, mostly to help the international visitors wind down. Ever ready, the production people, who were themselves starting to let loose in an attempt to enjoy their success, leapt back into action. Mobiles, gestures and a group rallying message was put out that it was soon time for the after-hours party to begin. This was a chill-out wrap session for anyone still standing. Still keen, DK was up for more so we got his bag from behind the bar and suddenly we were caught up in the back end of the remaining entourage who were meandering along to another restaurant lounge bar not far away. This one had an extensive spread of canapés and so forth. In this case, the food not the drinks, were being covered so I got a round in. The crowd had thinned considerably. A few of the visitors from overseas had started to pace themselves and were showing signs of fatigue, propping themselves on walls, sitting on high chairs. Some of the remaining people still fancied a drink, however, especially the production crew who were then in a position to properly relax. Inhibitions aside, I took out my camera, realising that some of the VIPs might have been getting weary and ready to move on.

I then spoke briefly to Hackett's partner Amanda, as well as a chap who called himself 'Bushman Pete'. Taking a few more photos of DK and Hackett, I was offered more email contacts. The evening celebrations went on for quite some time. We managed to get back to DK's hotel, where we parted after making a rough plan that he would join me in Wellington a few days later by taking the twelve-hour train journey.

Figure 2.1   Danger backstage (photo by the author)

Box Insert 2.2 This Is Your Life AJ Hackett (programme schedule)

This is Your Life AJ HACKETT 2007 (Alan John H, 1958)   Notes on the show structure
(70 mins) five parts plus credits
20th anniversary since Eiffel Tower jump (25 June 87)

Part One
Show starts predominantly with images of Hackett jumping from the Eiffel Tower in 1987.
(Hackett also wore a tail dress coat with a tuxedo shirt. But instead of a bow tie he wore a New Zealand greenstone necklace. Companion below waited with a Champagne bottle).
– First guest: 'Kelly Sori (Calasori Touré) French colleague for organising the Eiffel Tower jump.
– Virtual guests jumping from 'Auckland'. Rodney Hide, MP for Epson. Non-acquainted with Hackett personally. Admits to failing a past jump in Queenstown because he was too heavy at the time. He has lost weight so prepares to go for the first time with a video camera strapped to a helmet.

Part Two
Childhood to world fame, the Road to Paris
Mum (Margaret Josephine, Granny Jo). Pre-recording with still photographs of her as an adventurer and lone world traveller in the past.
– Studio guests: Childhood friends Trolley Gang / North shore Trolley Brigade.
1998 Sky Tower jump, footage
AJ mentions seeing bungy on TV, not the vine jumping of Pentecost Island but those Oxford guys.
– Studio guest: David Kirke. Paul Henry emphasises the DSC's parody of dressing up as the suicide stockbrokers of the 1920s Wall Street crash.
Rodney Hyde MP, jumps.

Part 3
NZ connections and early days
– Fiancé Amanda
– Studio guests referred to as the 'Crash test dummies'.
Susie H and Chris Allum (mentions that Hackett brought Bungy to the public, made it safe and accessible)
Also local celebration of the 20 years since they did the 19 metre jump from the Harbour Bridge Auckland in 1987 (before leaving for Paris). Police officer interviewed.
Tuma... Former All-Blacks Captain (in Normandy at Hackett's bridge site).
Another counterpart All-Black player in the studio.
Henry van Asch, former Hackett business partner (in Queenstown) doing BMX slingshot bungy jump.

Part Four/Five

Family man and national recognition
Margaux (later Jayde & Dean) 3 children in France
Studio guest: Julian Bruff 1988 Queenstown, carries Hackett's autobiography
Helen Clark from Parliament mentions being at the book launch.
Music in studio
Final studio guests: Mum and sisters
Kids reappear (linked in from France)

Part Six
(end credits)

Conclusions

Upon reflection, the show itself was cleverly scripted to be in keeping with Hackett's autobiography. Personality conflicts with former business partners, which he himself describes at length in the book were incorporated into the show so as not to create overtly awkward dramas. Having Hackett near tears, or embarrassed and ritually humiliated was fine but he was being celebrated as a national hero so an outburst on live TV, with someone saying something derogatory, would not have gone down well. Planning for the right combination of those who were in the studio, and those fed in from pre-recordings, as well as those left out (or who might have opted out voluntarily) must have been quite a logistical nightmare to organise.

The show serves to remind us of the importance of the media in popularising these activities, making them available to the wider public. And of course, we should not under emphasise the significance that this type of event has in the making of popular history itself. The use of old photographs and film footage, along with interviews and the gathering of famous people indeed becomes an instant audio-visual celebration of a national hero and thus a way of reinforcing the nation's own identity.

What can we make of the presence of our visitor from the DSC in the above descriptions? In an immediate sense, such an inclusion is about internationally validating this national celebration which in this case is conveniently linked with New Zealand's ties with the British Dominion and the Commonwealth. In more specialised terms, however, regarding the anthropology of innovation, one probable interpretation to frame the narrative has to do with information transfer, passing knowledge on – teaching, in other words. Indeed, DK has maintained his ties with Oxford University throughout his life. He defines himself as a perpetual student and is constantly searching to combine new physical practices together so as to challenge people's preconceptions of why they come to think that certain sports are natural in the form they take. Participating in high profile media events and involving new people in the activities of the Dangerous Sports Club, whether in formal or informal ways, would surely fit into most education models. Through the preservation of historical knowledge about the innovations made by people

Figure 2.2   Cave diving (photo by the author)

in the alternative sports communities, we are thus witness to one of the ways in which history writes itself.

This episode of *This is Your Life* also shows us that even the 'safeish' urban environment of a TV setting can be wrapped up in the intricate historical drama of the risks and dangers of adventure seeking. Indeed, the location of the TVNZ studio just metres away from the national Sky Tower landmark, itself a former AJ Hackett world-record bungy jump site, serves to remind us of the idea that buildings, especially but not exclusively iconic ones, have an agency, reciprocity and habitus (material distinction) for being built, 'lived' in, climbed, jumped, and refurbished or recreated. As a particularly relevant example, the Kawarau Bridge on the outskirts of the city of Queenstown has been accepted as the birthplace and ancestral home of commercial bungy jumping. It is the iconic landmark for the marketable brand of bungy jumping which Hackett and Co. enterprisingly took to the world. Unsurprisingly, it has its own fascinating history of dereliction and restoration because of the commercial venture that was established there.

Finally, this level of international commercial success should not be forgotten. If John Stuart Mill saw Jeremy Bentham as the great English subversive in the realm of innovation, what would he have made of AJ Hackett or David Kirke and the Dangerous Sports Club? Of course in utilitarian terms, both Mill and Bentham would have had difficulty in accepting the leisure value of alternative practices and risk recreation. Had they lived in our times, however, they would not have been able to dismiss the socio-economic significances of the massive growth in the industry of voluntary risk-taking behaviour, for pleasure and to refine bodily skills. From the perspective of the greatest good for the greatest number of people, the utilitarians would have undoubtedly begun to analyse whether more people benefited rather than suffered from such areas as adventure tourism or sport innovation. Taking into account as many variables as possible – health and well being, the creation of employment, the circulation of wealth, as well as to a certain degree the Marxist idea about sport acting as an opium of the people with the hegemonic consequence of maintaining social stability – the utilitarian view would probably have to uphold the conclusion that there was a place in the world for the invention of new games and activities – even if, these occasionally result in injuring or killing their participants.

Chapter 3
Risk, Rescue & Recreation

To gaze on the backs of crystal churns
And hear the hiss of offshore spray
To succumb to forces beyond those of play
And return by year by month and day
To feel the sting of salt rain pellets
And arch against a steepening cliff
To lose self and yet be aware
And know one's strength enmeshed with fear
Is to know what it's like; to have been there.

(J.K. Pearson 1977, vii).

Some people reap more benefit from fear than others. There are different degrees of knowing what it's like. Some have 'been there' more often. Fear is rarely experienced in isolation and so it occurs in combination with a number of sensations, emotions and understandings: excitement, exhilaration, panic. Risk, recreation and rescue are equally amongst them. The idea here is to focus on the micro-scale ways in which these last three topics unite. Elaborating upon such elements at the level of everyday life will act as a means to support conceptual statements that are not about the nature of any of these *per se* but about the embodied imagination. This chapter thus provides an ethnographic account of the more extreme and dangerous manifestations of coastal exploration. This includes climbing up sea cliffs but the focus will mostly be upon an activity that involves clinging to the rock faces of such cliffs and jumping from them in order to pierce through the surface of water after a brief moment of free-fall. Such cliff jumping (or 'tombstoning') along the shores of Britain's Cornish peninsula forms the main setting. The material for consideration derives mostly from participant observation and the more contrived *post facto* narratives composed by informants, sometimes years since they last took part in the activity.

As a contextual backdrop, the chapter also relies on less immersive research which brings in a wider range of settings, with a comparative emphasis on New Zealand. The rationale for the dangerous practice examined here in most depth positions itself within certain technical singularities, as compared with other recreations that are labelled extreme but which, by being increasingly socialised and made safety conscious, have become more mainstream. The civilising influence which imbues social safeguarding mechanisms means that it is inevitable that one should touch upon rescue and life-saving issues.

Spanning the Pan

The Devil's Frying Pan is a locally famous cove in Cornwall, UK, where young people have engaged with cliff hops, deep water soloing and other such leaps into the sea on a regular basis. This site is owned by the National Trust and is located near the village of Cadgwith on the east side of the most southern tip of the Lizard peninsula. For my informants in the village of Mullion, roughly six miles away, it is perhaps the quintessential cliff jump in the area, to which most newcomers to the practice are eventually introduced once they have gained a bit of experience and developed a minimum level of bravado from easier jumps. 'Trust me, ya need to build up to this one. It's not called the Devil's Frying Pan for nothing,' states Ally (aged 27), who boasts having made the jump twice in her 'youth' but would not dream of doing it again now. She continues:

> I think it gets its name from the actual shape of the cove and the way the water actually swells up and bubbles like oil in a frying-pan... that's the worst part of this jump 'cause even if it's a safeish jump, it's still a really eerie and sinister kinda place, no fooling.

My first face-to-face encounter with the Devil's Frying Pan really was an existentially informed leap of faith on many levels. Firstly, because it was a complete ordeal just to rally the enthusiasm to be taken by my friends. It was like pulling teeth. In May of 2003, I had tried to convince the 'Mullion Crew' to take me to the Frying Pan but they were simply not interested. They kept saying I was too old to be engaging in these types of crazy teenager activities. 'The advantage of reaching your thirties is that you don't have to do stupid things like that anymore. You clearly don't want to get any older do you? ... Mid-life crisis already, old boy?' These were the types of comments that Ally's partner Mike kept making.

His brother-in-law, Natt, a far more experienced extreme sports enthusiast, was quieter about the whole thing. Eventually he agreed to go to the Frying Pan with me but wanted to delay it until his shoulder, which he had injured a few months previously while snowboarding in Andorra, was feeling better.

Figure 3.1   The Devil's Frying Pan (photo by M. Burgoyne)

So I never made it that time and there were many such failed attempts. I was determined to go during a later visit at the end of July 2003. Upon leaving the pub one night, I thought I had convinced Mike to go on Thursday afternoon, after his work. I rang him after lunch and got more banter about being insane. He then said that he had scheduled a band rehearsal. I was beginning to think that this Devil's Frying Pan thing was cursed.

'Why don't you go with Natt? He's been there much more than me anyway.'

'But Natt would be at work, that's why we agreed we'd go during your afternoon off,' I replied.

'Why not find somewhere near Falmouth? There are some good jumps around where you are.'

'Who am I going to go with? I don't know the coves here well enough.'

Since I was really quite desperate at this point, I pulled the contradiction trump card. I asked for directions to the Frying Pan and said I'd do it alone the next day. I explained that I could not possibly return to London and look my research collaborator in the eye without having done the Pan. He then started to cave in:

'So you're really going to go then? Okay then, I'll take you. We'll rehearse later. Maybe DD [one of his band members] will come with us. He's a lifeguard and surf teacher so he'll be able to rescue your dumb ass from drowning. And he loves that stuff anyway, he's crazy too.'

So that was that, somehow my persistence had managed to convince him. It was a tense day of waiting, however, as I anticipated that a last-minute excuse might sabotage the plan. But the following afternoon, just after midday, five of us – plus baby and dog in tow – set off from Mullion. They were Ally, Mike, and their dog, with their friends Ron, Julie and their daughter Pearl.

The Pan would not give up its secrets that easily, however. This notorious jump also became a leap of faith because once we arrived, we had considerable problems in physically accessing the site. There was an overgrowth of gorse, nettles, and thorns all around. It was sheer determination and even obsessiveness which allowed me to reach it, driven by my conviction that I had to do this jump, and protected by a wetsuit which allowed me to pile through the otherwise impenetrable thicket of bushes. The Frying Pan seems to be such an important and symbolic jump partly because of its many barriers. Conquering these physical obstacles made the experience even more significant in my own limited biography of jumping. It should be clear though that it was the collusion of the physical and the social that makes the experience worth recounting.

Indeed, not being easily put off by the reticence of my informants was important. It is worth noting that all of them stipulated that the site had changed considerably over the past decade since they were last there, perhaps, one of them even suggested, as a National Trust deterrent for unsupervised climbing, swimming and jumping.

Not only was this jump a leap of faith for me because the others were themselves not prepared to participate but also because, given the difficulty of access, they were not even able to spectate either. In fact, no-one saw me jump. So one has to take it on good faith that I actually did. Though if you ask any of my four companions, I am sure that there is no doubt in their minds to the contrary. For one thing, they would testify, as they did to me, that they clearly heard the incredibly loud splashes when I hit the water. Given that I was upwind from them, they also explained how they distinctly heard my screams of terror, particularly on my second jump, which I felt I should mark out by yelling something. Since I could not think of anything clever after I'd leapt, I simply shouted, leaving them slightly worried, especially when I did not hear, and thus did not reply to, their enquiries as to my well-being.

My point here is that even though they never saw my jumps, the other senses have provided indications of the validity of my claim. Given that there was no one present to witness this jump or capture it on film, I was clearly doing it as a challenge to myself – for the pure experience factor. This was highlighted to me by Ron once we arrived on site. He jested that it was surely enough that I had now seen the place and had taken some photos: 'So you don't actually have to go through with it, we won't tell anyone, no-one will know the difference, right? Let's go then.' He was of course being facetious. But he was also touching on the importance that I needed to overcome the access barriers if I really wanted to understand what this was all about. The gauntlet was down.

Similarly, the jump was again a leap of faith because my friends were not immediately present to reassure me, and be reassured, that everything was going well. Nor were they able to encourage me or share any strategic information about the site. Not having anyone there to 'spot me', jumping blind as it were, was rather stressful. Hence it was much more part of an existential rather than an un-reflexive experience. There is a definite feeling that more things can go wrong when jumping alone, but also that it is a more individualistic, even liminal, moment. In a sense, then, even if it was not my initiation into jumping, I nonetheless felt that this was an ethnographic *rite de passage*.

In the end, all my jumps lasted a few seconds in total, a quarter of an hour with the climbing. Nevertheless, the event itself lasted several hours. It is worth noting that this type of solo jumping means nobody is there to share the actual experience with you on the day. Consequently, I could not find out from anyone else other than myself what the experience was like *in situ*.

Ethnographically this is a strange turn of events. I was participating in something in which my informants were not. But actually this did not matter so much because I now had their 'respect' and had potentially achieved a level of embodied empathy. I had done something that was once a significant part of their lives. And, maybe more importantly, the afternoon's jumping provided a good means of accessing certain social memories as well as soliciting loads of jumping stories afterwards.

The vignette above demonstrates certain methodological aspects in studying cliff jumping from a phenomenological perspective. One could always contrive situations to talk with and interview people about this activity. It is not, however, until it becomes a natural topic of conversation based on the day's events that one really arrives at a level of understanding of how the imagination exists in and through this fleeting embodied experience (Hunter and Csikszentmihalyi 2000).

Figure 3.2   Piskie Cove, Praa Sands (photo by the author)

Experiencing Essences

Before returning to such theoretical issues explicitly, it is important to add another layer of ethnographic thick description to the situation of cliff jumping. The activity is also sometimes referred to as tombstoning for a number of reasons, the imminent danger being one, as well as the shape of the body as one prepares to enter the water, whereby the arms are frequently crossed over the chest, resembling that iconic gothic pose of Count Dracula in a coffin. Less frequently, this practice also gets called 'coasteering'. Furthermore, it has many comparative elements with deep water soloing, which involves extended and unassisted overhang rock climbs over a body of water, most often resulting in a jump. The activity is becoming increasingly popular as an extreme practice in Cornwall, the UK and more generally.

The basic premise is simply to dive, or most often jump, feet first into some form of deep pool of water, often from as many different places and heights as possible. Jumping is a group activity and it generally involves two stages. The first is 'adventure swimming'. This is the search for new rocks, ravines or pools; basically anything surrounded by clear deep water. Such a search takes the form of traversing across the coastline, scrambling in and out of the sea, splashing through swirling gullies and sheltered pools. In terms of terminology, this is what certain people call coasteering and often it ends there. Some of those taking part believe that this part of the experience is as exciting as the actual jumping itself, if not more. Finding a new 'playground' amongst the coves and rocks is not always an easy task. Many swimmers face dangerous situations, encountering jellyfish, seals, as well as strong currents and waves that can hurl swimmers onto sharp concealed rocks. Adventure swimming or coasteering is partly a climbing activity. It often involves clinging against a cliff face to avoid the treacherous waves below and pulling oneself up to what would otherwise seem like an inaccessible spot. In many cases it is quite difficult to get up to these jump 'targets'. At times one can be many feet up, supported solely by a few fingers or toes, and this without the reassurance of safety ropes. Scrapes and bruises are the norm for this phase which many argue is when most accidents occur. As Dom, a seasoned practitioner from Helston in his mid-twenties, states: 'I virtually slit my wrist when falling onto a mussel, only to have to swim hundreds of metres back to the beach for any kind of treatment … and this just consisted of wrapping a T-shirt around my wound.'

Once the group has found a good spot, the preparatory stage of the jump can take place. Jumping off cliffs and rocks is not exactly an orthodox activity, nor is it a simple one. All cliff jumpers concur that the most important thing to do once a jump is agreed upon is to check out the surroundings for elements that might prove especially dangerous. This is a crucial part of the process and most will themselves insist on swimming underneath the jump site, often with goggles and flippers. Dom explains: 'I always check the landing area myself. There was one occasion where I left everything to my mates and regretted it completely.' They examine the site to see if there are any obtrusive rocks in the cliff face of the jump trajectory. Equally, they take a deep breath and dive under the surface to check the depth of the water as well as note any submerged objects or unusual currents. Once a jump has been given the all-clear and everyone has built up their nerve, it is time to 'go for it'. This is for many the best part. Despite the name, cliff jumping is not restricted to rock faces. Jumping will more often than not be from coastal overhangs, however, piers, boat masts, waterfalls and bridges sometimes act as substitutes. Jumping with seasoned enthusiasts can last all day. Jumps usually range from about 30 feet (10 m) to over 100 feet (35 m). Not surprisingly at this level then, a certain psychological strength, composure and determination – that many claim borders on the fanatical, if not the insane – is necessary.

Preparation is often more than an individual endeavour. A group of friends may be there to support, urging on as the first of the group attempts it. Or one could be under pressure from the others, sometimes as the last to do it after everyone else is swimming around in the water below. The 'psyching-up' process is complex and can last for hours, with many associated rituals and superstitions involved. For instance, there is a pair of friends who will only jump after they have laid themselves on their bellies over the cliff edge and stared at the sea for well over ten minutes. Others have such justifications for not jumping as having just seen a magpie, heard a seal or noticed a radical change in the wind direction. On a bad day a jumper might not be confident enough to do any jumps. On a good day, however, he or she might do dozens.

Although the activity is not unique to Cornwall, most of my informants very strongly believe that it is enshrouded in the Cornish peninsula's own particular seaside and surf culture. In relation to the materiality of waves in the context of this aspect of Cornish identity, I have elsewhere examined the relationships between sewage and surfing, protest and pleasure (Laviolette 2006b).

Despite being among the most unregulated of adventurous practices, cliff jumping now seems to be crossing over into a more formal and accepted public arena through competitions and corporate advertising. According to many avid enthusiasts, the Cornish coast provides an ideal scenario for jumping. It is scenic, with hundreds of isolated coves, bays, and steep rock faces that line a shore of relatively clean water, kept fairly warm by the area's characteristically mild and 'Riviera-esque' climate (Thornton 1993). Equally important to them, this coastline is relatively accessible, both in its physical proximity as well as because it is not particularly residential or industrial – that is, not built up or overcrowded and access is not restricted.

As far as the social profile of those who jump is concerned, it ranges from those with a privileged upbringing to those from family backgrounds with much lower levels of economic, social, and cultural capital. As regards gender, I would estimate that even though women do figure less prominently than men, the ratio is more balanced than might be expected. The most common inhibitory factor is age. Indeed for some, jumping starts when they are children (ten or twelve years of age) and drops dramatically after the teen years. Although less usual, in some cases people continue to jump into their thirties, forties and beyond.

Part of the somatic significance of this activity is perhaps not so much that it permits an intense adrenaline rush as that it allows for the engagement and exploration of all the physical senses. Touch (to a great degree, but often filtered through a wetsuit), sight, sound, smell, and the taste of salt water are all essential to the safe and successful enjoyment of the experience. Jumping is therefore in part about enhancing the potential for a full synaesthetic experience, in which one can merge the sensation of free falling with an endearing encounter of body, air, land, and sea. Hence, like many of the more intense activities of this nature, it has a high potential to further distort one's conventional notions of time and geographical perception. Events are rushed up or slowed in disproportional ways, so that sensations dealing with spatial-time come into play.

Another of the aspects used to distinguish cliff jumping from many other adventurous practices is that this activity has a minimal reliance on equipment, especially safety gear. This is a significant factor in the relative lack of regulation of tombstoning in comparison to similar dangerous games: 'Cliff jumping is unique in that it's a mish-mash of many sports. At the end of the day though, I'd say it was most like sky diving with a big watery crash mat instead of a chute,' states Rick (aged 27) from Porthleven, a waiter who was studying part-time. This minimal use of equipment demonstrates that jumping from cliffs is often about reducing restrictions and maximising the potential for a fully embodied euphoria. As Rick claims:

> There's something quite primeval, primitive, even animalistic at work. Of course you have to have all your wits about you but really jumping is one of those acts where your instincts take over almost completely … it's about letting loose and relying on gut reactions.

A more radical seasoned jumper recounts:

> I myself have been cliff jumping now for almost four years. My opinions vary from other jumpers' as far as equipment goes. Whereas some advise a thick wetsuit I am more the traditional jumper, wearing only a pair of shorts and a rash vest (which does not protect you from the water but the glaring sun). This, I find, is much more natural and the pain is more intense. The adrenaline rush is extreme but it comes with a high risk. Not only from hitting the sea hard but the various seals that attack you.

Such recall does not take the form of an excessively authoritative, unilateral narration of the events. Rather, as in many other contexts, the group's self-recollection stylishly unravels as jest and banter. This deprecation occurs in repeated playback of the day's inanities as well as of its bold accomplishments. Clever pun, ingenious parody, black humour and mock character assassination pepper the progressively pieced-together narrative. One person recalls a jump, only for another to butt in, embellishing the narrative, confirming it, contradicting

Figure 3.3   Newquay Harbour (photo by the author)

it, all through interjected put-down and ridicule. Whilst initially giving pride of place to the exploits of the bravest and most technically accomplished jumper, content-wise, this sociable bantering moves to recount the participation of each individual in the group. In effect, particular heroes notwithstanding, the bantered recollection composes and recomposes the group of cliff jumpers as an egalitarian cast of everyday heroes, deflating bombast and self-advancement from expert quarters, defusing persisting rivalry and tensions.

This levelling arises because the whole group has toyed with danger in order to experience the elements, produce the story and reproduce the jumps. It is in this way, at the complex frontier of play, danger and thrillscape, that a narrative is cultivated by the group for cultural circulation. Such narratives can aptly be labelled epic insofar as their protagonists commit to a hazardous and circular journey which, upon returning players to their starting points, fosters the crystallisation of a powerfully compelling memory rather than the application of any directly applicable power (Rapport 2003).

Light can be shed further on the emergence of cliff-jumping in Cornwall as a popular pastime by examining two related contexts: firstly, changing perceptions and valuations of landscape; and secondly, changing patterns in the signification and evolution of recreation. Along with the ascendancy of other dangerous games and adventurous activities on the Cornish coast, cliff-jumping occurs at the intersection of these two spheres where the enjoyment of landscape and the pleasure of recreation converge, merge and compete with each other.

But the point is, these are constructed narratives, socially regulated. When it comes to describing the experience itself, cliff jumpers frequently have difficulty in expressing or articulating the feeling they get from this practice. Responses are often rather curt. In Sharky's words: 'It's just a euphoric feeling when you're in mid-air, knowing there's no guaranteed safety mechanism to help you and no way back.' Most of them claim that it is beyond the sensation of other types of adrenaline rushes and ultimately one of the clichéd responses is 'you've just got to try it'.

So, after being told that several times, I did. My introductory jumping experience, at Piskie Cove, Praa Sands, was certainly eventful. I knew from experienced participants that my arms should be tucked close to my body or above my head. But not having the embodied knowledge or correct physical awareness meant that on my first jump I ended up splaying my arms so that my hands hit the water painfully hard, leaving them covered with bruises the next day. Needless to say it was a steep learning curve and I haven't made the same mistake again. I also chose to document the sensation of my first jump in the evening. The passage from my field notes reads as follows:

June 6, 2003

It was fairly obvious from their conversation that my two companions were seasoned practitioners. On the way to the cove they had been bouncing along the cliff path like schoolkids in their anticipation. This added to my own, already high, level of excitement. We got to Piskie Cove in perfect time at high tide. Without warning, Ron just jumped in. It didn't seem unexpected to Garry who quickly glanced at the ground of the take-off area without looking over the edge to see if his mate was alright. I stayed silent expecting him to run in as well. But instead he turned to me and said, 'Look, it's that simple,' then he was off too, giving a little shout as he pushed from the rock face. I took my shades off and left them on my bag. Concerned I might land on them, I decided to look down over the edge. I couldn't hear anything but one of them gave a little hand gesture which I took to mean 'all clear, get on with it'. So I took a few steps back and ran for the edge.

My thoughts on this first jump are that it feels quite unnatural. This is not a normal or regular thing to be experiencing or feeling. So it's an interesting juxtaposition to be having this 'exploration of nature' element as a significant part of the experience and discourse when really this physical sensation is completely at odds with what one would actually find as natural. I've never fallen from such a height before. Even as a youngster I never jumped from the ten-meter diving board in our local pool. I would not describe cliff jumping as anything close to a near death experience and yet this type of free-fall was one of the most unusual and unnatural sensations I've ever had.

Perhaps this is because it was so contrived from the outset. I was studying cliff jumping months before ever actually doing it. Or perhaps this is because it was my first initiation to jumping. But I'm assuming at this stage that one would have to jump almost every day for quite some time before one felt it was a natural sensation. Free-falling is not socially mundane. Surely most people don't experience this sensation with much frequency or on a regular basis.

After a short while my jumping mates began doubling the number of jumps that I was doing. I was trying to absorb it all, take it all in. To be honest, I was rather bewildered by the whole thing. I started showing obvious reserve and even felt myself shaking somewhat even though it wasn't out of fear as such. More like I started over-analysing things. Some water from our wetsuits had accumulated on the run up to the take-off point and I started worrying that without shoes or booties like those that the others were wearing, I might slip on take-off. But I had enough wits and ethnographic instinct about me to take a few photos.

Maybe the reason I started worrying was that I had been introduced to cliff jumping through narratives about it. Stories like this one by Dom (aged 24), one of Rick's mates from Helston:

> There was this one time, on a big(ish) jump; I really thought I'd had my last breath. I slipped just before take-off and so went hurtling, almost head-over-heels, downwards. I actually remember, I was on my side; it felt like I was in mid-air for minutes. I was even trying to almost fly away from the jump, y'know that feeling when you're outta control. You just flap around with all your limbs to regain some centre of gravity? Thought that might work ... But in the end, I was just waiting for a rock to smash against me. Luckily, it never came, but I hit the water with almighty force; jamming my jaw, chipping a tooth and spraining almost every muscle in my body.

As I have commented elsewhere, alternative sports provide an erstwhile poorly explored example about the relationships between the search for freedom, risk taking, the celebration of the body, and feelings of local pride and community (Laviolette 2007). The following quotation from Ben (aged 26), from Harlyn, reinforces the intricate connection between these themes when he describes this activity as:

> not for the faint-at-heart, but if done 'safely', not naively by some (mostly tourists), then there is no other feeling like it that I have encountered yet ... I have heard stories of those who have ripped open their skin on entry ... Maybe

this is a myth set up by a group of mates to keep others away from what they like doing.

Cliff jumping is thus related at some level to a feeling of local identity and belonging. Participants are often very protective of jumping spots and the local knowledge associated with the practice. This must be qualified, though, by adding that the enthusiasts of this activity are able to obscure what they do and where they do it by patrolling the coast. They are not bound to specific sites in any static sense. Even if they might in reality regularly be returning to the same coves and craggy overhangs, these beach loiterers not only strongly associate their shoreline explorations with movement but with a form of social freedom as well. They are therefore fine examples of those people who play in what the sociologist Tim Dant (1998) calls a transitory surf zone that emphasises fluidity, change, danger, and ecstasy. So, far from restricting themselves to specific spots, these participants generally share an overall sense of wanderlust; they hunt the coast for the best conditions, the least crowded beaches, the opportunities for spontaneous discovery.

Most cliff jumpers therefore feel that they are part of the same euphoria-seeking subculture – similar to, but also very different from, those inhabited by BASE jumpers and skateboarders for instance (Borden 1998). As is the case with frozen waterfall climbers, each sub-community of jumpers has a lexicon of names attributed to specific places or to venerate those people who have jumped in a remarkable way (Ferrell 2001). We thus find such designations as: Andy's Arse Flop, Lad Cove, Point X, Sharky's Echo, Dominic's Seal Squisher, Seagull Gully, the Beth Style Streaker, Piskie Cove, and so forth.

This subcultural element becomes particularly interesting when juxtaposed not only against the growing popularity of the activity but in terms of its commercialisation. An example here is the company COAST – Cornwall Outdoor Adventure Sport Training – a tourist organisation that promotes extreme activities for recreational leisure. It is a fully insured private company that arranges a series of sea and land based activities for a diverse range of age groups. The activities include snorkelling, canoeing and kayaking as well as climbing, abseiling, coasteering and cliff-jumping. Phil and Steve are the founders and managers of COAST. They are qualified in first-aid and as lifesavers. They have trained in white water rafting, windsurfing, climbing and power-boating. Steve gave up his career as a design engineer to pursue his interest in water-based sport. He claims 'while bungy or base-jumping have a fairly fixed fear factor, coasteering can be tailored to suit the individual's desire for risk. It can be as wild or as mild as you like'. Hence, in the same way that ski resorts offer nursery slopes for novices and black runs for experts, COAST have a variety of routes to suit most adventure levels, from the dabbler to the devotee. They claim, in their promotions brochure, that 'one does not need to be super fit or even daring to give it a go. Everyone can enjoy the easier routes, which offer huge thrills to the uninitiated – whilst remaining reassuringly safe'. They go on to state:

> However, if you are looking for the ultimate buzz, a craggy coastline challenge that will pit your wits against the ocean's awesome power, Coast also have the perfect route … A team spirit quickly builds as you help each other tackle the natural obstacle course which is as beautiful as it is challenging.

They also run corporate team challenges that are designed to promote ingenuity, team work and leadership skills as the participants operate together to complete adventurous tasks. It should be added that many purist cliff jumpers are somewhat cynical about this type of tourist-packaged danger sport. Generally though, most equally admit to being happy that such an organisation exists, as a means of looking after inexperienced tourists who would otherwise get themselves hurt and cause problems for other jumpers. According to Dan:

> it works as a 'round up the herds of novices and keep them outta the way' kinda thing … even the term coasteering isn't used by real local enthusiasts. It's a tourism marketing term invented by COAST and the people in the industry to try and give it a safe image.

This suggests that the danger factor is a critical part of the appeal for the most dedicated participants. Much of this danger and the activity's particular allure are related to the unregulated nature of the practice. It is part of taking calculated risks but not within the context of a formally, or even informally, organised sport. Rather, the intent that spontaneity remains as a key ingredient is hugely significant. That it is so reliant on this principle, however, does not make cliff jumping any less about creating sociality (Abramson and Laviolette 2007). One interesting aspect of this sociality and conviviality, which seems to push even further the level of danger involved, is when people jump together as pairs or even three or four at a time. The sharing of fun and fear, as well as the increased potential for collision with each other, reinforces the trust between cliff jumpers. Further, it binds them together in more than just a shared experience – it unites them through a socially constructed group narrative.

The instances described above are quite deliberately biased towards the point of view of the participant. Let us turn the tables and consider dangerous sports and the adventurous use of hazardous landscapes from the life-saving perspective. This will give a different angle on the ways in which communities are bound in a series of networks that often overlap. Indeed, Pearson's (1977) study in 1970s Australia and New Zealand demonstrated how, in being so tightly knit, the life-saving community was distinctly separate from the surfer's ethos which could not be so clearly defined as a community since its participants were more anarchic and individualistic. This set-up of juxtaposing as opposites two discrete subcultures was obviously a result of the forces of structural analysis still dominant in sociological thinking at the time. Undoubtedly, such a typology also reflects a certain ethnographic reality, indicative of the scene in the Antipodes.

Figure 3.4   Newquay Harbour team diving (photo by the author)

It is important to note, however, that in his introductions, Pearson acknowledges a certain degree of dissatisfaction with the necessity of imposing this form of classificatory order. In a number of ways, he insinuates that his subject matter is more about feelings, lived experience and physical creativity, whereby most forms of linguistic expression are inadequate. John Kent Pearson was a Kiwi sociologist who emigrated to Australia. He worked on surfing and left a significant legacy on the topic despite dying prematurely at the age of 39 from a research-related heart attack at a surf carnival. Jim McKay's (1983) obituary highlights Pearson's creative spirit, so much so that he chose to feature one of Pearson's poems in print as the closing to his memorial, which he also read out as part of his eulogy at the funeral. The poem, with which I began this chapter, prefaced Pearson's (1979) magnum opus book *Surfing Subcultures of Australia and New Zealand*.

Figure 3.5   Pendennis Point (photo by K. Kary)

999 For the First Time

The events below describe a walk around the Lizard Point with one of my good mates and long-term research participants on Sunday August 27, 2006 (Bank Holiday weekend). We'd spent the previous day exploring the area around Port Curnow in West Penwith, Cornwall.

At midday, after pulling into the car park of the Lizard Lighthouse Café, we headed straight for the most southern point in mainland Britain. We chose, on this second consecutive spectacular day, to walk mostly in a direction that would keep the burning sun to our backs. Consulting the map for a moment we began eastwards, aiming for the 'Hot Point' some two miles away on the bendy coast path. This would take us around Housel Bay in the direction of Cadgwith and the Devil's Frying Pan. I got particularly excited about the possibility of making it all the way to the Pan again, although the distance was rather unrealistic for our plans of a leisurely afternoon stroll. En route, we wound our way past the Housel Bay Hotel, continuing along between a precipice stretch known principally by locals as Klify and two wireless stations, referred to as Lizard and Marconi.

Of course encountering eccentric walkers and observing peculiar behaviour is often part of the fun of such escapades. The cultural geographer David Matless (1998) has chronicled the historical facets of walking and rambling in England. He upholds the need to examine the rural as a heterogeneous field, therefore conceptualising rurality in terms of a dialectic between the urban and the suburban, the city and the countryside. By investigating the various ways in which: '… different versions of what might be termed a "geographical self" are central to competing visions of landscape and Englishness' (1998, 14), Matless is effectively talking about the cultures of landscape in metaphorical and phenomenological terms. This perspective aligns itself well with those that I employ throughout this research. Any further summary of his findings is not especially relevant here, however, since it might detract from the story at hand. And more importantly, it would open the floodgates to the accusation that Cornwall's distinct character must remain outside the historical features of the English landscape. Interestingly, Matless himself only refers to Cornwall indirectly in his book, in relation to quoting a passage from John Taylor (1994) about photography and the tourist imagination or by making frequent use of people such as John Betjeman who was prominent in the development of an identity particular to the Duchy of Cornwall's literary landscape.

In the case of the particular eccentricity of our walk, it lay, quite literally, in the two separate instances of spotting some nudist sunbathers semi-concealed behind large boulders. We also went round the headland past the old Lloyds Bank and eventually started on the return trip after reaching Church Cove. On the way back, in order to get to the car park more rapidly, we cut up from the path through a field between a hedge wall and the east of the Lizard Lighthouse Café perimeter. On the gentle ascent we happened upon some people loitering near the Lighthouse boundary. One chap had some binoculars out, a mobile phone in the other hand and was preoccupied with something towards the cliffs at our backs. In the direction from which we'd just come, about 2,400 feet (800 m) straight across the bay is the small Klify promontory. The appearance of this man, casually dressed in wellies and a light but well-worn fisherman's knitted jumper, suggested that he was not accompanying these other two amateur ramblers with whom he was distractedly conversing. Slowing the pace down, we diverted off course slightly so as to investigate the commotion. Getting closer we realised that he had stopped these passers-by to ask for their mobile – the reception on his kept cutting out. Once he noticed us approaching, he asked us the same in turn, all the while fixated on the horizon and fiddling between his phone and binoculars. We were all sensitive to his agitated state so my friend Frank immediately went through his pack for his phone.

The guy continued his explanations. We worked out that he'd been there for well over an hour and was concerned about some people (two or three) who might be stranded. He handed us the binoculars.

'See that guy over there, hasn't moved for ages. Tide's coming in and he and his mate seem to be climbing up but they're not moving … lend us your mobile and I'll ring 999 if you'd rather not.'

By this time we had all had a chance to look over in an attempt to get our eye in. Frank mentioned that his reception wasn't great so we had better be succinct if we did ring. We considered the seriousness of an emergency call on a Bank Holiday Sunday as well as how to describe the location quickly. Other walkers stopped and questioned too. After a little while, there was some debate as to whether the climbers had ropes and gear or not. We dithered a little but our Samaritan insisted that he was prepared to accept responsibility for ringing.

The collective was thus persuaded and we agreed that the correct course of action was to ring 999. Better able to negotiate his own phone, and guessing at the intricacies of such a call, Frank did so himself. He got through to the main national emergency reception which patched him back to the Devon and Cornwall Constabulary Police. He was then passed on to the Falmouth coastguard. In turn, they connected him through to somewhere closer, such as the Helston or Mullion fire stations. Each process was complicated by the reception quality and having to explain the ambiguous situation of how much of an urgent emergency this actually was. After the series of re-routed calls, once they'd taken our contact number, there was the reassurance that a local coastguard officer would be on the way shortly and we should stand by to give further directions. So we waited. A few minutes passed and Frank's phone rang to confirm the call and assess in more detail the nature of the incident. A few more quick questions ensued which we answered in rapid consultation. The unanimous conclusion was that a helicopter rescue was probably not needed in the first instance – 'Ok, someone will be there soon'. By that time, something like 20 minutes had elapsed since we first stopped and our deliberation about ringing began.

More walkers paused to inquire and look. The differences of opinions were compounded further. One person, perhaps with better eyesight and a steadier hand than the rest of us, was quite confident that our stranded 'strays' were actually climbers with ropes and gear. She confirmed that there was indeed a rather well concealed third person on the ground in a dark cavernous section of the rock face. Un-camouflaged by being pointed out, this character equally appeared to be more and more active. The other two were higher up at different levels. They disappeared regularly from view in the folds of the rocks. One person disapprovingly commented that our three adventurers were 'not wearing any special high-visibility clothing'. Perhaps even anything but shorts, shoes and maybe dark helmets, it was hard to tell against the granite and gentle wave splash that shimmered in the intense afternoon light. From prolonged observation, neither of them appeared hurt either and no one was making any obvious distress signals.

After a while, there were seven or eight people who had stayed to watch, plus another half dozen who had stopped, asked questions and continued on their way. Most of these onlookers were fairly convinced that the situation was probably benign, or at least under control. Through discussion, surveillance and educated guesses, a process of collective reassurance had evolved.

'Some climbers slowly practising some routine holds?' was proposed speculatively.

'Perhaps a lesson with a guide leading the way, or b-laying whilst shouting instructions from the bottom?' hazarded another.

The instigator of the concern remained adamant that they were immobile for some time. In the intense heat and without shirts on, 'what with the tide coming in, it's better to be safe than sorry, right?' He reminded us that only weeks before, 'there was that case in the paper of the guy who couldn't swim and was swept to sea while fishing off some slippy stones'. As the tension mounted, we agreed again, hoping everything would be resolved quickly. Frank had had another call about the exact location. In anticipation, we were eager to see a lifeboat swerve around the tip of the headland, or anything similar. Suddenly a small all-terrain jeep popped into view from the direction of Lloyds Rd. It moved towards the wireless stations which are within metres of the coast path and a few hundred metres from the cliff edge, not far at all from the cave area in question. A man came out of the vehicle, put on a fluorescent-yellow lifeguard vest and proceeded rapidly down what seemed from afar as a rather steep descent to the actual cliff wall. From his movements, we could make out that the vegetation and stones were at a much less severe angle than they appeared, although he had obviously negotiated the precipice skilfully, so as not to slip over the edge or dislodge anything off the side.

He must have shouted to the climbers because the highest one began moving up as the lifeguard started getting close by. Although they might not have been within any easy line of sight, given the acute incline of the cliff face, at this stage they would have been within hearing distance of each other, especially on this calm afternoon. Indeed, after a couple of minutes of inching their respective way towards a sheer overhang drop, where the signs of grass, sea flowers or lichen were negligible, they would have been within metres of each other.

After a few moments of sprawling precariously over the edge, the lifeguard then proceeded cautiously but even more quickly back up. Driving off, everyone watching was relieved. A few people left. A couple more made signs of wanting to go. Before we could disperse, a few more still arrived on the scene and the explanation started up again.

It had been a long, hot and eventful couple of days with plenty of coastal path walking. So my mate was keen to get going before it got too late. We had some friends to meet still and he was going to a family engagement in the evening. Not to mention, since we had a long drive back up country the next afternoon, we were planning a fairly early start. Yet somehow those of us who stayed on as loiterers were all a bit mesmerised by the lovely late afternoon sun shadows closing in around an aptly named headland. In choosing it as their practice spot, our three anonymous climber friends had unwittingly given the Klify sea-caves a new adventure story, one which seemed to have had the potential to produce knock-on effects that could resonate in manifold ways.

Finally, the signal that we'd been waiting for without realising it occurred. Frank's phone rang again and it was explained that the situation had been dealt with. Frank responded, 'Yes we know, we were able to see the whole thing, sorry about that but ...'

Before being able to continue, he was interrupted by a type of response which implied that any further justification was not needed or in itself even warranted. 'Hey listen, no probs at all, that's what we're here for. Well done, cheerio.'

That was not quite the end of it though, since the story inevitably got amplified, first in the pub then later with a number of other people. The subsequent conversation about this life rescue mission with our mates is worth recounting, especially since many of them are part of the very same Mullion Crew who took me to the Devil's Frying Pan in 2003. It went along these lines:

'Alrighty, me 'andsomes? So what's up boys, been out rambling again today?'

'Yeah, fantastic day for it and guess what, we had to call the emergency services today. No really, for some climbers down the Lizard. This guy got all concerned that they were cut off from the tide, so we rang. Bit of a false alarm though.'

'What? So that was your first 999? Ahh, how cute ...'

As the drinks flowed and more people joined us, a slogan-like chant, sounding out our 'naïveté', even developed.

'Hey, get this, these lads have just had their first 999! Yeah, 999 for the first time! 999 for the first time!'

The embarrassment of our excitement, added to the fact that it turned out not to have been necessary to ring, were playfully being emphasised. More descriptions ensued and the piss-takes became more sparing. Eventually we were being reassured by our mates that it was the right thing to do:

'Don't you worry boys, that chappie will get twenty quid for his troubles, which in the end was probably not too much of a bother at all ...'

'Sure, but it is a Sunday Bank Holiday after all,' one of us replied.

'Yeah well, it must have taken a bit of ringing round to find someone at their BBQ who wasn't too pissed to drive out there. But then again, on his way back, he would have been able to buy some extra beer for whatever party he was dragged away from. So he would have been chuffed with himself, I reckon. What a nice way to end the weekend, don'tcha think?'

One of our mates, who was also registered as a volunteer coastguard in the area, confirmed that line of thinking. (Ok, he is the partner of the person who was making the argument so we do need to bear that in mind.) Nevertheless, being excessively cynical of what at first might seem like too limited a sample or too subjective an association would do his personal experience with such matters a huge disservice. He validated the point simply by saying, 'What a bummer, I had a music lesson, would have gladly gone out for that ....' He then continued, more to his partner than the rest of us, 'Could have even taken the boy and the dog out for a spin and some walkies afterwards.'

Other conversations about the importance of an urgent 999 call took place the same evening and next day with Frank's extended family. It became a great topic for small talk. Not only did it continue to bring agreement that we had acted responsibly but it also helped solicit other similar stories of people getting caught out. And, as is often the case in such socially embedded conversations, the moral frequently got turned back on the instigators: 'Let that be a lesson to you when you boys get out doing all sorts of crazy stuff.'

I'd been staying with him and his family whom I've known for years. They have frequently been so generous as to put me up for days on end without him even being around. They are quite aware that one of the reasons we're such good friends is that we both like to push the limits when it comes to outdoorsy things. One of the more humorous gifts that his mum received for Christmas one year was the photography book of the surrealist 'Extreme Ironing Bureau' (Shaw 2003). This was the source of a few giggles and pensively raised eyebrows. Such allegories (visually implied or like the spoken one above) about the flippant as well as the exceedingly serious sides of proceeding with caution have not been lost on the processes by which creativity and innovation have continuously re-shaped this particular project.

Indeed, even though I would be returning to a week's work in London the next day, I would also be catching the train back the following weekend for a fancy-dress music festival. The event, a fifteenth anniversary 'Crystal Ball', was in aid of a community/network of proactive environmentalists who have successfully married up surfing and the arts (see Chapter 4). Equally on the agenda, was some indoor climbing-wall practice in an old brewery.

One of the more direct messages I took home from these two extended weekend fieldtrips was the significance of the life-saving community in such coastal playgrounds. Less directly though, the reader might have noted how many of the participants fall into both categories of adventurer and rescuer, sometimes simultaneously. We shall return to this issue later. In the meantime, one last point to draw out is the ambiguity of this communal rescue event which raises certain questions that are worth thinking through regarding the veracity of certain emergency calls. That is, some degree of doubting the essence of what in this case should be termed a genuine distress call does have analogous counterparts. Hence, we need an additional illustration for how the 'caution in calling' could also hold true. This would not go amiss because the dilemma of crying wolf is not just a meaningless stereotype. Rather, it often has poignant validity which is context specific. Indeed, in the opening lines of the first chapter to his book about the Dangerous Sports Club, Martin Lyster (1997) starts off with the opening gambit that 999 is probably the first number that many children learn, under the auspices of hopefully never truly requiring to ring it.

A Pan-Hemispheric, Intertidal Interlude

Now as we've seen, in the 1970s Pearson provided an exhaustively comprehensive socio-history of this topic of life-rescue subcultures, particularly as it relates to the Pacific (e.g. 1979). Consequently, it is not my objective here to question, 'compete with', or revalidate his insightful approach and findings. Instead, I simply want to add some cross-cultural flavours to the mix and offer extra contemporary ethnographic material, this time as it relates to New Zealand's surf culture.

Analytically, the following example could appear as an anomalous curiosity. Alternatively, it might shed some comparative light on the structure and style of the 'precautionary principle' that I've just been hinting at. Given that the potential level of imminent danger was so high, one would be wise to question the scenario itself since it was an incident where the whole setting was perhaps even more immediate than the one previously described. The results thus seemed that much more absurd.

March 2008, Taranaki Surf Highway: Life saving incident at Opunake beach.

It had been one of those windy, rainy autumn days. The sea was choppy with what seemed to be a fairly strong rip pulling out to the south. There were few people on the beach in these conditions, only a few kids swimming or boogie boarding in the shallows. The waves in the sheltered south-west corner seemed clean enough though. On the way back to Wellington from New Plymouth, I saw this as a last chance for what might be a few months of having a go at a bit more surfing on the west coast. While pulling my wet rash vest back on and preparing to go in, a four-wheel drive parked up nearby. Two lads emerged and instantly grabbed their boards from the boot. They must have seen the same potential or had a similar idea. They headed off quickly into the water, paddling close to the emerging rocks on the left-hand side of the bay. They were only wearing knee-length shorts and even though the water was not cold, the conditions were not exactly tropical either. So an initial assessment was that they were especially strong surfers. Keeping an eye out as I went in, it became more noticeable that they had gone out too far, with

Figure 3.6   Warning poster (photo by S. Pawson)

too much machismo. They might be in a spot of bother soon, unless they were headed for some well-concealed sheltered break.

After about ten minutes, one chap appeared on the reef slowly struggling his way back to shore. The other was still in the water. He no longer seemed to be lying on his board. Looking around concerned, to see if anyone else had caught wind of the situation, I hesitated about whether paddling out would be wise. I was out on this old vintage nine and a half foot 'Atlas Woods' longboard. It weighs over 20 kg. My first thought was that I'd be more of a liability in the big choppy

Figure 3.7   Emergency 999 poster (photo by the author)

waves with such a heavy piece of equipment. Knocking someone out or smashing them into the sharp stones would not get me many hero points.

Spinning round, I made my way to shore to see if it was worth summoning the lifeguards at the BP Surf Rescue unit. Grabbing for the leash, I turned in their general direction only to notice a motored dingy race out through the chop (these are also known as Inland Rescue Boats or 'Rubber Duckies'). Turning back to the surfers revealed a surreally comical scene. The more visible of the two had stabilised himself in the gusty windswept conditions on a large tidal break stone. Yet somehow he was effortlessly waving his board over his head as a clear distress signal. His barefoot movements through the rocks had been slow and his mate was still drifting near the reef. Catching the occasional glimpse of the latter through the troughs of the spraying swell indicated that his head was still above water and that, however erratic, he had some grip on his board. The life-rescue crew collected the stranded surfer, leaving the other to make his way back through the reef boulders and around the stony bay. He returned within 15 minutes or so and the two boisterously jumped back into their vehicle and dashed off within half an hour of having arrived.

Maybe they were just tough skinned and pig headed but they were much less sheepish about this ordeal than might be expected. It was equally interesting to witness that they did not appear to receive any reprimand or telling-off from the life-guards for this stupid behaviour. So the incident does beg the question of whether it was an authentic distress call. In other words, could it transpire that this was something else, something other than it seems? It would be one thing if it was a bluff or a dare gone wrong. Reproachful yes, yet nonetheless valid as a call for assistance. But at least one alternative scenario remains; perhaps it was a covert test, a form of training session for the people of the rescue unit. Naturally though, when the stakes are so high, the interpretation should not remain so dismissively wry. Indeed, suspending disbelief can go too far – can itself be another form of danger – a moment when a mild hazard becomes even more severe.

One Dark Roasted Night

As a result of this civilising need to abide by some form of precautionary principle, especially as it relates to the dangers of the sea, one can witness many interesting developments that surround life-saving communities. Most straightforwardly, we can think of situations when carnivals and festivals are held, certainly to acknowledge the communal aspect but also to celebrate the idea of altruism. Another typical event to strengthen the social bond or act out minor rivalries is the rescue competition, as a means of rewarding dedication and commitment.

If certain rivalries become more intense, or when some life-saving communities become too large and socially prominent, they can dissolve into smaller entities. Competition then gets manifested in different ways, sometimes with the result of rescue specialisation. At Lyall Bay in Wellington, New Zealand for instance, there exists a peculiar history of two independent rescue organisations within metres of each other. These are: the BP Surf Rescue unit called the Lyall Bay Surf & Life Saving Club Inc. established in 1910; and the Maranui Surf and Life-Saving Club which opened the following year. Institutionally, they have had different charters, membership ranges and distinct management structures. Nevertheless a recent incident on 1 August 2009 (when a fire damaged the latter's club building) has put into question the level to which they can really be seen as that socially separated. At a more encompassing cultural level then, through examining the impact of the sudden closure of the Maranui on the larger community, one could suggest that these independent clubs are interconnected in many ways. It is also worth noting that there are 77 rescue clubs nationally (Jackson 2006). Such institutions are therefore prominent features in the New Zealand landscape and are therefore part of a larger landscape of care.

The fire took place in the middle of the night because of an electrical fault on the ground floor. The building was not destroyed but the smoke damage was significant. The main fire damage was to the kitchen on the floor above where the Maranui Café is located. The café has itself been run independently from the club and had been a favourite eating place since it opened its doors in 2005. It would not be an exaggeration to say that together, the club and café are Wellingtonian icons. The structure is itself a landmark of the city's identity and is listed by the Historic Buildings Trust.

Immediately after the fire, there were attempts around the city, mostly but not exclusively by other cafés, to temporarily employ the café staff. One café in particular kept the Maranui's 'Sunday breakfast tradition' going, even though it was normally closed at weekends. Also in this case, and for a time when the neighbouring art gallery started serving coffee and snacks, the community spirit went one step further, with proceeds being donated to a 'Save the Maranui' campaign. Such a rally had become necessary because of insurance complications whereby the particular type of calamity that occurred was not covered. A placard put up in front of the café while it awaited its future expressed some of the social sentiment. It thanked the community for its support, with the following poem appended:

> I've listened to Aussies with wonderful tales,
>   of their bridges and cities that never have gales
> I've heard tall stories of wonderful clubs,
>   with their thousands of members and quite close to pubs,
>   but for all their fine beaches and sunshine and sand,
> I know of the finest spot in the land,
> For old Maranui still beckons to me,
>   where the Freyberg Street sewer sweeps down to the sea.

Figure 3.8   Maranui Placard, Wellington New Zealand (photo by K. Kary)

Many individuals and local businesses have equally supported the redevelopment by other less direct means. And other entrepreneurs have started up initiatives during the indecision phase. A few initiatives have shown signs of benefiting. For example, the morning after the fire, beachgoers and so forth were shocked to see what had happened in the night. Some had heard it on the news, of course. The following conversation took place at a nearby café:

'Hmm, so business should be good here for a while then?'

'Hope so, ya, not that we mean any disrespect to the Maranui.'

A few days later, said café was searching for extra part-time baristas and other casual staff. Also seizing on this market force asset, a hot-grill trailer caravan was put together in front of a house overlooking the bay. After a few weeks of self build, this movable snack-shack stationed itself at the beach car park near 'the corner', a favourite surfers' spot which runs alongside the airport where a break is produced by an artificial reef created by a road that circumnavigates the main runway. Additionally, one new boutique deli-café opened near the bay. Rumours circulated that it might have a late night 'license' which some people identified as a niche in the immediate area.

One of the hallmark 'trademarks' of the Maranui is that it is directly on the beach. This probably lies near the heart of the planning difficulties that Wellington City Council has had to face in terms of competing desires for change or a return to the way things were. The general ethos of community support has not gone without numerous controversies and indeed the refurbishment process has been riddled with complications. Legal design debates, repeatedly reported in the press, have surfaced because of the complex lease and ownership structure whereby the

Maranui SLSC (surf and life-saving club) leases the top level to the café but leases the 'property' (or beach access) from the Council. These issues have been publicly and privately debated, slowing down further the refurbishment plans.

Of the Maranui Public Meeting about the future of Lyall Bay on 22 Oct 2009, Tom Scott, a regular cartoonist for *The Dominion Post*, wrote the following into one of his sketches: 'Why return to that draughty, creaky, noisy, old, admittedly quaint building that's utterly unique to this coastline, when you could have this gleaming featureless edifice that could be anywhere?' (T. Scott, 8/10/09) Accompanying this cynical parody, Scott has sketched a view (north to south) of the bay from the road, just off the pavement, looking to the café and beach. The narrator is a nerdy Town Planner. The centre piece of the cartoon is a modern glassy/cubist architectural design plan which he speaks to as a form of sales pitch. In profile, this 'establishment' figure is enthusiastically addressing a complacent chef and a Maranui lifeguard who stand next to each other on the left-hand side (east) of the picture. Behind the narrator, on the sketch's right side (west) is the burnt café which looks fairly fine but is clearly boarded up and 'in limbo'. The speech bubble hangs above the plan, in the skyline horizon of an open passage to the sea, heading towards the Antarctic.

Because of the issues over insurance and the many political deliberations, the building remained boarded up for some time with only minimal access. The objects in the café and club were cleared out quite slowly. High in the public concern were the irreplaceable photos of the club dating back decades. Most of these reportedly escaped unscathed. Other stuff, however, was more severely affected: some vintage surfboards, and 'modern' life jackets for example. Many of these are heritage reminders and some effort seems to have been made to repair them. Others were left by the refuse skips for passers-by to collect (e.g. a burnt bike), presumably as a gesture of goodwill for anyone who might like to have a keepsake to rejuvenate; to take on a project and thus contribute in their own individual way to keeping some memories alive.

Conclusions

Including the three interludes above has not been with the intention of highlighting the importance of life-saving communities. Rather, the idea is to add a layer of nuance to what might have become a normative cliché. That is, although we can divide the class of people with an adventurous predisposition from that of a subcultural group dedicated to rescuing those 'individualists' who go astray, or are subject to misfortune, the overlaps are so recurring and habitual that such a distinction runs the risk of becoming banal. In Bourdieu's (1977; 1990) terms then, I would suggest that the people in each of these two 'subgroups' share so much of the same habitus that it might not be worth seeing them as separate in the first place. Admittedly, this would be going too far. The material in this volume, particularly in this and the next chapter, suggests that the overlaps are often temporally related so that one's habitus swings back and forth over time. Post-structurally though, we would have to say that it oscillates between more than two comfort zones. While habitus defines the field of play along with the written and unwritten rules of the game, Bourdieu's concept of the social field is interesting in allowing us to think about the feel for the game, all those reasons which we can find for justifying why the game is even worth playing in the first place.

Contextually then, when play is serious it includes the rescue mission and there are thus many diverse reasons for playing in hazardous places or in similar liminal environs. This raises the issue about distinctions being produced by access to technologies and training, which immediately creates a hierarchical relationship between extreme sports enthusiasts and those who rescue them but with whom they share certain sympathies. What this tells us about risk and danger as socially mediated is the way in which social consensus creates a particular kind of social reality that must be represented and adjudicated by some authority (who has access to technologies and experience). Essentially this is a point about egalitarianism shading off into democratic action that necessarily produces inequalities. We can trace this back to Kierkegaard's (1849) ideas about anxiety, when he posited that this sensation was the consciousness of lived possibility that involved reconciling the existential experience of death as a termination of life, with the awareness of death as a stage of life. Acts that produce anxiety then provide opportunities to truly experience life as transcendental of its lived, perceived limitations. Of course, given that it is Kierkegaard there is a religious basis in all of this but it nevertheless resonates with the argument about how risk and dangerous pursuits create awareness of living as an experience.

Robert Desjarlais has argued against the ability of people to have an experience unless they are able to incorporate it into their lives. So 'experience' necessarily means that one is able to reflect upon what is happening and to base future actions on having had certain events take place in their lives. Similarly, Joan Scott (1991) has been interested in intellectual and scholarly practices that produce evidence of what had heretofore been invisible. Even though she is concerned primarily with difference, her approach is relevant for anyone trying to show the evidence for the existence of a sensibility through which people instantiate their own existence, often through narrating what has happened to them. Other scholars have demonstrated that many of the reasons for embracing the dangerous are linked to significant changes occurring in the areas of recreation and landscape usage (Hudson 2003; Gyimothy 2008). Such changes are increasingly beginning to form a fundamental part of western modernity's ongoing socio-cultural reformation of spatial and behavioural marginality as a means of reshaping ontological structures of risk.

Arjun Appadurai's (1996) use of the imaginary is relevant at this stage because he is concerned with the creation of trans-local sensibilities enabled by resisting promiscuous representations that have penetrated given locales. This ties in with some of the local understandings described in Cornwall with respect to tombstoning, danger and the sea. It clearly shows the limitations of particular imagined ideologies to become catchy for a particular people in a particular place, thus helping to explain why cliff jumping is so prominent in Cornwall and not Blackpool, for instance. The argument via Appadurai is that it is the dangerous activity itself that allows for self-identifications and meanings to be instantiated by practitioners.

The material above is not intended as a direct means of supporting or challenging any of these more grandiose framings of risk. By highlighting the embodied character of a particular genre of dangerous practices through first-hand ethnographic accounts, these observations are there to strengthen the supposition that it is within their visual, sensual and narrativised transformation that oxymoronic dualisms such as risk vs. recreation, deep vs. shallow play are at their most powerful. It is during such moments of change and transgression that one can best witness a range of novel imaginative associations which exist in linguistic, corporeal and material terms. Their novelty is in the possibility that these associations offer us a different way of identifying perpetual intellectual paradoxes. Doing so often helps open or free up new spaces. In this case, these are the embodied spaces of intuitive understanding that remain relentlessly bound together when viewed through a lens that divides safety from hazard or even when simple dialectic mediators are brought in to weaken the rigidity of such categories but which ultimately keep them in opposition.

To suggest, as Castoriadis (1998) has done, that the imagination is embodied and does not just exist in the mind, does not contradict that there are social realities of collective fear, risk and danger. The idea that through some phenomenological agency, the material world itself possesses many layers of the social imaginary makes certain levels of the risk society argument even stronger (Beck 1992; Furedi 1997). What it denies from the general argument, however, is the extent to which many risk theorists have historicised a radical break around the global repercussions of modernity. Hence, the position put forth here, which I'd argue is in keeping with a dialectics of alternative theory building, posits that there are no singular cause/effect ways of prescribing whether humans are now more or less prone to risk; whether globalisation has embedded the world into a greater degree of catastrophic cultures of fear or danger. Simply put, those grand narratives which have a view over such debates about an unprecedented new world order of indoctrinated disaster anxiety often bypass the human reality on the ground. Collectively these largely mount up to saying that there are no easy 'either/or' theories to explain the multitude of ways in which the human imaginary constantly negotiates the fictional and real dangers that people set up for themselves as well as those which the world offers freely.

Chapter 4
Through Seascape and Sewer – Shallow Green to Full Brown

Yes, this is the eternal renewal,
the incessant rise and fall
and fall and rise again.
And in me too the wave rises.
It swells; it arches its back.

(Virginia Woolf 1931, 297).

In reading Virginia Woolf's *The Waves* and *To the Lighthouse*, one is easily caught up in awe regarding the ever changing seascape – its power, its beauty. Somehow it evokes both fascination and fear. This chapter addresses Woolf's notion of waves as an eternal source of renewal. It explores the metaphor of renewal as part of three interconnecting facets, an environmental debate, an embodied set of practices and a discourse based on shifting Cornish identities. Surfing, waves and water pollution protest are all part of a wider interest in places of motion and change, as well as a changing political landscape that is increasingly accounting for, as well as linking, issues of Cornish identity with local concerns for the state of the environment. Youth culture and its association with seaside leisure pursuits is now, more than ever, recognised as part of an embodiment of extremes that is somehow less excessive in Cornwall's schism of socio-cultural distinctions. That is, the embodiments that are part of 'greening the extreme' nevertheless carve a middle ground between the highbrow cultural traits of language or art and the historical working attributes associated with mining, fishing and farming.

Drawing on the reference to the embodiment of waves that Woolf makes in the quote 'and in me too the wave rises', this chapter explores the impacts that radical modifications in bodily practices have upon the changing social worlds of leisure. It also plays with the issues that straddle the extraordinary and the mundane in a sphere that encompasses the elements of a revered contact with nature and everyday economic subsistence, a realm where pleasure and protest aptly come together. Here protest results from both privilege as well as victimisation. Focusing on Cornwall's seascapes through the haptic experience and sensorial perception of extreme bodies, this chapter addresses many ecological concerns, examining how the politics of water pollution and protest relate to understandings of leisure and pleasure. Implicitly, it speculates about how the anthropologies of sport and the body could begin conceptualising seascapes as social, material and imaginative spaces. Considering underwater environments and the boundaries between air, water and the body as interlinked spheres suggests the existence of certain frontiers in the social sciences. In this case, there would be a need for fresh investigations capable of reflecting upon worlds which many people visit and play in but which are only metaphorically lived in, at least socially.

Activities to do with the coastline and the aquatic environment such as fishing, boating and seaside holidays have been mainstays of the Cornish peninsula for generations. Building on the material of the previous chapter as well as on the legacy of marine leisure, this chapter explores both the fluidity and materiality of waves, tides and coastal seascapes through a metaphorical framework encompassing symbolic as well as literal issues of pollution and embodiment. It examines Cornwall's distinct surf culture with regard to concerns over the effects of sewage and other malignant discharges on public health and the quality of the seashore environment.

Extreme water sports are an increasingly prominent factor in the formulation of Cornish identity. Hence, this chapter outlines the ways in which certain environmental pressure groups, charity campaigners and corporate surf companies have become involved in attempts to safeguard the ecological sustainability of coastal leisure pursuits. It does so primarily through ethnographic case studies concerning protest-art exhibitions and environmental campaigns. On the surface, the symbolism of fluidity and pollution may appear contradictory. But through an exploration of the materiality of waves, this chapter illustrates the dialectical ways in which water and the sea relate to shifting local identities and to creative forms of extreme subversion.

Empirically speaking, most of the data I have gathered on adventure or alternative sports in Cornwall is ethnographic in nature. Much of it was collected during the summers of 2003 to 2006. My connection with the peninsula is far more extensive, however, dating back to 1998. I am also involved with the environmental pressure group Surfers Against Sewage (SAS), particularly through an ongoing attempt to develop a project entitled SEWER (Surfers Engaged With Extreme Research). In order to raise money and publicity for SAS, one of the intended activities under this rubric is to plan a series of sponsored jumps in and around the Tamar River, ideally from off the Brunel Bridge. The material for this chapter is primarily focused on people associated with SAS as well as a wider network of surfing informants. This is predominantly a white, middle-class cohort of people between the ages of 16 and 45. Regarding gender, I would estimate that, even though women do feature less prominently, the ratio is more balanced than might be expected, being in the order of 60/40. This is most likely the result of dealing with an environmental organisation rather than an extreme sports group. Women, however, are highly involved in Cornwall's extreme sports scene and might only figure slightly less because of the requirement for manual labour in many of the permanent jobs available for 18- to 30-year-olds. In this sense, the 'brain drain' in the area acts as a gender drain to a certain extent (Beine et al. 2001). The age profile can of course be explained by the fact that this is fundamentally a youth culture. The other discrepancies perhaps say more about the region's demographics than about its surf culture. Notwithstanding, Becky Beal and Lisa Weidman (2003) provide a more comprehensive discussion about gender and the social exclusion involved in California's skate subculture.

Mainstreaming the Extreme Body

In 1999 Henry and Sophie Ashworth launched the Extreme Academy. The concept behind this enterprise was to create a hospitable ski resort on a beach. By transposing the idea of an alpine resort to one of the largest beaches of Cornwall's north coast, they hoped to combine the laid-back local lifestyle with all-weather adrenaline sports, particularly surfing and kite-boarding. They converted Watergate Bay's original 'café and bucket and spade' complex into a Beach Hut Bistro Bar, with a large clothing and equipment store. The Extreme Academy quickly gained a national reputation for innovation. In 2000 the Ashworths won the Devon and Cornwall Millennium Award for Best Entrepreneur Business. A £500,000 refurbishment of the beach complex added a second storey in 2002, creating an upstairs floor for facilities to host public events as well as its sports school offices. This new complex has transformed the beach into a mixture of classroom, wild playground and trendy 'hang-out spot' for tourists, offering lessons for people who wish to experiment with new sports or improve their skills. The venture has continued to flourish by expanding the range of activities on offer. Mountain boarding and kite-buggying are now also possible options. The success of this organisation illustrates just how extreme activities have shifted from the exotic and the 'eccentric', to the exemplary, the mainstream even.

The space of extreme leisure has thus become a sensually creative realm. The extreme body manifests itself in this realm in numerous and diverse ways, such as the appearance of extreme sports, adventure tourism, body modification, radical sexual practices and patterns of substance abuse, to name but a few (Lyng 1990). Such hedonistic states are increasingly weaving themselves into the fabric of people's social relations. They have so altered the parameters of society that they generate new cultural forms that are grounded in the recognition of shared sensual experiences. These mark groups out at experiential levels. Such relationships therefore have their own social structures. They offer expertise, experiences and distinctions that are significantly different from those housed in more conventional social contexts.

With the modernisation of traditional sports and the marketing of new ones, sport has dramatically enhanced its potential impacts on the expression of personal and social identities. Sports have been increasingly associated with recognisable styles, fashions and subcultures, and thus with what Alan Tomlinson calls the 'performing self': 'a performing self has embodied the intensifying connectedness of sport and style in an expanding culture of consumerism. The obvious focus for such developments has been the body' (2003, 405). The relationship between the body and culture has become a growing area of concern for the anthropology of sport and scholarly research in general. Many disciplines have begun to examine the sensual and corporeal foundations of our social and individual experiences in the world. As the importance of this hitherto largely ignored social and sensual realm becomes recognised by contemporary academics, the body is moving from its degraded and distrusted position within both Judaeo-Christian theology and Western philosophical traditions to the forefront of social analysis (Howes 2003).

A continual emphasis upon economic capital as a measure of success, granting access to the symbolic structures of contemporary capitalism, has significantly eroded alternative social structures through which people can gain a sense of moral and social worth. Yet the construction of epic narratives via the intensification of lived experience offers such an alternative arena. Here people encounter an intensified sense of participating in their own lives through the creation of sensual and fluid ontological systems (Bauman 2000). Although still held within the economic structure of capital, such systems nevertheless manage to generate alternative models of success, respect, morality, courage and conviviality that exist beyond everyday social and cultural norms.

Extreme bodies have always had a certain place within culture. Violent conflict, sacrifice and many ritual practices have a profoundly intense bodily dimension, which marks out the times and spaces of their occurrence as 'liminal' states (Turner 1974). These either challenge or justify the social and cosmological systems of that culture. Within the fragmented ideological structures of post-modernity, however, many contemporary manifestations of the extreme body occur outside of a prevailing ideological order. This process brings about profound changes in the way in which the western world experiences the social body. Such a body has indeed historically acted as a vehicle or medium through which morality can be performed in the form of protest and civil disobedience. Hence in terms that would have been all too familiar to people such as Henry David Thoreau ([1849]1993), the action of protest in itself is consistent with activities that are extreme and for which the need arises in extreme social circumstances.

Between a Rock and a Fluid Place

Sewage pollution is that extreme circumstance for many water sport enthusiasts. Without question, the people described here like to take certain risks. For those enjoying adventure sports, the knowledge of contact with a degree of danger is one of the things that appeals most. At the same time, however, these players like to retain a degree of control. They know that paddling-out through a ten foot wave, or jumping off a rushing waterfall could result in injury. Yet in such cases, they can judge the risk involved for themselves and make informed choices. What has become an unacceptable risk is the threat of high levels of untreated sewage. As Peter, a thirty-something SAS campaigner, musician and sports clothing shop owner based in Truro suggests:

We aren't talking protection from the uncontrollable hazards you are choosing to expose yourself to, if you want to risk life and limb in a death defying feat, go ahead, it's your choice. But, there are risks that can and should be minimised or even removed from the equation—and here we're talking sewage!

Interestingly, there exists a significant legacy for Cornwall to be seen as a protest nation. Recent examples abound: the 1997 march to Blackheath as a 500th anniversary re-enactment of the crusade to London by Trelawny's army; the 1998 economic protest blockade that closed access to the Tamar Bridge to raise national awareness for the region's severe financial inequalities; and finally, an incident in 2003, where 'the Camborne 3' organised Operation Chough against English Heritage. These Cornish vigilantes removed 18 signs from historical sites as a protest against 'English cultural aggression'. An article for *Adrenalin* Magazine on Cornwall's search for political autonomy observes how regional identity increasingly relates to sport and leisure. It cites Bert Biscoe, a Councillor for the Cornwall County Council and the chair for *Senedh Kernow*, the Cornish Constitutional Convention which campaigns for a locally controlled regional assembly. Biscoe affirms, in relation to shifting attitudes towards Cornishness, that 'surfing really helps "put us on the map" and with the Cornish surf team competing in the yearly Celtic Nations Championships, Cornwall is and always has been a legendary nation in the eyes of some' (Biscoe quoted in Gilchrist and Evans 2003, 92).

The connection to Celtic identity is further strengthened through the spiritual folklore of St Piran, patron saint of Cornwall, after whom the Cornish flag is named. St Piran is said to have arrived in Cornwall by surfing across the Irish Sea on a millstone. According to the legend, his original community was jealous of his powers of healing and carrying out miracles. Consequently, they tied a millstone around his neck and threw him off the Irish cliffs. Through divine intervention the millstone was transformed into a buoyant rock so that it floated. Outcast from his homeland, St Piran set sail for Cornwall, where he landed at Perran Beach, to which he gave his name and where he first introduced Christianity to the local Britons. The Cornish peninsula is certainly recognised for having had its own Celtic language and possessing a complex religious heritage.

Additionally, it was a principal cradle of engineering and industrialisation in the UK, harbouring one of the world's largest mining industries during the eighteenth and nineteenth centuries. With a coastline of over 240 miles, fishing has also been central to this territory's socio-economic identity, now mostly known for its art and literature and for the promotion of coastal tourism. Despite this diverse legacy – to which many claims of distinction are ascribed – this constituency is still one of Europe's poorest, receiving remedial European *Objective 1* funding in 1999. To an extent, many of Cornwall's claims to social difference are grounded in its economic impoverishment, which results from the area's rapid de-industrialisation, socio-political marginality and dependence on a fluctuating and seasonal tourist trade.

As part of this post-industrial era, capsized ships and submerged wrecks feature prominently in the south-west seascape. One of the largest maritime research organisations in Europe, the Institute of Marine Studies at the University of Plymouth, runs a range of nautical archaeology modules. Many of the staff and students are involved in identifying sunken vessels off Britain's coast and in its rivers and waterways. In addition to their diverse scientific angles, such studies also bring to the surface the idea of the ritualistic sacrificial destruction of the hull of an undesired boat due to lack of structural integrity. Deliberate sinking to ensure that a vessel cannot obstruct the waterways might have once been understood as the mercy killing of an old vessel. But as with any accidental wrecks, I would like to offer an alternative interpretation – that such sacrifices are part of a process of transforming the life histories of navigational artefacts.

In this sense, decommissioned hulks offer a precious resource for aquatic archaeologists, historians, marine zoologists and so forth. There is no shortage of academic interest in diving for sunken treasure. The idea of treasure is of particular significance here because legends regarding piracy, wreckers and submerged treasure are well-established parts of Cornwall's past, to the point where ancient salvage laws still apply to boat wrecks. The 1997 sinking of the *Cita* off the coast of the Isles of Scilly was a fairly well-reported case in the media. Shipwrecks additionally offer a mysterious playground for leisure divers and adventure seekers while sometimes constituting a nuisance or health hazard to certain enthusiasts of water-based extreme sports.

Aquatic Art

Wrecks are also treasured as a resource of identity which can easily be transformed by creative people. Such artistic recycling and the relationship that it holds with sacrifice, death and the resurgence of identity exists in the work of many art practitioners in the South-West. The transformation of beach waste, derelict boats and submerged vessels serve to socially bemoan the decline of the seafaring industries. One implication behind artworks made of coastal debris is that they have begun to stand for a collective form of social remorse and memorialisation. For instance, the Newlyn artist and gallery owner Helen Fieler has a particular interest in artworks made from abandoned marine vessels such as Don Howling's piece *Creep Table* which Helen now has in her gallery. For her, such artworks are about reincarnating disused materiality. They are also about breathing new life into the issues of Cornish identity. By exhibiting pieces made from nautical waste, Helen is pointing out a nexus of social relations that exist between the material culture of the past and the present. In this sense, she is referring to 'the ways in which coastal communities are adapting to changing socio-economic conditions'. She was responsible for making public a local desire to reclaim a derelict fleet of fishing boats in Newlyn in 1999, of which *Creep Table* became a focal point by featuring in an exhibition called *Transformations* held at Oxford's Pitt-Rivers Museum for 18 months from March 2000.

Now living in Carlyon Bay with his partner Lindsey and their two sons, the maker of *Creep Table* has strong family ties with traditional ironworking. His father Don Senior is also a blacksmith in Cornwall. Don and Lindsey (and presumably their sons Logan and Sean) are passionate environmental campaigners who are heavily involved with SAS. Lindsey teaches yoga and Don regularly makes trophies for extreme sport competitions. He also takes part in a team on the television programme *Scrapheap Challenge*. They see recycled art as mnemonic but not necessarily as memorials to a dying way of life. Rather, they indicate that recycled art is a medium that is imbued with its own agency, which does not want to be seen or 'looked at' as if it were dying. Quite the opposite, they claim that the recycling of derelict material for creating art is a positive statement about a growing concern for the environment – a statement which is sometimes part of giving objects a completely new lease of life, as well as a new sense of motion.

This view is consistent with an overall attitude of defying normativisation. Hence in general, and perhaps especially in Cornwall, surfers and other adventure sport enthusiasts are no more bound to place in any static sense as they are to conventional employment. As we have noted previously, they invariably associate their lifestyle with freedom and movement. Surfers do often have to return to the same breaks, however. Indeed, they are playing in what the sociologist Tim Dant (1998) calls a 'transitory surf zone' that emphasises fluidity, change, danger and ecstasy. The majority of these participants rarely restrict themselves to specific spots: they share a general feeling of wanderlust and hunt the coast for the best conditions or the least crowded beaches.

Dant's points are obviously salient. I nonetheless take issue with one of his later affirmations that the windboard sailor 'is not a political actor' (1998, 89). This may be the case for his material on the relationship between play and leisure in windsurfing. Nothing, however, could be further from the truth for surfers in Cornwall, whereby sewage and their protests against it are part of the very *habitus* of the peninsula's sea-side beach culture. By referring to *habitus* in these terms, I wish to open it up to a more fluid interpretation, one that frees this concept from the more unadventurous definitions which bind it solely to the realm of the everyday experience. In this sense, a protest culture has to exist both in and out of the everyday (Highmore 2002). In such terms then, *habitus* thus regains the possibility of connecting to the exceptional circumstances intrinsic to social movements.

It is therefore useful to expand upon the political links between pleasure and protest by considering some research on environmental surf art that I have been conducting with SAS. This environmental pressure group was founded in 1990 by a handful of local Cornish surfers who were concerned about the discharge of raw or partially treated sewage and toxic waste into the sea, harbours and inland rivers. They have since grown to a nationally recognised organisation comprising some 4,000 members.

A passionate surfer and supporter of SAS, Jonty Henshall of West Penwith makes a variety of recycled sculpture. Of relevance here are those of his pieces that range from decorative sea birds to a bookshelf made from a sawn-up life raft. In the summer of 2003, Jonty made a podium that was used to auction off the surfboards of the *Longlife* Art Exhibition at the Bark House Gallery in Newquay. This event, which toured around the UK, was a charitable and promotional means of raising money and publicity for SAS. Frequently appearing as recent items of material culture, surfboards provide a good post-modern example of the ways in which Cornwall's navigational and marine heritage are being recycled into contemporary icons of youth culture. That they are modern western inventions is of course a misnomer since they are steeped in a rich international legacy of appropriating for leisure purposes the thin strip between coast and open water. The earliest explorers of Polynesia had described surfing as far back as the sixteenth century (Finney and Houston 1966).

I began examining surf art as it related to this environmental campaign as well as the SAS infamous annual ball which takes place near the cliffs of St Agnes. The 2003 ball theme was 'Atlantis', and one of my key informants, Frank (aged 30) from Redruth, went in fancy dress disguised as a wave. In commenting on the rationale for this outfit he reluctantly said, 'it's an expression of the Cornish love for both art and the sea'. An important perspective to tease out at this stage is that much of the SAS ethos is versed in discussing the performative nature of both the proficiency inherent in surfing, as well as in orchestrating effective protest campaigns. Indeed, many of the campaigns are media-savvy demonstrations involving installation and performance art.

Longlife was an exhibition of artistic designs on surfboards inspired by the threat of coastal pollution. It toured a dozen venues in the country, from Northampton to Newquay. The works were created by ten artists, who designed a variety of art surfboards which they donated, in support of this cause, to an auction at the end of the tour. The objective was to raise money for SAS and to increase their public profile. The artists included Maia and Damien Hirst, the graffiti artist Banksy, the professional surfer Laird Hamilton, Paul Kaye of Dennis Pennis fame, the American Surf Culture designer Jamie Carson, the musicians Richard D. James of the Aphex Twin and David Hewlett of Gorillaz and Tank Girl. The auction raised in excess of £70,000.

When the exhibition visited Brighton, I went with Frank, who had recently moved there for work. He commented that his favourite board was the only one that truly captured any local sense of place particular to Cornwall. This was Richard D. James's board depicting a craggy rock face. Incidentally, he added, the artist was one of only two out of the ten to have any real connection to Cornwall. In the context of this exhibition, art and leisure are clearly acting as metaphors for protest against environmental degradation. The art surfboards and their relationship with water, tides and waves are additionally icons of identity, particularly in serving as potent material metaphors that embody an extreme temporality. That is, they stand for notions concerning a 'slow pace of life'. If Cornwall really is a land apart, this relates to the laid back, surfer lifestyle that characterises the 'd'reckly' timeframe separating Cornwall from the rat-race existence of people who live 'upcountry'. An interesting tension arises in this case, perhaps even a possible social contradiction; that is, the way in which adrenaline sports which rely on a speeding up of experiential encounters with the world can exist alongside, not just the stereotypical image of surfers as a laid back subculture, but also alongside a larger cultural construction of relaxedness.

Unfortunately, an area where surfing becomes hypocritical and contested has to do with the one essential piece of equipment. Chris Hines, formerly the Director of SAS, was encouraged under the leadership appointment of the Eden Project's CEO Tim Smitt to leave the management of SAS to others and join the Eden team as Director of Sustainability. One of Chris's pet projects has been to tackle the paradox of using petro-chemical products in the pursuit of surfing. As a deliberate ploy to shock the surfing community into action he has said the following: 'Surfers pride themselves on protecting the sea and being eco-warriors but still ride some of the most toxic pieces of sports equipment'. The Eden Project team have worked with a Newquay-based company on the design of new environmentally-friendly boards (this is the main subject matter of Chapter 5).

In 2008, Chris Hines was awarded an MBE for his services to environmental issues. The following year he again changed his employment path by leaving the Eden Project to help initiate a new development known as Blue Gyms. This is a project about social well-being that deals with the importance of fitness, mental health and playing by the sea. Instigated as a nationwide campaign to encourage members of the British public to exercise near water, it is a Peninsular Medical School initiative, supported by the Environmental Agency, Natural England, and the Department of Health. Launched in August 2009, the main interface is provided virtually through an interactive website with a diversity of functions: newsletter, many different notice boards for information about regional/national events, sister organisation links, blog comments, photography and digital film galleries and so forth. Chris Hines is the main spokesperson and he summarises the intent of the project as well as his interests in it with the following statement on the promotional video clip:

> Blue Gym is about using the coastal waters and inland water ways for mental and physical well being; and strengthening of our communities … water has always been at the centre of my life, from growing up next to the rivers of Dartmoor, through my career as Surfers Against Sewage, and my love of surfing. I'm still in three and around water as much as I can be.

But before leaving the Eden Project, Chris Hines through his SAS connections helped instigate an alternative follow up to *Longlife*. October 2008 saw Surfers Against Sewage put together a second version of that exhibition and auction. This time called *Drawing Boards*, the collection of 14 surfboards consisted of eco-friendly prototypes. Tracey Emin, Sir Paul McCartney, Kurt Jackson, Nick Walker,

Figure 4.1   *LongLife* **Auction Stand (photo by the author)**

Figure 4.2   Mural, Penryn Cornwall (photo by the author).

Figure 4.3   Eco surf-board, Eden Project (photo by the author)

Figure 4.4   Sand mermaid, Fistral Beach Newquay (photo by the author)

Beejoir, Pure Evil, Eine, Mau Mau and Gavin Turk are amongst the artists to feature. And instead of having the auction in Cornwall, the directors of London's Bonhams agreed to host the event as the centrepiece to their Urban Art auction in London on Thursday, 23 October. The boards were on display at Bonhams' New Bond Street gallery for the event. The *Drawing Boards* artworks even featured on the Urban Art auction invitations and images of the collection also appeared as distribution material as part of Bonhams' publicity. The intention was both to help raise more awareness for SAS campaigns as well as to attract attention from wealthy international bidders. The long-standing association with counter-culture movements such as urban art that surfing has maintained over the years, along with the inclusion of leading contemporary artists as well as street artists, meant that the collection was seen as one of the UK's most substantial urban art events at the close of 'the noughties', the first decade of the twenty-first century.

Elsewhere I have explored in more depth these relationships between art, recycled identity and performance (Laviolette 2006a, 2006b). Suffice to say here that the materials to be considered regarding surf art range far beyond nautical relics or boards. Body art, in the form of tattoos, piercing, scarification and similar types of modifications, is quite prominent amongst surfers. Peter (34) provides a compelling anecdote for the relationship between the art of tattooing and the desire to express environmental protest messages. His 'Keep it Clean' slogan, written across his back under a large blue-green wave, illustrates one way in which the body acts as a political canvas. It is worth mentioning that Cornwall's connections with fishing and the maritime industries make it a place where nautical tattoos are not uncommon. Additionally, its highly charged political situation also means that 'nationalist' or at least 'patriotic' tattoos are also prominent.

Of course Alfred Gell (1996) discusses at length the ways in which tattoos in the South Pacific act as a second skin for the individual and social body. Tattoos in Cornwall are thus similarly part of an extensive and complex nexus of aquatic and ideological art, a way of adorning the body with layers of protective meaning. Correspondingly, the tattooed or wetsuit-encased body would extend towards the floating device that allows them to walk on water. In this sense, we can speak about the tattooing of the board, which in many cases is seen as an extension of the body. For many surfers, the board acts as an extension of their legs and feet, a type of prosthetic bodily appropriation. This is not just demonstrable through the observations of movements and the comments that surfers make about their boards but also by looking at the boards themselves and how they change over time. One result is to note the versatility of ways in which, by their frequent decoration and modifications, attempts to make these items 'putatively' benign exist. Such personal incorporation of surfing implements into extended patterns of physical corporality and individual aesthetic taste is a typical case of objectification. This adds to the level in which surf boards gain meaning as things by being able to acquire biographical histories with markedly exceptional dimensions.

It has therefore been quite problematic to challenge the level of this purification process, since the argument about the extension of the self into the board means that one ends up challenging the purity of that self. Perhaps this helps explain some of the resentment that many surfers have expressed at the pronouncement that their boards are un-ecological. It is a slap in the face not only in revealing a contraction in values but also because it becomes an indirect yet profound form of personal attack.

We must add to the mix, however, that there are age and gender discrepancies as well as a basic categorisation of surfer types which need to be specified before making conclusions about the board-surfer relationship. For instance, the distinction between the 'soul' surfer who might have other rationales at heart and thus be open minded vs. the competitively driven, often younger (male) who is preoccupied with performance.

Pollution: Symbolism and Sewage

In accord with these ideas, the symbolism associated with the surfer's wetsuit could be said to act as a prosthetic extension, a third skin, a protection device not only against the cold but against the elements as well, especially against fouled water. Wetsuits encase the body in a protective outer layer. Three-millimetre-thick neoprene/titanium wetsuits are the norm for surfing and cliff-jumping, particularly in the summer, because they do not overheat, and are adequate for wearing to the pub afterwards. Cold water suits (5mm) provide maximum protection for winter surfing and diving from the rocks during cliff climbing and jumping. However, they are considered bulky and awkward in most conditions. Boots and gloves are sometimes recommended for diving and cliff-jumping, but again these are considered as intrusions, so most surfers go barefoot. Many state that this is to allow for a full contact with both water and board.

In ideal conditions such contact is sought but waves and the beach are not seen as benign or even limitless resources, as we are witnessing through the advent of 'Surf Rage', the surfer's equivalent to road rage, where antagonism and fights result from competition over breaking waves (Young 2000). Neither is the sea seen naively as the magical cleanser of waste. It also brings to shore both debris and sewage. *An Mor Daskorr* is a phrase in Cornish that captures this idea of cyclical return. Shipwrecks, plastic, chemicals, poison, pollution – what we throw in the sea, the sea returns – *An Mor Daskorr.* In West Cornwall there exists another dialect word for flotsam, jetsam and wreckage debris: *Scummow.* Interestingly, this term has developed some positive connotations, because it has increasingly become associated with things washed up by the tide which inspire creativity. For example, an artist-led collaborative project working with Cape Cornwall, Mounts Bay and Humphry Davy School has produced a film under the name *Scummow.* This 20-minute documentary, directed by Denzil Monk for the 2004 Golowan festival, illustrates the salvaging process through which the sea becomes the giver of materials for beach art, sculpture, music, dance and film.

A BBC Radio 4 play under the title *Scummow* in 2010 this time tells the story, not of debris washed up by the sea but of a shipwrecked drifter. This theme of *Scummow* coming to mean the washing-up of human seafarers, who in their rescue attempts also bring potential grief, danger or peril to their saviours, has had many literary, theatrical and film adaptations from Shakespeare's *The Tempest* to Victor Hugo's *Toilers of the Sea*. To name but a few relating to the current setting we have some well-known examples such as: Winston Graham's Poldark novels which were turned into a BBC television series; the Cornish Theatre Collective's *Bohelland*; Daphne du Maurier's *Rebecca*; Kneehigh Theatre's *The Wooden Frock* as well as their adaptation of *Tristan & Yseult*.

Waves and sand are not only crucial in returning waste but are also involved in the actual process of transformation. On the sea bed, through the motion of waves, the sand abrades coarser materials, transforming them into new forms. This highlights an association with the endless process that the tides have in smoothing over sharp edges – in rounding things off. The salinity and motion of the sea has acted as the great natural recycler across cultures and times. Problematically, however, the sea as the ultimate human dump is the very concern of those who seek to take pleasure from the waters of coastal places. Sand also gets used in its own right, sometimes by alteration into rather permanent materials like glass. At other times, it is turned into fleeting beach art.

Anthropologists interested in indigenous art have provided elaborate discussions about how sand drawings temporally embody and convey complex mapping information, mathematical patterns as well as secret ritual knowledge restricted to certain spiritual elders (e.g. Morphy 1998). Thus an interesting material chain engulfs the process by which beaches, micro-deserts of sand with latent aridity against life, equally retain a potential for trapping fresh water, allowing plant re-colonisation and thus providing oases of life in parched environments. Metaphorically then, we are faced with a series of ancestral relationships between beaches, deserts and decay. Playing on this analogy, I would say that this referentially alludes to the hydrological cycle and the 'wisdom of waste' (Tuan 1968).

An important connection to Mary Douglas' *Purity and Danger* (1966) exists in relation to the materiality of waves in the context of surf culture. Particularly relevant too is the work of Sharon Beder (1989) *Toxic Fish and Sewer Surfing*, in which she exposes the clandestine state of affairs behind staged public relation campaigns that are designed to mask increasingly dire scenarios. Dominique Laporte's (2000) Foucauldian analysis *The History of Shit* is also pertinent, as is Gay Hawkins' (2003) chapter 'Down the drain: shit and the politics of disturbance' in her co-edited book *Culture and Waste*. Hawkins draws heavily on Michael Taussig's (1997) work to suggest that, in their symbolic and political forms, excrement and death parallel each other in stately discourses about their disposal. In this sense, sewage and death, especially through their link with water-based activities, unsettle boundaries between the body and its others, the nation and the environment, truth and concealment, public and private, and of course purity and pollution.

For instance, the website for the new British Surfing Museum in Brighton informs us that a group of surfers, both men and women, were captured on film as early as 1920 on a beach in Cornwall with their 'primitive' surf boards made out of modified coffin lids about five foot long, crafted by a local undertaker. Indeed, the relationship that the Cornish peninsula has with death, dying and rebirth is significantly distinct in its own right (Laviolette 2003a). It is nevertheless important to reiterate that the other side of issues of pollution is a less literal interpretation, which figures prominently in symbolic conceptions.

The fact that water surrounds most of Cornwall's borders alludes to a powerful visual metaphor about the role of crossing over water to reach the end of life (Anderson 2002). In this sense, many elderly migrants who take their retirement in Cornwall are often anticipating and preparing for death, crossing a threshold and embarking on a pilgrimage to the great beyond. There are many examples of members of the extensive Cornish diaspora, as well as outsiders with a history of family visits, who return to Cornwall upon their retirement. In this way, a popular belief exists in which people see this region as a place where it is good to grow old. And it follows that it is seen as a good place to die. Thus the migration to the extreme west may act as a preliminary to death or 'death's door'. As an 88-year old female Breton informant put it: 'for France it's Brittany, for England it's Cornwall, beyond there's nothing of this world'. In this case, these western regions are more than peaceful, picturesque peninsulas.

Alternatively, what might be at work here is some resistance against death. Along these lines, the tidal shore is an area in constant flux. Informants frequently comment on how waves and water not only constantly renew Cornwall's coastal seascape, but also have the potential to wash away the past and the present: that is, to heal and to cleanse. Regardless, we are in the interesting realm of spiritual pollution. Indeed, many aspects of western culture communicate images of elderly people as dry and arid (Kramer 1988). The voyage of life is a slow process of desiccation which culminates in burial or incineration – 'ashes to ashes, dust to dust'. As such, the journey towards death in Cornwall figuratively parallels a return to the womb, a final journey to the primordial essence of life.

In this respect, let us consider the work of Judith Hubback (1990, 1997), a local scholar and novelist who examines the symbolism of how women relate to the sea and the Cornish coast. She evocatively demonstrates the relationships between pollution, death and the fluidity of the shoreline:

> the shore is revealed in a gradual way during the flux of the tide, opening to light and air the many beautiful creatures and plants which both prosper and are at risk from natural predators such as wading birds (the goodies) and unnatural enemies, such as oil pollution and the detritus of plastics (the baddies). The natural factors can be considered as analogies to the changes in a woman's life when it moves, like the tide, not too fast for her. The unnatural ones are akin to events which are at enmity with organic development, such as unexpected disablement or sudden death. There is something in the usually crude-coloured plastic containers, thrown out when they are empty and have no future, which feels totally alien to the character of the shore, where colours mostly harmonise well: sea weeds wilt … and then the tide brings them up to the beach but they never look as absolutely discrepant as plastic cans do (Hubback 1997, 102).

The feeling is thus that Cornwall offers certain escape spaces for cleansing oneself from spiritual pollution – here people conceal themselves from the inevitable. The region and its waters become safe havens in which people search for embodied mystical healing experiences (Day and Lunn 2003). This extends itself to the realm of Cornish identities, which also relentlessly fight off their own demise. Such identities frequently strive towards survival from the extreme. Hence, for many local residents like Mr Pascoe, a retired farmer from the outskirts of Newquay, Cornwall's beaches and popular immigration towns by the coast are polluted by the decay that invasion brings. His attitude suggests that most apprehensions towards holidaymakers are not, as it might appear at the surface, related to xenophobic distrust. Tourism is not always frowned upon locally. Quite the opposite, most residents believe it to be an essential component to the region's economic survival. What is unwelcome, however, is the leisure industry's suppression of the local in favour of development schemes that do not fit with tradition, that is, projects which drown 'agencies' of belonging.

In this sense, Cornwall often becomes defined through the dilution of 'localness' that occurs from both excess infiltration as well as from the loss of its own population. One can consider this form of grievance as a fluid social commentary about social distinction, a method of generating cultural cohesion around a fragmented discourse that seeks ambiguity (Bourdieu 1984). Consequently, cultural dialogues about the departed abide by a situation in which migration and diaspora have come to characterise and caricaturise the unfixed nature of 'Cornishness'.

In this context it is important not to overlook Cornwall's recent socio-economic developments, where there have been a number of success stories including the Tate St Ives, the Eden Project and the Cornwall National Maritime Museum in Falmouth. With the launch of the first fully fledged university in the Duchy (the Combined Universities in Cornwall) the peninsula itself seems to be undergoing a sea change. Another indication of how the tides are turning can be found in the example of the many conferences and development projects. A conference held at the Newquay Hotel in 2003 entitled *Passion, Power and Possibilities: Challenging Conventional Wisdoms of Regeneration in Cornwall* provides one example. This conference was organised by the Cornwall Business School and the Cornwall Rural County Council. It explicitly addressed these issues of a territory at the threshold of change in its historical development. The Heartlands regeneration project is another larger scale initiative. Heartlands is a community-led vision to transform Cornwall's most derelict urban area into an inspirational cultural landscape. By celebrating and reigniting Pool's local traditions of innovation, invention, creativity and enterprise the project will contribute to re-creating an optimistic place to live, work and play.

Fusing past, present and a progressive twenty-first-century future, the Heartlands landscape will see the creation of an inspirational public green space, outdoor classrooms, and event and performance spaces, all supported by the latest developments in streetscaping and landscaping. The site will incorporate public art in stone, sound, light, and water features. The key focus within this reclaimed landscape will be the restoration of the derelict Robinson's Shaft minehead complex into one of Cornwall's three World Heritage Site interpretation centres. The managers of Heartlands therefore hope to highlight the aims of both the Big Lottery Fund's Living Landmarks Programme and the local aspirations for community redevelopment.

The project's holistic approach to the design process considers the widest possible 'users' requirements to create relevant and unique visitor experience. The aim is to create a scheme where the various elements within this heritage site are harmoniously connected and belong to the whole. In this sense, the notion of play features prominently in the 'Integrated Design' approach so that young people are not alienated but instead actively involved in creating the vision for Heartlands. In this regard, popular themes to date are: adventure and climbing; slides and towers; water and bridges; ball games; and no fences. A suite of innovative and integrated play opportunities that young people can explore and engage with throughout the area is being sought. This requires the participation of young people in the development of bespoke play design elements such as 'sculptural landforms' and public art interventions for play.

Figure 4.5   Sand dune surfing, Northland New Zealand (photo by K. Kary)

Play interventions that are creatively interpreted to meet young people's requirements for excitement and opportunities for risk taking, independent exploration and problem solving also need to be strategically linked to the post-industrial history of the site. Here the designers plan to bring together a combination of developmental play and natural play features which explore the natural and built environment throughout the scheme – emphasising industrial architecture, grassy slopes, woodlands, shrubs, water, climbing rocks and 'den' making options. Also emphasised in the strategy is the idea of exploring different kinds of play; for physical play, quiet play and play that ensures children with a disability and their carers have equity of experience.

Conclusions

Part of the embodied nature of adventure, lifestyle or risk sport is that they encompass more than the intense adrenaline rush experience that is commonly reported in the popular media. Phenomenologically, activities like surfing, cliff jumping and cave diving also allow for the complete engagement, intensification and exploration of all the physical senses. Touch (very much so but sometimes filtered through equipment like wetsuits), sight, sound, smell and taste are all

Figure 4.6   Windsurfer fixture (photo by the author)

Figure 4.7   **Cornish wind turbines, SAS 'Earth, Wind and Fire-Ball', 2004, St Agnes (photo by the author)**

essential to the safe and successful enjoyment of the experience. Surfing, scuba-diving and jumping are in part about enhancing the potential for a full synaesthetic experience, in which participants can merge the sensation of gliding over waves, caving underwater or free-falling with an endearing encounter of body, air, rock and sea. Similarly here, the sociologist and the artist Claudia Bell and John Lyall have explored the concept of the inverted sublime in terms of bungy jumping.

There is, therefore, an intermingling of the physical senses. But it is not the phenomenon of synaesthesia as such that is most importantly at work here. Instead we should talk of 'dysaesthesia' or 'ana-aesthesia': a distortion or transformation rather than a blurring or blending of the senses. Indeed, particularly underwater, the experiences of touch, smell, taste, sound and sight are not as normally perceived. As a viscous medium, water alters people's physical perceptions. It gives a different type of experiential exposure. This is especially the case after a 'wipeout', when surfers find themselves tumbling through the washing-machine effect of powerful waves. Everything is spun around and becomes distorted. We can therefore also speak of the importance of kinaesthesia here, since these activities distort conventional notions of time, spatial perception and motion. Events are rushed up or slowed down in a disproportional way so that sensations of time shift temporarily.

During these moments it is not just the senses that are affected. Emotion and a certain empathy with one's surroundings become apparent. Take, for instance, the following comment by the professional Cornish surfer Mark Harris:

Every swell seems to have a different mood. When you're surfing, you seem to be able to tap into that mood. It's like meeting an old friend. And I think every surfer has a special place where they like to surf the most because that's the place where everything seems to gel together, you known, everything flows. You don't need to think. You're in tune with the mood of the ocean (quoted in Evans 2003).

In this sense environmental sensitivity and ecological awareness are paramount. A main aim of extreme play is to harness the natural forces of the elements, to make a fleeting playing field. By transforming kinetic earthly powers into sources of joy and exhilaration, extreme players are both greening the extreme as well as blurring the structural boundaries between such binary opposites as pleasure and pain, risk and recreation.

The following quote from Fluid Concept's website illustrates the point:

The beauty of the day awakens to the call of the sea—as it slips its fluid motion across the crystalline sand—a hoot can be heard in the distance—as the conception of a dream gives birth to the reality of a slight perfection—simultaneously a slice of fiberglass bites into the morning blue.

It is indeed the idea of having fibreglass in this mix which speaks about the beauty of the sea that some surfers now have issues with. It spoils the green image of the sport. This topic makes up the focus of the next chapter. This materialising of amorphous activities on waves and in the surf is part of a shifting political landscape in which new criteria such as coastal leisure pursuits become part of what helps to define the extreme body. Activities that were once shunned as tourist-related symbols of the outsider have started to be appropriated into regional discourses of belonging. They have equally been internalised and objectified into regional practices of belonging. And significantly, they are associated with growing environmental concerns and awareness. By flowing through a certain Douglasesque structural association for a moment then, it is possible to suggest that surfers and sewage, waves and waste, pleasure and protest are in the process of being used as renewing sources of social relations. This would indeed be part of 'the eternal renewal'.

Chapter 5
Re-Materialising Liminal Objects

KAURI TREE ... (Agathis australis), a species of pine which is unique in that its habitat is confined solely to the Auckland Province in the North Island of New Zealand. The tree is remarkable for the fine quality of its timber which has been considered the first softwood in the world. The trunk rises frequently to a height of upwards of 100 feet, a straight smooth barrel imperceptibly decreasing in girth, until the first limbs are reached.

(Raymond Firth 1922, p7).

As we've just seen in the previous chapter, surfing and surfers have recently been identified as perpetrators of a certain double standard or form of hypocrisy. They generally abide by an ethos that pronounces the glorification of alternative lifestyles and a loving respect for nature, yet eschew acknowledging certain fundamental contradictions – most significantly that the one essential piece of equipment in the contemporary pursuit of riding waves is amongst the worst culprits of environmental disregard of all sporting equipment. The modern surfboard, made up of a toxic cocktail of plastics, resins, glues and fibreglass, has been held up as a model demon of un-sustainability in a world of growing ecological awareness. Hence, a niche for an eco-friendly design has opened up.

On the world scene, a handful of people have accepted the challenge of trying to produce a prototype for a green substitute which is as light, durable and high performing as the synthetic brands that dominate the market. But the early designs of benign counterparts face many challenges of public perception. Despite surfing's historical origins, when boards were made of natural materials and few were in global circulation, the last 50 years have seen the development of standardised mass production techniques. Led by the international market forces resulting from an exponentially increasing demand, this period has witnessed the establishment of formulaic manufacturing procedures by a select number of multi-national corporations. With their considerable vested interests in marketing expertise, financial backing and access to research and development funds, these companies have set a precedent for low production costs. This has perpetuated itself into a highly regulated market which is kept in stasis by the relatively high start-up costs for entering the industry, at least at the level of national or international commerce (Kampion and Brown 2003).

This chapter outlines the development of certain task-networks amongst environmental pressure groups, charity campaigners and corporate surf companies who search to overcome the contradiction of using a toxic piece of sporting equipment by devising an ecologically sensitive alternative. The unit of analysis is therefore those who have made it their mission to search for a sustainable surfboard design. My findings are primarily based on comparative ethnographic examples drawn from research on the distinct surf cultures of New Zealand and Cornwall, where I have mostly been examining the social impact of such environmentally conscious organisations as Surfers Against Sewage, the Eden Project, Surfbreak Protection Society and KASM (Kiwis Against Seabed Mining).

In the vast literature on surf culture, which as a rule defines wave riding as an art-form – a poetic expression of bodily movement through a powerfully shifting environment – it is interesting to note that surfboards themselves have only been the source of attention in popular and promotional texts, not academic ones. The exception is a study from a Masters thesis at the University of Hawaii which was published in the mid-1960s (Finney and Houston 1966). In this sense, within the frameworks of anthropology and material culture studies, these objects are subcultural items that fit the quintessential mould of being completely taken for granted, intellectually back-grounded, discursively ignored. One thing we've learnt is that the objects which are the most noticeable and are of most value are not always those that are most obviously life shifting or socially significant. In fact, because they structure our cultures in ways we do not immediately notice, because they remain unquestioned, the matter in the background of our everyday lives should not only remain in the equation, it should be paramount within the calculations. Indeed, studies on such pop items as scooters or Walkmans have taught us that it is often the overlooked things of everyday life that harbour the most interesting bits of cultural information (Barthes 1968). With this in mind, I want to place surfboards alongside the many ludic artefacts of international significance which have nonetheless remained invisible to scholastic inquiry.

I would equally like to suggest that surfboards possess many particular features that define them not just as forgotten items but as liminal ones, an analytical category which itself has received scant attention in either anthropology or material culture studies. Given their many distinct characteristics, thriving in a shifting transitory zone between land and sea, as well as their affiliation with both corporate branding and yet epitomising many counter-cultural western values and principles, surfboards have persistently been in-between things. As liminal objects, they are transcendental inducers, experientially facilitating altered states of cognitive and corporeal perception. Moreover, they are also quite possibly at a significant crossroads in terms of their manufacturing.

The lack of anthropology and material culture studies for considering objects as liminal entities in their own right is an intellectual conundrum that is all the more perplexing given the significant development of Gell's theories concerning the agency of artworks and technologies (1992; 1998). Indeed, perhaps it is the fascination for, appeal in and even the agency embodied within Gell's own framework of agency that has overshadowed our ability to imagine that the type of agency an object possesses might be a liminal one. We would also have to assume that Turner (1969) defined liminality so exhaustively that our capacity to think of it as anything other than a concept applicable to threshold spaces, groups in communitas or individuals undergoing a rite of passage has been severely limited.

Yet in art history and fine art, the term seems to have more currency, as it does in science and technology studies, where numerous projects have openly examined the ways in which material innovations in the realm of health care often act as intermediaries during the liminal moments that separate life and death, or how new intelligent technologies exist between the world of human desires and that of the things designed to animatedly respond to those desires. Yet, even if it is mostly in these areas that the idea of liminal artefacts has existed, it has still not been conceptualised in any comprehensive way. Consequently, through the prosaic issues surrounding the design of surfboards, I hope to demonstrate that there is no reason why anthropologists should not begin to consider the conceptual implications of thinking about objects in terms of the liminal characteristics that they might have or the liminal states which they might help induce.

Anthropologists may find themselves thinking of Roy Wagner at this point and his major contribution to symbolic thinking *The Invention of Culture* (1975). Wagner writes about the invention of culture as if there were a culture, so the theorisation of the surfboard as a liminal object needs to maintain that the board is not so much invested with liminal agency as it is a mediating object that enables the invention of culture such that it can be deciphered by the observer. The object can only be liminal in the sense that difference is continuous rather than overlapping. In putting forward the idea that mediation is a way of enabling the knowledge which is understandable, so that it is not mere translation but creates a context within which something can be understood, William Mazzarella (2004) is useful to us here.

Double Take

Famous for his prolific ethnographic accounts concerning the Pacific island of Tikopia, many people may have forgotten (or never been aware) that Professor Sir Raymond Firth, cited above, began his academic career as an economist interested in his own country of birth. The quotation that starts off this chapter is from his MA thesis on the socio-economic facets of the Kauri Gum Industry in New Zealand which he submitted in 1922. The Kauri, the second largest growing tree in the world, was massively over exploited in the nineteenth century, so that only small pocketfuls remain in a once large range covering the Northland area from Auckland onwards.

The species features prominently in Maori lore and culture. An ancestral guardian of the forest, it is a living manifestation of cosmological origins, standing quite literally as a force that helps separate the land from the sky. To colonial settlers and European explorers, however, it was mainly seen as an abundantly available resource of considerable value which helped fuel the industrial revolution. More than a century since its large scale deforestation, the Kauri tree has become a complex and contested element of bi-cultural national identity. It features prominently in contemporary discourses about education, heritage and tourism through site tours, museum and conservation practices as well as the sale of a wide range of products made from both its wood and the bright orange resinous gum that fossilises in the soil after oozing from the trunk onto the ground below. From furniture, sculptures and paper weights to bowls and necklace tikis, the distinctly coloured items made from the Kauri's high quality timber or its crystallised gum are highly visible in all sorts of shops around the country.

Now one of my own surfboards, a 7 ft 10 inch mini-mall, is made out of Kauri veneer. I happened to find out about this board while browsing the online auction site Trade Me, the New Zealand equivalent to eBay, an internet service for bartering and bargain hunters. In addition to a couple of images, the relevant details were that the board was shaped by Paul Shanks and the seller was located in the Auckland region. This was useful because I would be travelling through the North Island and could pick it up if need be. As luck would have it, I failed to win the auction because the closing deadline was in the middle of this travel period when I was camping and did not have regular access to the internet. The unmet reserve for this item was $650.00 NZD and the highest bid a week before closing was $340. Before leaving Wellington for an escapade of just under two weeks, I had put in a bid for ten dollars more with an auto-bid for up to $450, then left for a few days and forgot about the precise closing date. Checking from Auckland a couple of days after the auction had finished, I noticed that a few other people had proposed some small incremental bids but had stopped at $390. The auto-bid system had thus put me in the lead but with a sum that was nowhere near the reserve.

As a result, the board had been removed from auction. But in my email inbox there was message sent on behalf of the seller. It said that he was prepared to drop his reserve to $600 and give me first refusal as the highest bidder. There was a three-day period within which to accept before the offer would be withdrawn. Over two days had passed already by the time I had checked my messages. My first thought was indignation: What a cheeky so-and-so, his auction had barely reached $450 and here he was trying it on for $600! So I figured he might re-list the item after the three-day window had elapsed. Leaving the city for a further short excursion into the Northland area, I decided to regularly keep my eye on the surfboard trades from various internet cafés.

A few days passed and no new re-listing appeared. I had gambled wrongly and was regretting not having accepted his offer of $600. Then it dawned on me that it might be possible to work out who he was from the details on his seller's profile. Knowing a first name and a place of residence within the North Auckland region left me hopeful that a surname could be deciphered from the trader name. So back in the city for the last evening before returning to Wellington, I tried the phonebook trick and rang a few numbers under the assumption that I had worked out the puzzle of the seller's second name, asking whoever answered if they had recently been advertising the sale of a wood surfboard on Trade Me. After making six or seven calls I gave up, embarrassed about disturbing people with such a strange request. Oddly enough, it seemed that I had got close at one point when a woman answered saying that this sounded a lot like her son-in-law. She gave me a forwarding number. I rang and the bloke she mentioned answered. He did not seem as perplexed about the whole story as the others but was more concerned about how I had reached him. He became curiously vague after I explained and then evaded revealing much at all about any of the surfing equipment he had previously sold. From his responses and queries back, I ended up thinking that it was him but that he was either no longer interested in selling the board, or annoyed that I had subverted the trading protocol of not contacting people directly.

A week or so later, from the seller's specifications about the auction item, I chased up some information online about the board designer. I wanted to see if ordering another Kauri board might be possible. I found out that he had been a national surfing champion who ran a little custom-made board business out of Whangamata. He was also a prominent environmental activist, the president of an organisation called Surfbreak Protection Society (SPS). It was therefore easy to find contact details for him. After a series of email exchanges, he rang me and left an answerphone message with his phone number. I rang back, mostly to speak about SPS but also to enquire about the costs for shaping a similar board.

Around the same time though, about three weeks after the auction had closed, I discovered that the original seller of the Kauri board had another completely different item for sale on the Trade Me site. This allowed the possibility of posting him a question about whether he still wanted to sell the surfboard he had listed a few weeks earlier. He replied making the same offer he had made in the reduced reserve email. Since this was about half the cost of a new one, and because I had not committed to ordering a customised one, I accepted, mentioning some forthcoming travel plans when we could arrange a cash-on-delivery pick-up.

We met in Albany Village, a part of Auckland's outskirts that neither of us knew but which was convenient for both. In showing me the board quickly in a busy car park, he gave me a brief background on its history. He had bought it for his girlfriend who only used it a few times and was hardly likely to use it much in the future. Nor would he. 'Shame to see it go but we've just no time for the beach these days, now that we've moved from the coast to the big city … it's better off in the hands of someone who'll use it'. He continued by explaining that the move had been the result of a sudden work-related opportunity, only months after she had decided she needed some decent surf gear as a motivator to learn properly. I told him about being especially interested because the board was made from Kauri veneer. He mentioned that they got it from a custom surf place and it was from Paul Shanks's Special Forces series. As a way of soliciting some response about their purchasing motives, I explained that I had contacted Shanks once the board had been removed from auction, commenting upon his affiliations with environmental lobbying. This did not stir any further reaction however. That is, he did not volunteer any information about whether he or his partner had been attracted to the eco-principles behind the design, adding simply that she had been

Figure 5.1   Kauri surfboard (photo by the author)

taken by its aesthetic appeal. He added that it was quite easy to ride for a 'novice' because it had considerable buoyancy and width. He then repeated that they had paid double what he had put as the reserve. Since it was 'still in perfect nick', they had agreed before listing it that they weren't prepared to let it go for less than $600, although he admitted to thinking there would be considerably more interest than there had been.

I would venture that this object was fairly easy to let go of, most probably because the owners did not identify especially strongly with the surfer lifestyle. In the short time in which it was in their possession, it did not facilitate the self-realisation of learning the skill of wave riding sufficiently for them to envisage its continued relevance in their lives, once their circumstances of living by the sea had changed. It had been an easy purchase and a relatively easy sale, especially since its value had been aesthetic rather than based on ideological tenets. But for the maker of this unusual piece of surfing equipment, Paul Shanks, the item's value reflects his values. It is a model example of objectification, whereby his crafting of it is essential to the fabrication of his social self (Tilley 2006). Shanks has been involved with the surfboard industry since the late 1960s. Initially working for the board shaper Brian Weaver in Waitakere, Auckland, he set up his own company a few years later in the same suburb of Glen Eden, a good location for surfers since it is in proximity of the famous Piha break on the west coast. By the mid-1970s he moved his business to Whangamata, another renowned surf area near Auckland, this time to the south-east. This was also the coastal town where his parents had the family batch (small holiday retreat) so it is where Shanks spent a lot time on holiday as a child developing certain skills in and on the water.

As a board shaper, one of his favourite materials for working with is the wood veneer derived from the scrap remnants of deforested Kauri tree stumps cut in the nineteenth century. There are many reasons for this: the wood's unique colour and texture, and the provenance from a majestic tree, of course. Additionally, one of its physical properties is that it is a material which does not change shape when it comes into contact with water. This has made it ideal for seafaring uses and the choice of this resource for making boat hulls has been one of the reasons for mass depletion. Using the wood waste of this period of exploitation has therefore become a powerful socio-political comment about the lack of foresight regarding environmental issues in the past. And this visual statement is one that is made visible to those in the surfing community – those who might not have questioned the elements and processes which go into making their 'sticks'; who might have become complacent about, or have taken for granted, the manufacturing chain that allows wave riding to exist in the first place.

Tree Planks and Toxic Blanks

Thought to have developed most fully in ancient Hawaii, surfing also existed in several island cultures of the Pacific prior to European contact. The art of riding waves was not only recreational, it was also a training exercise for Hawaiian chiefs, a means of conflict resolution as well as a spiritual and symbolic affair, whereby different ritualistic prayers for good surf or surrounding the building of surfboards have been recorded by ethno-historians (Finney and Houston 1966). Surfing therefore began as a complex Janus-faced activity, with both leisurely and ceremonial facets. Indicative of this in-betweenness, of this liminal character, the boards themselves were hierarchically separated in these early days: the 'Olo', ridden by the chiefs or their 'Alii' entourage of the noble classes and the 'Alaia', ridden by the commoners. The wooden boards were made using three main tree species, the Wili Wili, the Ula and the Koa. Their length ranged depending on social class: 10–12 feet long for commoners and 14–18 feet for the nobles and chiefs. These class distinctions were also manifested in gender divisions, even though surfing was commonly practised by women. The creation of masculine power dynamics through the demonstration of endurance, strength and skill pivoted to a great degree around heavy longboards in pre-contact Polynesian cultures (Ford and Brown 2006).

The effects of the puritanical ethos that went along with global colonialism saw the activity dwindle. Douglas Booth chronicles how this occurred even in a country like Australia, which we highly associate with the early advancements of surf culture:

> Beachgoers claimed that heavy and cumbersome boards posed a hazard to their riders and the surf bathing public, and they initiated 'ban the board' campaigns. Prominent Manly councillors lent their support to a proposed ban on 'menacing' boards ridden into bathing areas. The Surf Bathing Association of New South Wales (SBANW) also rejected surfboards (2001, 38–39).

It wasn't until the inter-war years that an international revival would take place, resulting in several big changes in board design. These dealt with the materials used as well as size, weight, fin types and the variation in shape to accommodate different wave conditions. During this era of rapid innovation a number of people, all men and mostly Americans or Australians, have been identified as the main pioneers in the developments. These include: Hobie Alter, Simon Anderson, Tom Blake, Dick Brewer, George Downing, George Freeth, Wally Froiseth, George Greenough, John Kelly, Jack O'Neill, Bob McTavish, Joe Quigg, Bob Simmons and Dale Velzy. From the early 1930s until the late 1950s, surfboards were generally made of balsa wood, with redwood pine as a favoured alternative. The Malibu longboard was still the preferred style which ranged in length from 10 to 16 feet, the non-hollowed pine boards weighing up to 100 lb. The major commercial innovation of developing foam blanks that were then coated in fibreglass is accredited to the Californian Hobie Alter who began searching for a substitute to South American balsa once it got harder and more expensive to obtain because of the growing demand and production competition. The short board revolution of the mid-1960s amplified the use of foam blanks as the industry's norm (Kampion and Brown 2003).

Local surfing histories vary considerably and reveal their own peculiarities. In the case of Aotearoa/New Zealand for instance, shorter carved planks about 5 ft long, known as kopapa, were commonly used on the east coast of the North Island before European contact. Waka canoes were also used extensively across New Zealand and the South Pacific for certain forms of wave racing. Historical reports also indicate that some Maori iwi groups in the Canterbury region rode large devices that could support up to three people. In the lowest parts of the South Island, the Murihiku used kelp bags (pohas) or roughly shaped logs (paparewa) to ride waves which they referred to as kaukau (Jackson 2006). In an extended and comparatively late period of colonisation, New Zealand witnessed a prolonged lull in leisurely seaside pursuits. But at the turn of the twentieth century, a boom in surfing, sea bathing and life-saving practices took place. One significant repercussion was the co-evolving significance of the seaside family batch, a small holiday retreat minimally furnished and often without running water or electricity. Batches sprang up around the country and surfing became a common practice for many children from the 1920s to the 1950s.

A pivotal figure in the transition from the modern era of New Zealand surfing history, dating from the 1950s to the late 1980s, and the current post-modern period, is Paul Shanks, a former national champion who lives in Whangamata, south of Auckland on the east coast. He is the president of the Surfbreak Protection Society which he co-founded in 2006 in protest at the development of a marina which requires the alteration of the Whangamata Bay sand bar, hence possibly affecting the local surf break. He was officially drawn into the affairs of political and legal legislation a decade before forming SPS 'over the issues of water quality and the territorial rights of established surfbreaks'. It was around this time in 1998 that these ideological interests in the environment became formally manifested in his business as a surfboard shaper when he turned his attention to using alternative materials.

Regarding the legacy in social anthropology of being expertly fascinated with kinship and genealogy, it is interesting to note how some people describe their identity as a surfer in terms of whakapapa – lines of extended family relationships and descent. In a document submitted on behalf of his SPS organisation in 2008 to the Board of Inquiry of the Department of Conservation regarding the Proposed New Zealand Coastal Policy Statement (Policy 20), Shanks introduces himself as an expert witness in the following way:

Figure 5.2   Whangamata marina expansion (photo by M. Gunson)

I am a Surfer. A surfer must have a reasonable grounding in geography, geology, meteorology, hydrology, micro-biology, chemistry, aero-dynamics, environmental law and adherence to the principles of kaitiakitanga to/of a Surf break. A Surfer must know the history of surfing, in his hometown, in NZ and also the rest of the world, because these disciplines have had a major impact on surf breaks and Surfing over the last century. Hawaiian Duke Kahanamoku, Olympic swimming Gold medalist introduced modern Surfing to NZ at Lyall Bay, Wellington in 1912.

I am a Surfer, there is no formal qualification to be a Surfer ... Who am I to claim to
be a Surfer?
– I represented NZ Surfing 3 times in International events 1972–1977;
– NZ Senior champion 1990;
– Assistant coach twice NZ junior teams to world titles 1993 &1995;
– Husband of Jan Shanks, life member of Surf NZ;
– Brother of Mark, 2 times NZ finalist national Surfing champs and coaching
  coordinator for Surfing NZ;
– Father of NZ junior women's reps Amber and Heidi;
– Father of Heidi twice NZ junior champ, 1994 Open women's champ;
– Father of Samara, Surf-shop manager;
– Brother of Jeanne, 10 times NZ open women's champ;
– I have been in the Surfing business/industry since 1971, owning and operating a
  business in Auckland and Whangamata, retailing, manufacturing, wholesaling and
  exporting.

Similarly, the artist and carver from Raglan, Aaron Kereopa, comments that he
was fortunate enough to be adopted into a Hawaiian family. From this he has been
able to appreciate and comprehend the similar thematic patterns of Pacific cultures,
especially in terms of mythology and the narratives of navigational travel:

When you combine that with our common approach to our tupuna (ancestors),
whakapapa (genealogy) you have a rich tapestry that I end up translating onto
the surface of the boards I work with. When I first started this journey I would
use broken boards, take them out for their last surf then strip them out. From
there it is a matter of working out what will fit in that space, what will work in
with the thickness, the curvature, length and rails of the board. To me it is like
they are a living piece, a waka (canoe) (cited in Panaho 2008).

Many surfers, particularly those who are actively involved with environmental
organisations, are increasingly feeling compromised by having to use boards
that are ecologically damaging in what should be a 'natural' environment. The
surfboard's three base materials are extremely toxic and there is an annual global
production of nearly 750,000. Internationally, one can find several examples of
local board shapers such as Shanks who have specialised in the niche market of
environmentally conscious surf equipment. Indeed, this is not a new phenomenon
but has been going on over the last 40 years or so. The main problem has not
been with the vision since the social memory of surfing is not so old as to have
forgotten the roots of the activity as one reliant on wood as the initial material
of board production. Rather, the issues have been threefold: lightness and
performance; affordability in relations to mass production and consumer demand;
and the international popularisation of the activity which has turned it into a fairly
minimalist and low-cost leisure hobby as well as an increasingly competitive
professional sport.

As we have seen in the previous chapter, one of the main proponents for developing new eco-board prototypes that can satisfy the needs of a huge global market has been Chris Hines. He has made several public statements about the search for ways to clean up surfing's image such as: 'This board is a challenge to surfers and to the industry ...' Over the years, while Director of Sustainability at the Eden Project, he and his team have been involved with exploring several design options. They have worked in partnership with a range of Cornish-based companies on the prototypes for making boards in an environmentally-friendly way on all the levels concerned, from the sourcing of base materials and colouration pigments through to each manufacturing procedure.

A Cornish company called Ocean Green began producing custom boards that were one hundred percent 'bio-derived' – that is, made entirely from renewable materials. The idea was to replace the traditional board production process with a sustainable alternative which had equal or better qualities, thus giving surfers an ethical consumption choice that would be consistent with the overall respect for the environment shared by many. Initially they started by experimenting with hemp cloth, balsa wood and potato peelings instead of fibreglass and polyurethane foam blanks. Combined with natural resins, rather than polystyrene epoxy, the hemp cloth laminated coating produced boards that were undoubtedly more environmentally sensitive, while remaining fairly light and strong. Another of the advantages is that balsa trees grow rapidly.

Pat Hudson, who works as the sustainability research officer at the Eden Project, has pointed out that one of the main drawbacks with the balsa-hemp design was in the expensive production cost. Not being within a reasonable range of the cost of normal boards removed their commercial viability, meaning that they remained an exclusive product for a limited consumer base. Also, the balsa-hemp trial boards were especially susceptible to fungal attack and damp rot. So after some comprehensive research into the ecological footprint of the materials involved in 2005/6, a new approach has been taken by the Eden team. One alternative which seems hopeful is not to strive towards producing the utopian ideal of sustainability but to aim instead for a realistic compromise which might leave a positive global impact. The result has been the design of Biofoam surf blanks. These were launched by HomeBlown in 2007, a company that has manufacturing facilities in the UK, US and South Africa. They estimate that the shipping of raw materials for local production is 18 times more efficient than shipping pre-made blanks. The result has been that it is now possible to order eco-boards at prices competitive with those of the normal market products. These blanks have close to 50 per cent of their foam sourced from plant-based agriculture products and the production results in 36 per cent fewer carbon emissions and a 61 per cent reduction in non-renewable energy use than the standard board made with polyol resins (Brun 2007).

We can see that this new approach also includes the proviso of being more 'scientific', thus being able to produce more convincing evidence for persuading both manufacturers and the public of the need for change. In this respect, it has been calculated that professional surfers, for instance, go through more than a board a fortnight as they snap in two, develop pressure dings or simply lose flexibility. Some minimally damaged boards get repaired and re-enter the market as second-hands but many are disposed of into landfills where they take centuries to decompose. Conversely, the eco-version can simply be composted. Pat Hudson has commented about the green alternatives, that in theory they can 'be thrown onto the compost heap to decompose naturally and quickly'.

This raises the question about the death of the object and what seems to constitute the need for generating a discursive attitude of alienability around surfboards. There is an important point to drive home here about the relationship with modernity and disposability in terms of responsibility for an object until it turns into something else (Eco 2007). Whereas the modern position is that once the use value has expired, one's responsibility for it shifts to someone else, so that we can forget about it and are no longer connected to it. Without wanting to be too cynical, we do need to acknowledge that often boards go through several lives. They get gifted, repaired, sold at car boot sales or on internet auction sites. Older ones get collected or transformed into furniture and artworks. Many simply get tucked aside as a voluntary or unwitting display of the laid-back lifestyle associated with beach culture. In other words, surfboards are actually objects which are difficult to separate from the identity of the practice.

This dilemma has been identified by many scholars working on the redeemable features of refuse and rubbish. For example, the compilation *Culture & Waste* by Hawkins and Muecke (2003) addresses the production of value for things taken out of the formal economy thus raising such questions as: why would we want to encourage a throwaway society component which has long-term value even after its originally intended use has waned? As a keen surfer, Hudson is of course aware of the rhetoric, especially since he recognises that professionals are only a tiny fraction of the market. They are therefore not the targeted users for the green prototypes, nor at this stage in the developments would they even be seen as the standard norm for the more expert surfer. So even though they go through lots of boards, the impact of the professionals is minor in comparison with the huge number of beginners to moderate surfers for whom optimal performance boards are not especially necessary.

Regardless, the problem of performance perception of the eco-board is highest amongst the most competent practitioners, many of whom are themselves old-school shapers or the ones who run the businesses which order materials or products from suppliers. In general, this group is either complacent or opinionatedly antagonistic to the need for developing sustainable surf gear. Granted, it was during the early phase of the developments for the eco-board solution, but one time in 2005 I dedicated a full day in Newquay and St Ives to tracking down a shop that would stock or order an eco-board. Most often I was given a blank stare. On a couple of occasions, I was laughed out the shop by a bunch of lads who followed with comments such as 'what was that all about' or 'bloody hippy'. Only at one shop in over a dozen did the salesperson pay attention to my interest and said he would pass on the request to his manager, adding: 'the more we hear such requests, the more our suppliers will realise that there's a market for such things'.

And of course why stop at boards? The Billboard Surfboard Bag is a new venture in providing an eco-alternative to manufactured vinyl board bags. Its waterproof vinyl is made of reused, colourful motorway billboards. The dual benefit of saving an otherwise discarded material and limiting the production of new vinyl-based plastics not only makes the board bag an environmentally friendly option but gives it a much more distinct and individual aesthetic.

There is of course another reason to gain the support of the professionals with regard to such alternatives – they are often idolised by many young beginners. This is where it becomes essential for the promoters of the eco-boards to get the sponsorship and endorsement of corporate multi-national surf companies. Since these organisations are increasingly sensitive to market demands for green products, they are beginning to respond by changing suppliers or associating with certain environmental campaigns. Many environmental pressure groups have themselves become sensitive to this bandwagon phenomenon and have responded in a variety of ways to make sure their corporate affiliations do not become smokescreens.

Canvases and Emergency Objects

It is not just designers who have been involved with promoting the use of alternative materials in surfing. Artists are prominent amongst the groups that have been recruited to help lead the way in changing the public's mindset. As discussed in Chapter 4, especially with reference to a couple of high profile examples in the UK, there is a fairly long history of surfboards being used as the canvas for contemporary and street art. For instance, the Californian board shaper Jeff Ho, made famous through his central position in the Venice beach surfing and skateboarding scene of the 1970s, became internationally renowned for his extravagantly coloured artistic designs (Peralta 2004). There is no direct way in which one could argue that the Ho & Zephyr Productions surfing and skating products can be associated with the onset of environmental awareness in the realm of board sports. Nevertheless, it is the maintenance of the excessively counter-cultural façade in the rapidly developing corporate appropriation of extreme practices which is the point worth emphasising here.

Another example of the growing attempts to promote green awareness in surfing includes the *Full Circle – Surfboard Evolution* exhibition which ran at the Eden Project over the summer of 2008. Displaying rare and historic surfboards dating from the late 1800s to the present day, it was the first exhibition in the UK to look at both the environmental impact of surfboards and the change in their design over a hundred-year period. By highlighting significant historical developments, the exhibition was put together with the intent of showcasing new ideas in material selection for the future of the industry and the practice. This idea of a cyclical return connects well with the theme of liminality in that undergoing the phase of anti-structural 'in-betweenness' allows for a return to the structured social setting, albeit in an enlightened way which might serve to challenge or change the status quo.

An artist who has deliberately played on this connection between the return and ecological concern is Ben Cook. Again in 2008 at the Eden Project, Cook set up an homage to Joseph Beuys's *The Pack*. Inspired by Beuys's 1969 installation, the piece was meant to highlight the need to consider change in mainstream as well as alternative communities. Beuys's installation consisted of a Volkswagen camper van with 24 sleds emerging from the rear doors. Each had strapped to them a roll of felt for warmth, a lump of animal fat for energy and a torch for direction. Beuys had described the piece as an 'emergency object', representing the need to resort to immediate and reliable means of survival during instances of modern technological breakdown. Beuys had drawn on an incident of crisis when his dive-bomber was shot down in Crimea during the Second World War. He subsequently alleged to have survived the crash as a result of being rescued by nomadic Tartars who wrapped him in fat and felt to nurse his wounds and keep him warm.

As well as the sleds and felt being swapped for surfboards and wetsuits, *The Pack* 2008 sees the animal fat replaced with tablets of surf wax and the flashlights with tide tables to symbolise survival and direction. Behind Beuys's initial installation and Cook's re-enactment is the idea of exploring the human capacity to adapt in the face of technological failure, a concept that blends well with the Eden Project's overall vision as well as their search for sustainable surfboard prototypes. Both the sledges and the boards are depicted as being in a liminal state of waiting, of readiness. They are about to undertake a potentially perilous journey – a phase of transit through the wild between one place and another – between one time and another.

Cook is explicit in the rationale he gives for the environmental agenda behind many of his artworks:

I want to question the current consumer-led fashion for an insistence on a pure white surfboard blank. Surfers are close to nature. They're dependant on it and immersed in it, and they ought to be the first people to question prevailing technology. They should also be the first people to adopt new sustainable materials.

The reasons behind the artistic use of surfboards are rarely so clear cut or overt in terms of environmental concern. This is not to say, however, that other types of surf art address poignant issues less equally. Dealing with the relationship between identity and local materials is certainly crucial with regard to influencing the public's perception. For instance, Brian O'Connor, an artist from Southland had one of his two paua shell laminated boards bought by the National Museum of New Zealand, Te Papa Tongarewa, in 2001. In 1987 O'Connor established Southern Paua, a little business in Riverton which specialised in making and selling paua shell souvenirs. In 1998 he moved his business to Kaikoura, an area just north of Christchurch which was becoming increasingly popular with tourists because of whale watching, decent weather and consistently good surf. His four sons and wife are all dedicated surfers and keen on snowboarding as well. One of his future projects is to make a paua snowboard. He is one of a number of New Zealand artists and craftspeople passionate about using the nationally iconic paua shells. The O'Connor surfboard is just one of the many pieces made from paua shells which are held in the Te Papa collection.

The paua shell surfboard is a standard shortboard size of six foot, two inches (1.89 metres). O'Connor has been a surfer since the mid-1970s and in 1990 started making his own boards. Creating a board with paua shell seemed be a natural thing to do for an artist interested in surfing and he was surprised that no contemporary artist had thought of it until the twenty-first century. He has emphasised its functionality as a board, saying that it is:

> definitely rideable. It's an uncomfortable feeling knowing you're sitting on a big
> fishing lure, but it's an amazing experience to see the sun reflecting off the paua
> in the water … I knew it was possible, and I thought it would be out of it, and
> nobody had done it before.

To make the paua board, he applied all the normal procedures for shaping surfboards. That is, he took a standard foam blank. In the middle of the blank is a thin piece of wood that runs the length of the surfboard. This is known as a stringer, and it provides strength and weight. O'Connor shaped the blank to his own specifications by shaving layers off it with a tool called a planer. After applying resin to the board, he fixed stripes of paua laminate, which were simply held in place with double-sided tape. After coating the entire board in fibreglass, the usual process of sanding and polishing is required.

The board features in the *Made in New Zealand* exhibition which has been on permanent display since 2001. It is a piece that considers sustainability in the sense of cultural and heritage issues rather than direct ecological foot-printing. If, however, one of the main hurdles to overcome in the environmental debates surrounding surfing is public perception, then the O'Connor piece is a highly visible contribution of major significance.

Box Insert 5.1 Skateboard Art

Another high profile example along these lines, this time in relation to skateboard art, is worth commenting on because of the intertwined historical relationship between skating and surfing. Artists from Wellington's Weta Workshop and Totem Decks held an exhibition *Board Culture* on artistically designed skateboards at the Underground Arts and National Tattoo Museum. The exhibition was scheduled to run for two weeks in the Spring of 2008 but due to its popular appeal it ran for an additional few weeks. The long tradition of skateboard street art has generally been in the form of painting, graffiti spraying and occasionally, sticker pastiches. This exhibition broke with that convention by displaying etched images engraved into the wood. Even though the 'sustainability' message about them was articulated in terms of cultural not natural heritage, it was quite obvious from the visual and material evidence that the simple/pure aesthetic deliberately incorporated certain eco-values. Indeed, the sourcing of the timer as originating from best practice renewable forestry plantations was heavily emphasised in the marketing of the exhibition and by the curator.

The exhibition was not only successful in New Zealand. On the evening before the opening, the manager of The Underground Arts and National Tattoo Museum, Steve Maddock, was surprised by a call from the British Museum inquiring about the purchase of some of the works. He was delighted when the British Museum curators confirmed that they would buy some of the intricately laser-etched skateboard decks of his subcultural exhibition. 'Some of these designers are huge. There are people who have worked for Disney, Marvel, Weta and Warner Brothers … It's amazing having these artists involved. This is one of the biggest exhibitions we have ever had.' Among other items, the exhibition featured decks created by some of the people at Weta such as Greg Broadmore, Leri Greer and Christian Pearce. Other contributing artists included award-winning American cartoonist Frank Cho (*New Avengers*, *Liberty Meadows*), New York pin-up artist Alberto Ruiz, Disney animation designer Ron Cobb (*Sleeping Beauty*, *Star Wars*), and filmmaker Wojciech Wawrzyniak (*Love Hurts*).

Regarding the British Museum's interest in the exhibition, Maddock specified 'they wanted the decks with Aboriginal designs on them'. These were selling for $1,000 to $2,500 AUD each, whereas the others ranged from $300 to $800. The exhibition was secured on the recommendation of Weta workshop's director Richard Taylor, who has been a long-time friend of Steve Maddock's and supporter of the Museum's promotion of non-mainstream art. Despite the backing of such high profile people, the Museum remains little known outside the alternative community. Regardless of this recent success though, as a tattoo artist himself, Maddock has remained adamant that the Museum would remain a staunch supporter of the local alternative arts scene. His rationale for extending the exhibition was to allow Wellingtonians a chance to see the decorated decks, now sanctioned as a part of the world's cultural heritage by one of the most internationally recognised institutions.

Conclusions

Simmel's ([1911] 1997) musings about the adventurer are relevant for our purposes on many levels but I want to use them here because of the explicit connection that he makes between the adventurer and the artist. Not only is the adventure like a work of art, but in speaking to the meaning of life in a way that is torn out of everyday experience, the adventure captures a privileged microcosmic reflection on humanity's place in the world. As he says:

> A part of existence, interwoven with the uninterruptedness of that existence, yet nevertheless felt as a whole, as an integrated unit – this is the form common to both the work of art and the adventure. Indeed, it is an attribute of this form that makes us feel that in both the work of art and the adventure the whole of life is somehow comprehended and consummated – and this irrespective of the particular theme either of them may have (1997, 223).

In illustrating a classic paradox between nearness and remoteness, both adventure and art share transcendental qualities that can be captured in concrete ways. It is the tension between its closeness to life and its distance from the everyday that provides a logical coherence to the adventure which is distinct and potentially memorable.

This therefore allows us to consider the ambiguity of both the functions of surfboards and their current transition, when a large-scale design shift might be about to occur. Water sports are an increasingly prominent factor in the formulation of identity, and in several ways such leisure activities are tying into ecological discourses since the surfboard becomes a quintessential liminal object in being in that moment of history when they might be changing towards a new ethos of sustainability.

Surfboards are also liminal objects because they are literally and figuratively about the flattening of experience, although not in the derogatory sense. Only minutes of any session are actually spent standing, the rest of the time is for sitting, lying down or duck-diving. They are devices that allow their owner to float on the water taking in endless hours of contemplation and meditation, staring at the horizon, observing the swell. Even when standing, the surfer's gaze is not predominantly directed at the water below but instead probes the beach or rocks in the distance. In facilitating transcendental experiences surfboards are thus classic liminal objects made more so by the in-between area which they move through, beach and sea, domestic and public, concealed and revealed. For the apt surfer, they equally allow for the irregular possibility of mediating the entry into a space created by the curvature of the wave crest before it breaks, the 'green room', a unique environment of sensorial distortion. Moreover, they are a piece of equipment that transgresses modernity into post-modernity, allowing their owners that subversive identity of being outside normative society.

Figure 5.3   Etched skateboards (photo by the author)

To return briefly to Raymond Firth for a moment then, it is important to emphasise the economic significance of the struggle to make equipment prototypes into a social reality. The material above illustrates an interesting contrast: the nature of independent versus commercial adventure. It shows that these two facets are intimately linked and yet simultaneously on opposite ends of the spectrum. The latter seeks to reduce real risk to minimal levels, in order to create an enduring enterprise with a clean public image. In this sense, adventurous activities are far from being dangerous or 'close to death' (Buckley, Cater and Godwin 2007). Thus the business end of the alternative sports industry reminds us of the need to consider both the form and the function of the equipment used. Without worrying about the debates over functionalist determinations, we can – by seeing the complex networks outlined above and considering their intricate entangled relationships – certainly appreciate the need for micro and macro level analyses. Indeed, in thinking about the bigger picture, we need to bring together many variables concerning the complexity of understanding the socio-political (including financial dimensions) alongside perceptive or psychological discourses, as well as debates about the symbolic and considerations over the material cultures of the activities involved in thrill seeking.

The boards provide a bridge between the previous chapter which focuses on surfing bodies and the following chapter on the notion of ritual and symbolic adventure. Surfboards are thus an interface between the participant and their chosen peak experience activity in a way that other equipment such as shoes or snowboards simply are not. They are more akin to the fundamental importance of rope in bungy jumping, rock climbing and the acrobatic traverse of tight-wire walking, for instance. The Heideggerian (1988) point about becoming, as the board enables the production of knowledge which allows this new identification with skill and social position, applies well at this point.

We can further speculate theoretically that the debate about eco-surfboards stands as a metaphor for a paradox that most people and cultural groups deal with in terms of the multi-faceted structures within which identities exist and change. This is particularly revealed through the relationship that holistic innovation has with our attention to consumption in an increasingly global capitalist economy. The base assumption, perhaps worth investigating further, is that an increasing world-wide awareness of, and concern for, environmental issues is currently taking place. If such is the case, does this mean that human perceptions of materiality are likely to evolve as a result?

Chapter 6
Eclipsing Reason – Ritualising Hazards

'Hey, there's something falling down in there,' said the chief clerk.
Gregor tried to suppose to himself that what had happened to him might some day also happen to the chief clerk.
There was no denying that anything was possible.

Franz Kafka (1915, 7).

Now from the descriptions in previous chapters, it should be getting clearer how I got to this point of thinking that a study of euphoric places and adrenaline practices might make an interesting topic to explore. One part of the answer dates back to a single identifiable incident or observation, midway through my original fieldwork, which it must be said was not on this type of subject matter at all but instead related more generally to issues surrounding identity and the social construction of landscape. Although I did not realise it at the time, I was witness to an unofficial ritual on a day of historical magnitude which would add an unanticipated dimension to my future research.

On 11 August 1999 at 11:11 am, the south-western Cornish peninsula was at the epicentre of a total eclipse of the sun. This event provides a telling example of the appropriation by different groups within the region; most specifically a confusion between commodified leisure pursuits on the one hand and the cultivation of a local aura of mystery on the other. The esoteric nature of the eclipse meant that identity politics could take a new shape in its re-emphasis, at least in an allegorical sense. By iconographically associating Celtic and prehistoric imagery with celestial and astrological signifiers, this event fed into a discourse about a radiating regional distinctiveness. It provided a context whereby attempts were made to illuminate the territory's socio-economic hardship, while simultaneously endeavouring to shadow out the conditions of modernity that have been responsible for the region's increasingly desperate plight since the industrial revolution.

If certain themes like hospitality, death, healing and tradition provided some coherence to this discourse, the eclipse itself was made comprehensive by an overarching ritualistic meta-narrative. By its very nature, this event revolved around symbolic issues of ambiguity, liminality and rebirth. Examples of such issues include: the national media promotion, the choices of parallel activities, the visibility of the event due to weather conditions, the effects on the natural world (birds, flowers), the security for eyesight and the fear of blindness, the spiritual outcome of a world being cast into daytime darkness with the associations here with temporary gateways to the otherworld.

Picking the right spot to see the eclipse was a major source of concern for all my research informants. A number of them gathered at a friend's place in Falmouth. Another group, hoping for a bit more privacy, arranged to meet at a dramatic clifftop near Padstow. I also had the opportunity of joining a few people I knew at a music festival on the Lizard Peninsula. Instead I chose Carn Marth near the village of Lanner and the town of Redruth. This was the location chosen by many local people from this ancient mining area. Contrarily, the neighbouring hill of Carn Brea, which is a well-known tourist attraction, was largely ignored by residents. Unsurprisingly, it was instead the site of choice for several thousand visitors. Despite having several days of good weather prior to 11 August, leaving forecasters hopeful that the event would be clearly visible, the climate across most of Cornwall on the day was densely overcast. One of the members of the pagan community who refers to himself as the Grand White Druid of Cornwall even held a specific ceremony to incite good weather across the region. This was well reported in the media, both before and, presumably to his dismay, afterwards.

The two thousand or so witnesses at Carn Marth were thus unable to discern where the sun and moon actually were in the sky. Instead, most of the people I spoke to afterwards remarked how it was seeing the camera flashes going off in the surrounding towns of Falmouth, Newquay, Redruth, St Ives and Truro that had left the biggest impression on them. Largely because most people were unable to see this event in its full grandeur, it has since become a notorious part of Cornish history. As one person exclaimed, 'it's typical of the way you can't expect things to work out the way you imagine or hope they will down 'ere'.

In terms of group dynamics, the eclipse offered a major occasion for both sociality and antagonism. Parties were thrown all around and for many local residents the event provided a chance for them to invite friends and relatives from around the world. The date of 11 August 1999, also referred to as the Millennial eclipse as well as the Celtic eclipse, presented a chance to see something extraordinary and for the region to be seen in extraordinary circumstances. The Duchy of Cornwall thus entered a quasi-liminal state for several days. As a result, the atmosphere was not one hundred per cent convivial. Indeed, a major debate surrounded the promotion of the eclipse as a means to boost tourism. It was waged, on the one hand, by many residents hoping to renew people's interest in visiting the south-west. One such informant from the village of Lanivet even made the pun that 'Cornish hospitality is like Cornish cream: the richest in the world'. At the other extreme were those who wished to exploit the event to the full. Such residents equated the notion of a rich welcome with an opportunity to 'bleed the tourists dry'. Generally, the tactic of trying to maximise any potential economic return from this 'one off' event was also intended by some to subvert future tourism. The take-home message pitched by certain residents was thus 'Cornish hospitality, the most expensive in the world'.

A mentality of ritualistic purification for the region was also responsible for fuelling Cornwall's hyped-up international role during the eclipse. The event provides a telling example of how the region's appropriation by various, often contesting, groups launched the Duchy into a confused state of ambivalence by attempts to accommodate a hodgepodge of contemporary mythological issues.

The themes that conveyed themselves most coherently at the time orbited around how the moon's shadow over Cornwall for two minutes would provide the opportunity for a turning point at both personal and social levels. By highlighting the importance of rurality, prehistory and folklore, the promoters and participants were often unwittingly and sometimes consciously involved in a process of producing a regional aura of distinction – reinforcing the creation of social difference – elevating Cornwall to an otherworldly status. Jeff, an informant in his late thirties (who was raised on the outskirts of Newquay and visits regularly from London), seemed to be speaking for many when he said:

> The eclipse is all about dying and being reborn. Unlike other artificial occasions, it's a natural form of emptying the old and bringing in the new. Time to start again, a once in a lifetime chance at self-purification ... the potential for this isn't the same in other places. Only here is all this astrological stuff going on. I mean the date and time of the eclipse [11:11 on 11/08/99] is more than coincidental, it's all about a new beginning which is so meaningful here because dates, time, the sun and moon were so crucial to the development of this countryside. In prehistoric times, occasions of this magnitude would have so completely marked how they perceived the world and their understanding of nature. What we're going to witness would have changed their world-view for generations and that's surely a big reason for these stone megaliths ... it's the kind of thing which made this all possible in the first place.

Ritualistic Diddle – The Crowd that Jumped Under the Moon

The act of jumping off steep cliffs first came to my attention during that morning of the sun's eclipse. As the peninsula entered into the moon's shadow, three men in their mid to late twenties, to celebrate the occasion, stripped down to their shorts and started jumping into a flooded quarry on Carn Marth, near the town of Redruth. When it had become apparent that they were about to do so, a few dozen people quickly gathered around the artificial lake created by an open cast depression in the ground. One of the lads quickly swam around the landing area and shouted to his two mates above that everything seemed fine. He then got out and walked up around the edge of the 30-foot-high ridge. They waited huddled together for a couple of minutes and once it started getting dark, they proceeded to jump in one after the other, with a delay of about ten seconds between them. They each jumped three times from the ledge, dried themselves off with their T-shirts and then left unceremoniously. None of the onlookers interjected and no one was encouraged to join in or follow suit once they were gone.

After taking a few photographs I quickly forgot this incident but soon witnessed more people jumping into the sea from a cliff face along the coast path which had a sheer drop into a deep cove. Only a few days later, when walking along the Newquay harbour, I saw a small group of five or six teenagers jumping from the top of a toilet block that protruded from a cliff edge at the side of the harbour car park. I began asking my friends and informants whether they were aware of this strange practice: 'Oh ya, it's a big thing down here. The press and coastguard started calling it tombstoning to try and put the kids off … but I reckon that's probably made it even more popular'. It wasn't long before my own first experience a few months later, by which time I had also become aware of some of the more serious accidents that sometimes occur, some of them fatal.

One informant I spoke to about cliff jumping told me that at least one death per year is caused by the practice. He said it was the most hazardous activity practised by the young people in the region. Indeed, in that year a series of three deaths around the UK received high-profile attention in the media. One of them occurred in June 2003, while I was doing fieldwork on this very topic, when a 24-year-old youth did not resurface from a 100-foot jump into another flooded mine quarry, this time at Kit Hill in Callington. Another well-reported case occurred in 2005 when a professional Australian surfer, on a day off because there were no waves, broke both his legs when misjudging the depth of the water. By 2007, the statistics from the Maritime and Coastguard Agency stipulated that the emergency services were being called out for an average of one rescue a week. These incidents had led to over a dozen serious accidents nationally and a yearly death rate of four.

Drawing upon such examples of jumping and falling from cliffs into flooded quarries or the sea reveals that part of the non-utilitarian logic of such practices is ritualistic on many levels. In an admittedly structuralist way of creating an artificial opposition, it is easy to see that one type of manifestation of these activities is glorified as totemic, its adventurous spirit is celebrated as part of many forms of identity. At another extreme are a series of social representations of danger which are socially feared, legally illegitimated and to many extents, culturally tabooed. Depending on the levels of mitigation that take place, risk and danger thus flow between various states of totem and tabooed-ness.

Now certainly in popular parlance and even amongst many researchers interested in symbolism, theology or non-western belief systems which include magic, witchcraft and animism, ritualistic activity is equated with some form of rehearsed ceremonial event. It is something that follows strict guidelines: prepared, controlled, then led by certain spiritual leaders and elders. Conversely, anthropological definitions have tended to consider ritual in terms of its role in marking drastic changes, in rites of passage that substantially alter one's worldview, for instance. Such a position suggests that ritual ceremonies are infrequent and unpredictable events, even if certain stages and elements are constantly present.

Figure 6.1   Eclipse 1999, Carn Marth (photo by the author)

In *The Ritual Process* (1969) Victor Turner wrote about the significance of spontaneous rituals with these tenets in mind. In fact in his definitions, liminality and communitas are the spontaneous anti-structural counterparts to the profane social structures of everyday life. Here the focus on guarded ceremonies is shifted towards what takes place behind the scene or at the edges of an established spiritual doctrine. Hence, the act of communion in the Catholic faith, typically seen as a ritual, is not considered as such in Turner's model. He argues instead that it is the arduous journey of a pilgrimage which should be seen as the true ritual or rite of passage. As well as the cathartic potential to affect powerful ontological questioning – where a significant metamorphosis of worldviews is an inherent part of the process – this position also highlights the significance of real or symbolic danger to ritualistic processions and activities.

Under this guise, the main symbolic ingredients of the ritualistic event are metaphorically transformed so that they no longer stand for what they do normally. Hierarchies and statuses are temporarily inversed for instance. Significantly here, Turner addresses the liminal state of a range of things, celestial events amongst them: '... liminality is frequently likened to death, to being in the womb, to invisibility, to darkness, to bisexuality, to the wilderness, and to an eclipse of the sun or the moon' (Turner 1969, 95).

With the Carn Marth jumpers, it is clear that the flooded quarry was inverted so that it could stand for the coastal sea-cliffs, what Turner would have called the essentiality of 'the empty centre' or what Le Breton (1996) refers to as 'the extreme elsewhere', a scenario whereby the core of the jumper's social world actually exists at the periphery of society, not in its perceived middle. Also inverted was the usual reliance on the cliff jumper's second skin, the wetsuit, which in this case did not feature since the participants jumped in their pants. Finally, another inversion was the public display of what is usually an activity practised amongst mates, with only the occasional onlooker permitted to eavesdrop. Granted, when tombstoning takes place on quaysides, piers or harbours, a substantial crowd can sometimes gather to spectate but on the whole this is the exception to the majority of jumping events which occur in seclusion.

Turner is especially relevant to our thinking on this matter because he has directly applied his theories on ritualistic processions to the area of leisure and play (1983). In this research he has made the connection of the anti-structural/ liminal aspect of ritual to a phase of social freedom when contemplation, prayer, speculation and invention are possible. In this sense, the liberations made possible by leisure activities are a freedom *from* as well as a freedom *to* (the 'from' equating with the release from the manipulation of social structures and the 'to' is important as it exists in relation to being able to impact upon these social structures to change, modify or reinforce them).

Somewhat contrarily to Turner's postulates, the French anthropologist David Le Breton (1991; 2000) has stuck to the colloquial definition of ritual and has conveniently devised such events into the duality of archaic vs. modern. That is, he separates out those rites of passage of traditional societies, which are controlled by the elders, and opposes these against the individualistic rites of passage of contemporary society, where risk-taking behaviour is entered into in an ad hoc, spontaneous manner. Even though this framework is simplistic, his research material is crucial to us here because not only does he apply the model directly to play and leisure but does so more immediately since he also examines risk play and dangerous leisurely practices. Le Breton's conclusion is that these participants are playing symbolically with death, every successful attempt to overcome it results in a reinforcing of their self-appraisal.

We need to consider play theory at this point, particularly its relationship to those rituals in which a life-threatening or fearful scenario is simulated and stage-managed under a variety of controlled circumstances. Unlike the orthodox play theorist's view, such as Le Breton's, that these activities help prepare the young for the real dangers of life, teaching them survival and endurance skills, the voluntary participation in such hazardous practices is equally a way in which we can get to gain a vicarious semblance of control over a world that all too often is beyond our capacity to cope with. Generally, risky rituals have tended to flourish in life-worlds that have become stiflingly controlled, overly safe and too routine for people to ever feel there is much at stake. Or that anything truly depends on what we do and feel.

The thesis about hegemonically controlled risk from Beck, Furedi and so forth is certainly insightful, yet the control is often amorphous, magical, spiritual or symbolic rather than originating from the State and the powers that be. Le Breton's work is credible and valuable in emphasising the often overlooked ritualistic dimension. However, in providing the quintessentially 'primitivist' view of ritual, he not only risks limiting the discourse around hazardous games but he is also in danger of forgetting about the importance of cross-cultural comparison, something which is clearly lacking in his analyses to date.

So again if we go back to Turner (1974) as a reference point, we learn that culturally specific metaphor is inherent to symbolic rituals. In their recordable narrative content, these are similar to quantifiable data which we can compare, contrast and perhaps more importantly, from which we can evaluate the influence of cultural change. For him, the importance of the ritual's dynamics is such that the rite of passage and its symbols are active together and generate new forms of meaning through their evolving co-activity. This perspective stresses that the ethnographic study of cultural metaphor requires us to look at the ways in which tropes move in semantic, embodied and ritual space. Locating these movements brings us closer to grasping the purpose of this communicative instrument as a crucial element in a complex and fragmented world. In his words:

> … those of us who take them too seriously, become blind to the creative and innovative potential of symbols as factors in human action … Comparative symbology does attempt to preserve this ludic capacity, to catch symbols in their movement, so to speak, and to 'play' with their possibilities of form and meaning (Turner 1983, 126).

Georg Simmel's ([1911] 1997) work on the adventurous imagination is vital in this regard. We will remember how Simmel suggested that ordinary life is defined by sameness and continuity. The adventure, in contrast, markedly disrupts the flow of one's routine. It is a moment outside of the mundane. Effectively in Turner's terms, it is akin to a liminal or liminoid episode, temporarily standing at the margins of chains of thoughts and experiences that link the everyday events of ordinary life. The adventure would therefore occur outside the context of regular living and yet be an indispensable part of it. As such, it demonstrates unreal and surreal qualities, distant, sometimes dream-like as compared with familiar day-to-day events.

Again another distinction that Simmel identifies is the ill-defined boundaries of ordinary events. Transitions between things are less well clear cut; activities blend into one another seemingly by happenstance. Conversely, people ascribe to the adventure much sharper and more memorable beginnings and ends. The adventure is thus somewhat disconnected from its surroundings. It represents a moment taken out of time with an organic wholeness which gives it a precise inner sensibility that allows it to stand as a causally separate occurrence. Again the parallels with liminality are unmistakable.

The relentless enthusiasm that some people have, even after a serious accident, supports this position about spatio-temporal distantiation and the liminal nature of voluntary risk taking. Retelling a story about his most serious cliff-jumping mishap, Dom (referred to in Chapter 3), said the following:

That was the most frightening experience of my life, but even with many less dramatic near-death experiences like that, I'm not put off. People love to hear these stories and the feeling of success is too great for me to stop, even though I know I'm going to feel pain every time I pull on my wetsuit.

This passage highlights a significant relationship between performance, pleasure, and pain. Indeed, if you knew him and read between the lines, you would realise that he means 'girls love to hear these stories'. An interesting facet of the physicality and embodiment of the Cornish coast is the relation of place to the body, risk, and sexuality. Indeed, these themes have become associated with the peninsular sense of identity and part of the region's subversive ethos exists in this relationship. The extreme sports circles are very much related to the club, rave, and art scenes. During the 1960s and 1970s, St Ives artists generated numerous links between the human figure and the hazards or sexuality of the Cornish landscape (Laviolette 2003b). This has reinforced a hedonistic conception of leisure that especially marks the mood of the Cornish seaside as a place where adventure and reinvigoration as well as sexual promiscuity and fornication have become holiday sub-themes. Surfing hotspots like Fistral Beach and the Watergate Bay in Newquay, or the nudist coves near Porthcurno and at St Austell's Carlyon Bay allow for these types of celebrations of the body, so that they have become synonymous with both risk and the *risqué*.

This is perhaps not all that surprising, especially when we consider that such relationships are reflected in a lot of the contemporary literature on bodily risk which is often related to the threats and dangers associated with certain sexual practices and behaviour (Douglas 1992; Caplan 2000). The sociologist John Fiske has therefore produced a model of the beach that defines it as an ambivalent and unpredictable zone that encompasses 'a physically anomalous category between land and sea ... Nature/Culture'(1989, 44–5). Hedonism, anarchism and thrill-seeking thus occupy a spatial area that seamlessly takes in the centre of society as well as the liminal fringe of both nature and culture. In this sense, deep and dangerous play is often starkly and symbolically played out on the social margins.

As a result, the act of falling provides a fleeting resolution of the existential struggle between such structural dualities as centre and periphery, the local and the global, freedom and constraint, modernity and nature. The body is rarely more unregulated than during these few moments of free-fall. So it is both the most natural and unnatural sensation since being truly free is quite unnatural. Despite the prevalence of Foucauldian perspectives about the controlled body that the social sciences have drawn from for the past 30 years, the types of techniques of the body described here can also be seen as therapeutic, emancipatory and ritualistic vehicles for transporting the embodied imagination. Scenarios in which the hazardous use of landscape, when linked to positive encounters with danger, allow adventurous acts to exist in the liminal realm of the in-between as opposed to the extreme finality of the *au-delà*. Falling is thus a rite of passage, from youth to maturity, from insecurities to emancipation. In giving meaning to, and subverting the abstraction of, the body it allows for experiential immediacies of the moment.

If, as Freud (1919) has suggested, the liberation of repression is to die a little, then so too is the act of moving from adolescence to adulthood through the practice of free-falling. That is, cliff-jumping is also to die a little – to engage in a gradual process of sacrificing one's youth, one's adolescence. These types of activities, as rituals of the social imagination, have thus come to incorporate both risk and *risqué* features. They form part of a non-haphazardous system of totem and taboo. Hence, in remembering the existential insecurities that arise from Kafka's (1915) *Metamorphosis*, which addresses the themes of impossibility and the transformation of reality, we can draw a parallel with the transformations that result from deep and dangerous play. Does the absurdity of the protagonist's situation in Kafka's short story not force us to question normative ontological or epistemological frameworks? In providing a context for impulsive and unstructured ritual, the consideration of falling is a clear reminder that we need to be more attentive to the significance of spontaneous rituals. It illustrates how the inherent creativity of a body hurling through the air, as the result of an embodied imagination, can swindle the view that rituals should only be understood to exist as rehearsed processions.

'Get Away Closer'

8 to 11 April 2007. On my last weekend in Cornwall before moving to Wellington, New Zealand.

Late swim in Poldhu, Mullion – as a semi-liminal, 'spontaneous ritual'.

There was quite some resistance from my friends when, on my last evening in Cornwall before moving to New Zealand, I decided that it was imperative to go for a swim at Poldhu Beach in Mullion. This, I proclaimed, was my last chance to go into the sea in the northern hemisphere before leaving the UK. There were a few reasons put forth to demonstrate some reluctance towards the idea. For a start, it was freezing cold out that night and it was made clear to me that I didn't have a wetsuit or even a change of clothes. While in the process of finishing some socialising with some close friends, we had somehow got onto the subject of how to mark the migration. I was with Frank, who, as the sober designated driver, was most prone to objections over the swim idea. He and I were about to head off to the pub in Falmouth to meet some other mates, where he could then indulge in a pint. He suggested that this sentimental talk of going for a ritual swim before leaving was fuelled by having had a few too many drinks already. This I took as a sort of a challenge which also meant that if it was to be done, we had better be quick about it since the window of opportunity was closing fast. If we left the village past 10 pm, he would either not stop at the beach or would simply drop me off, leaving me to my own devices.

As a gesture of support for doing this ritual swim, our host Mike rushed upstairs to find something for me to change into.

'Are you sure?' I asked. 'I could always just go in my undies'.

'Don't be daft,' he replied, scavenging in an airing cupboard. 'We've got loads of extra swim-gear lying around.'

'Hmm, nice.'

'No, no. Not like that, silly; clean stuff, well mostly, fancy a bikini? Ahh, that's it, perfect – here.'

He handed me a pair of extra-large synthetic football training shorts, algae green with pockets. The kind that can also double up as swimming trunks since they have a concealed key compartment and net-lined pants sewn into the waistband. As he did so he rapidly fired off the associated story. They belonged to Derek, one of his best mates, whom I'd met several times. Derek had left them behind after their last game of 'killer beach football', just before leaving the village and moving up-country with his partner. Picking up on the nostalgia value of these less than fashionable, tent-like shorts, I again asked if he was sure, reminding him that I might not have time to post them back to him before leaving for New Zealand.

'Whatever, next time, just use 'em. Now git, before you miss last orders, Stanley's [AKA Frank] got ants in *his* pants,' was the reply that followed, along with a loud chuckle at the pun.

During this exchange, a lot was also quickly communicated between the two of us non-verbally. Stretching out these super-elasticised trunks in front of my hips revealed just how massively oversized they were for me. The implication I intended with this gesture was that they were double my size and that my torso could fit into each leg socket. He replied with a knowing laugh and an alpha-male beating of the chest which I later interpreted as an ethnographic innuendo meaning something like this: 'Even though they're way too big for your skinny legs, you'll eventually grow into the Big Man's shorts'. An indeterminable bachelor, Derek has been a larger-than-life character for most of his years growing up and living in the village. His marriage and sudden departure had left a mark on pretty much everyone, even, or maybe especially, those who weren't his biggest fans.

Consequently during this short, spontaneous gifting of shorts, there were many layers of masculine gendered sentimentality taking place. Not just my own, though. The inter-subjective nature of this lending event was about a profound adage: knowing how, as well as what, to borrow, lend and return. This was coupled with another unspoken life-saving principle: knowing when to take care of both receiving and giving care. In such terms, this 'functional' loan would thus be better described as an informal type of ceremony, albeit a low-key one. We can understand it as an exchange event which would act as a parting memento of a particular kind, one that was socially binding as a stay-safe pledge. In other words, it was a way of saying, in a materialised form, a number of valuable things such as: 'Keep 'em safe/keep yourself safe in case we can't meet up again anytime soon'; 'Now you know the story, guard it, quite literally, with your life'. In the process of being loaned/gifted and accepting to take these shorts of considerable biographical significance, we were thus saying to each other 'See you anon, 'til next time'.

This was quite a direct version of a reified gift exchange. But during this parting visit to some of my friends in Cornwall, it was accompanied by a less tangible yet no less significantly real semantic gift – a spatial idiom – 'Get Away Closer'. I've increasingly come to understand this term in the last years as a commentary on the necessity of leaving a place temporarily in order to truly begin understanding its importance to others as well as to oneself. In an analogous form, I would interpret it as signifying something to the effect of 'you only really begin to appreciate how important something is when you've lost it or when it's gone'. So on several occasions during my final visit to the field for an indefinite period of time, I was baptised with this idiom which I must admit I had never heard, or at least never taken any notice of, beforehand.

'Right boy? You off New Zealand soon, I hear. Don't you worry 'bout that, you'll be getting away closer once you're back. Then we'll get down to business and finally teach you what we're really about down 'ere.'

This friend must have sensed my discomfort at this last bit of the comment because that was it for the rest of the weekend, he kept blurting out 'Get away closer, boy!' The comment seemed to be an invitation to undergo another ethnographic rite of passage, this time in terms of properly leaving instead of simply moving 350 miles away. The discomfort that it aroused did not run especially deep but it did stir up a certain self-questioning, mostly because it was the kind of statement so reminiscent of what Paul Stoller was so disgruntled to realise while doing his research, that his informants were constantly deceiving him: 'I was lucky because I discovered early in my fieldwork that people were lying to me; some of us are not so lucky, especially if we do not engage in long term fieldwork' (1989, 127–128).

What my informant and, in a different way, what Stoller are reminding us of is something most anthropologists would probably concur with, at least for those adopted into and who adopt their field site as a second home; that there are many stages of nearness and separation which researchers go through, during as well as after their initiatory period of ethnographic field study. Consequently, the significance of leaving to return is tied up with all sorts of issues to do with friendship and a certain symbolic kinship that sometimes take place between researcher and some informants. In a sense then, the paradoxical simplicity of the saying 'get away closer' seems to encapsulate these many layers of being familiar with, yet removed (or liminal) enough from, a cultural situation so that when it comes to describing it, one has reached an unbiased understanding. Or at least, one has attained a level of bias which is sufficiently knowledgeable and reflexive.

Tragedy and the Disembodied Free-Fall

'An accident may easily and naturally befall me on a mountain cliff' (V. Gordon Childe 1980, 3).

The world-renowned Marxist prehistorian Professor Vere Gordon Childe retired from his position as Director of the University of London's Institute of Archaeology in 1956. The following year he returned to his native Australia for the first time in over three decades. Whilst hiking in the Blue Mountains near Sydney to collect material for a book on the geomorphology of New South Wales, he fell to his death at Luchetti Lookout near Govett's Leap on 19 October 1957.

Rumours quickly circulated that he might have deliberately taken his own life. Troubled with increasingly complicated health issues, fearful that his intellectual capabilities were deteriorating and (perhaps indicative of his staunch socialist values) mindful of becoming a burden on the state, such a conclusion seems more than plausible despite the coroner's verdict of accidental death (Thomas 2003). A letter sent to Professor W.F. Grimes, his successor at the Institute of Archaeology, published as the Editorial to the first issue of the journal *Antiquity* in 1980 all but confirmed speculations about deliberation on Childe's part. Grimes had further added that during a conversation with Childe just prior to his retirement, that the unexpected reply to the question 'What are you going to do when you retire?' had been 'I know a 2,000-foot cliff in Australia. I intend to jump off it'. Over the years, Childe is alleged to have made similar, seemingly flippant comments, to a number of friends, colleagues and acquaintances.

Now jumping off cliffs, high bridges, buildings or other similar structures in order to commit suicide as well as to 'show off' is an activity that has a rich history. We will remember the Wall Street stockbrokers' mass suicides during the crash of the 1920s which the Dangerous Sports Club parodied with their choice of attire when they did the first bungy jumps in 1979. In his book *The Art of Suicide* (2001) Ron Brown mentions the famous case of a daredevil in the nineteenth century who jumped off the Tower Bridge in London as a public stunt and who did not survive. Andy Warhol also captured some of what could be called the 'aesthetic' facets of precipitating danger in his screen print *Suicide: purple falling man*. This piece was part of the somewhat controversial series *Death & Disaster* in the early 1960s, controversial largely because of the apolitical nature of Warhol's work and maybe even his morals.

More recently, the documentary *The Bridge* (2006) by Eric Steel also depicts the 'popularity' of jumping as a means of attempting suicide. The filming at San Francisco's Golden Gate Bridge during the year of 2004 reports an average of one person every fortnight throwing themselves off the 220-foot-high suspension span with the intention of killing themselves. The Golden Gate remains the most frequent site for suicides in America and thus ranks amongst the most prominent in the world, along with such places as Govett's Leap, the Aokigahara Forest at the base of Mount Fuji, Niagara Falls on the US/Canadian border, Eiffel's famous Parisian

Tower, the Grafton Bridge in Auckland, the cliffs of Beachy Head in Sussex and the Clifton Suspension Bridge near Bristol.

Another well-known tragedy which caught the public imagination, this time at the turn of the new millennium, was the frequently reprinted and for a time heavily censored depiction of 'the falling man' in New York. Hundreds of people jumped or were blown out of the twin towers of the World Trade Center on 11 September 2001. Of course we are no longer dealing with suicide for those who jumped. Rather, it is a clear example of being pushed by circumstance. Some might even say that when faced with the inevitability of death, these jumpers were making a type of leap of faith, either for the unlikely chance of survival, or to catch one last breath, to live one last moment.

This level of the absurd perhaps illustrates part of what Camus in *The Fall* (1957) and Jean-Paul Sartre in *Being and Nothingness* (1956) were addressing in their own existential ways. Given that at least one person is reported to have been killed by being hit by such a falling victim during 9/11, we see a tragic irony in the actual result of these jumps, not that I am suggesting the possibility of foresight in this case. Additionally, we have the rejection by some people that their loved ones could have given up hope and actually deliberately leapt. This is captivatingly captured in the *9/11: the Falling Man* documentary when attempts are made to identify the protagonist of this affair and locate his family (Singer 2006).

One of the things that was so captivatingly disturbing about the falling man was the symmetry of his descent. This is one of the reasons the American press was censored from reprinting the image for a long time after the catastrophe. But the case of the falling man had not been an isolated instance in terms of the form of the drop that some take. There are other less famous accounts of people plunging in this way. Take, for instance, the following description of a suicide in New Zealand in the 1990s:

> *Witness's description*: 'At about 12:03 hours I noticed a male climbing over the protective railling [sic] on the top floor of the City Council Building. He moved out to the edge and then jumped. There was no hesitation from the time he mounted the barrier to the time he jumped. The victim appears not to fight the fall. He held a perfect swan dive the whole way down keeping his legs straight and arms extended. At no time did he kick his legs about in the usual manner. The victim landed face first on a small concrete path. He bounced and shifted about 10 foot sideways from the initial impact. When the victim was climbing over the protective barrier he was on his own. At no time was there anybody on the top floor with the victim'.

Since the confrontation with death is an ultimate condition of existence, the relationship that free falling has with the possibility of physical injury and death marks it out as an act of foreboding, a true existential moment. In his book *The Culture of Speed* (2007), John Tomlinson talks of the inherent connections between danger, machine innovation and socio-cultural acceleration. He highlights some interesting features that bind the social construction of rapidity to the prevalence of the risk society, when violence as well as the creation of moments for reflexivity or even existential realisation are made possible. Summarising the work of Paul Virilio, he says the following about the immediacy of the politics of violence:

> Virilio has developed a complex and wide-ranging analysis of the relationship between speed, technology, cultural representation (particularly cinema) and what he calls the 'pure-war' of twentieth-century modernity ... Virilio argues ... that the increasing speed of modern weapons delivery systems, linked to high-speed communications technologies is producing a shift in the very ontology of warfare. Wars are now not so much about gaining, holding and pressing the initiative in terms of *territory*, as in terms of *temporality* [emphasis in original] (Tomlinson 2007, 58).

Here we see that it is not the sublime that is accelerated but rather the conditions of modernity, through efficiency and an aggressive abolishment of frills as well as an alienation from labour-time and nature. The escape from these hegemonic structures, which in more extreme cases can also be forms of oppression, is one of the things that liminal rites of passage are orchestrated to permit. These obviously come in many shapes and sizes but hurling oneself away quite literally from such constraints is clearly an immediate and visually powerful symbol which exists in a number of cultures, across a vast expanse of history. Examples include the El Colacho baby jumping festival performed by Spanish Catholics, the bull jumping of the Hamar tribe in Ethiopia and the Alaturbi Turkish jump into the Black Sea (Rosen and Kassoy 2009).

Jumping with the desire to end one's life – attempted suicidal jumps – share certain things in common with free-falling and similar leisure-oriented thrill-seeking jumps. On a simple structuralist level then, there could be two strands of jumps. On the one hand you have the person who wants to feel life at its extreme, i.e., jumping off a cliff for the pure rush and exhilaration, and on the other is the person for whom life itself has become too extreme.

The notions of performance and appearance play an important part, both involving a considerable amount of planning, preparation and determination. In the cases of jumping to celebrate life and those of jumping to die, the jumper is taking a risk of failure – the extreme sports enthusiast runs the risk of failing to execute the jump properly, for its proper enjoyment. These are persons who are hoping for extreme life experiences. They want to prove to themselves that they are fully alive, that they are in control of contingencies, the elements, themselves – mind and body. Some of their main exhilaration comes as they survive and master the perils, during those moments once they realise that they have executed the task correctly and perhaps even in their own novel way.

Suicidal individuals also run the risk of failing to kill themselves, thus facing an unbearable humiliation as well as serious injury and/or other psychological harm. These are persons for whom life itself has become too extreme, so much so that they can no longer stand to be alive. That is, they no longer want anything to do with the 'extremity of life' and are searching to opt out. At the heart of each individual action there is another meeting point – the rush. Indeed, many failed suicide attempts report a kind of release and euphoria that comes over the faller with the knowledge that life is ending. Extreme sports jumpers equally articulate their experiences in terms of searches for freedom and adrenaline rushes. The free-fall of jumping experiences can therefore quite literally be an end in itself as well as without end – endless. Consequently, at the heart of each individual action there is a meeting point – existential extremity.

These more individualistic opposing perspectives have more ambiguous counterparts such as the pseudo-accident and the charity campaign jump. The latter are a form of symbolic social statements about the worthiness of a life-giving principle through the desire to help others by engaging with dangerous practices which can potentially entail a risk of death for the 'giver'. Here spontaneity and a blurring of the distinction between accidents, jumping to live and jumping to die are frequently involved. Of particular artistic relevance in this case is the engraving *The Suicide* by the famous nineteenth-century cartoonist Thomas Rowlandson in the volume *The English Dance of Death* (Combe and Rowlandson 1815). The art historian Ron Brown (2001) describes this aquatint as an allegorical depiction. In it, Death sits passively and relishes in the fact that his victims are doing his work for him: a man drowned in his attempt to save someone from a shipwreck, whilst his lover hurls herself into the turbulent sea to join him in death. Indeed, she chooses to kill herself but this choice is thrust upon her by the circumstances.

Regarding some material on suicides in New Zealand (for the years 1920, 1924, 1926, 1928, 1932, 1980, 1982, 1988, 1990 and 1992) a few brief generalisations about jumping as a means to end life can be made. What first becomes immediately obvious is that while jumpers are in a distinct minority of suicides, the mentally ill are over-represented amongst them. There are 18 cases for the years 1922, 1924, and 1926 and it is surprising that the number of people who jumped is so low, particularly because of the economic depression in western countries during that time when jumping was prominent in other countries. Here we take a fairly liberal definition of jumping to mean a suicide that involves a significant height. The categories are: (i) jumped from a bridge, building, cliff, wireless tower, or tree; (ii) drove car over cliff; (iii) jumped down a mineshaft, well, light-well or stairwell; and (iv) jumped overboard from a ship at sea or from a moving train.

In terms of jumping from a bridge, a significant height of a least 30 feet had to be involved. Jumping from a bridge into the Avon River some ten feet below was not factored in as fitting into this category. In 1990 there were ten suicides committed by jumping from heights and two more who, although they self-destructed by other means, had made previous attempts on their lives by jumping from heights. The link with mental illness remains strong but proportionally less since self-euthanasia becomes more common. One particularity is a case in 1982 when there were three Wellingtonian jumpers in the same day and in one of those instances there seems to have been a copycat suicide. Two cases are more typical in being related to mental illness but the other most probably is not. The jumpers were overwhelmingly mentally ill in most of the instances from the suicides in the 1990s.

Conclusions

The importance of the sea for shaping cultural identity and sustaining many aspects of the economy is certainly vast. But the sea has also been the taker of life through the perils of fishing, shipwrecks and diving accidents. Furthermore, it has been the vehicle by which emigration was made possible in the eighteenth and nineteenth centuries. Hundreds of boats carried thousands of people from Europe to Australia, the Americas, New Zealand, and South Africa.

In Cornwall, the phenomenon was so prevalent that a kinship category was created: the cousin Jack and cousin Jenny scenario, who were of course taken away to the New World by the sea. Elsewhere I have discussed in more length the links between death and Cornish identity through the material metaphors concerning emigration, immigration, heritage tourism, and the hazards of Cornwall's industries (Laviolette 2003a; 2006a). Indeed as one informant elegantly states, the Cornish peninsula has often been seen 'as a place where places end but never begin'. Britishness, Englishness, and Cornishness reach their final destination in many of the Duchy's places, no less at Land's End, the most western point of the 'nation'. As Alfred Tennyson commented in his personal travel journal: 'Funeral. Land's End and Life's End' (Tennyson 1949, quoted in Martin 1980, 320).

The above contextualisation sheds some light on the ritualistic reasons why people increasingly participate in hazardous sports and adventure tourism that involve the coastal seascape or bodies of water of historical significance such as harbour quays as well as flooded quarries and mineshafts. They do so because they wish to embody a significant ontological reality of the margins. They do so to fully embody the environmental essence of landscapes where, increasingly, modern actors feel they are banished by modernity. They do so for the life-giving adrenaline rushes that brushes with danger produce. They do so to consume the extreme as well as to mutely rail against consumption, modernity or the status quo. Adventure tours and risk recreation therefore take part paradoxically in epic journeys to search for life and meaning amongst the absurdities of modern society. That is, to search for the secure control of life already bounded and objectified as style, difference and identity within a fluid and fragmenting post-modernity (Bauman 2000). This paradoxical position in geo-cultural space – tied to the consumerist order, but tipping over into its extreme opposite – becomes increasingly emblematic of rallying against being fully immersed in the risk society. Consequently, increasing numbers of people apt to engage in dangerous games and adventure tours are turning seemingly pointless acts of recreation into pointedly critical acts of collective environmental self-definition and creative redefinition.

Chapter 7

Conclusion
Landscaping Leisure and the Accelerated Flâneur

By imagination I do not mean simply to convey the common notion implied by that much-abused word, which is only fancy, but the constructive imagination, which is a much higher function, and which, in as much as man is made in the likeness of God, bears a distant relation to that sublime power by which the Creator projects, creates, and upholds his universe.

(Catherine Crowe 1848, 182).

The urban cityscapes of the Parisian arcades were perfect examples of an imaginative 'panoramic architecture' devised to orient the individual's movements through the marketplace. In light of all the social changes brought on by the French Revolution, the most significant of these were the result of budding capitalism which involved the need to create new social spaces for vending and purchasing purposes. These were passageways through neighbourhoods that were covered with glass roofs and lined by marble panels so as to shape a sort of ambiguous interior-exterior environment. Through the literary inspiration of Charles Baudelaire [1821–67], this generic space and the character of the *flâneur*, a marginal occupant of such a space, were initially theorised by Walter Benjamin in the 1930s and published posthumously (1980). Both authors wrote about the growth of a new upwardly mobile class as one of the key groups to embody the public experience of modernity:

> The street becomes a dwelling for the flâneur; he is as much at home among the façades of houses as a citizen is in his four walls. To him the shiny, enamelled signs of businesses are at least as good a wall ornament as an oil painting is to the bourgeois in his salon. The walls are the desk against which he presses his notebooks; news-stands are his libraries and the terraces of cafés are the balconies from which he looks down on his household after his work is done (1980, 37).

Inevitably men, flâneurs would stroll through the city to kill the time afforded them by wealth and education. Their tendency for nonchalance meant that they would objectify the masses, treating the other passers-by and the surrounding architecture as riddles for interpretative pleasure. The act of the flâneur symbolised privilege and the liberty to move about the city observing from a distance, not interacting, consuming the sights through a controlling but rarely acknowledged gaze, directed as much at other people as the goods for sale. An anonymous face in the multitude, the flâneur was free to probe for clues that were unnoticed by other people, simpletons, caricaturised as domestic beings. In making apparent the spatial inversion between public and private, Benjamin brought the outside in and placed the inside out. This inversion was intended as a social subversion whereby leisure became one of the main tools behind creating an enduring persona for the flâneur as someone not confined to an increasingly State-manipulated domestic sphere but who had the capacity, freedom and cultural capital to live in the world.

Mobility is of course central here, as is the kinaesthetic dimensions of movement and ultimately the physical experience of the urban. Benjamin defined modernity as a break from the past, focused on the gaze and liberty of movement. We should also note that mobility and movement are inherently connected to the phenomenological project. It is through such an emphasis that certain anthropologists have come to think through and conceptualise the idea of being *At Home in the World* (Jackson 1995) or how migration can be a form of identity creation (Rapport and Dawson 1998). In this sense, the emphasis is not on the formulation of identity as necessarily being focused on where someone is from, but more importantly on where they are going.

A notable feature in this regard is that the flâneur, this supreme being of leisure, was the personification of in-betweenness, especially in terms of a perambulating demeanour which was halfway between sleep walking and an intoxicated consciousness of reform. This characteristic of course lent itself well to the surrealists who captured the flâneur as a kind of mascot for moving poetry. For Benjamin, dreams were indices of freedom, whereby our socially constructed dreamscapes could be tapped to provide visions for utopian change.

The flâneur was therefore a form of transcendental presence who encompassed what Thorstein Veblen (1899) had later labelled as 'conspicuous leisure'. Veblen's musings were heavily influenced by the populist movement in America which was prominent from 1887 to 1908. With some socialist influence, they divided the world between those who were producers and those who were not. Populists were antagonistic to the values of the dominant leaders of the business community and shared a sense of urgency and an edge of desperation about the demand for reform. And it is this connection between a desire for change, increased leisure and the ability for movement through different spaces that connects the flâneur to adventure. But despite being mobile in a number of senses, the flâneur is nonetheless the embodiment of idleness, at least with regard to the production of socio-economic value. So we need to introduce another component before we can apply the relevance of this category to the topic of adventure. This additional element, also a product of modernity and the industrial revolution, is acceleration, rapidity, speed.

The contemporary manifestation of the flâneur can perhaps best be understood in our times through the idea of immediacy and therefore as an 'accelerated flâneur',

Figure 7.1   Climbing wall, Arvika Festival, Sweden (photo by the author)

facilitated by globalisation anxieties, postmodern architecture and the ruinous decay of buildings, as well as the modern ambition for heightened leisure and freedom from restraint. For attention to the actual social experience of modernity's fascination with acceleration, one must move away from traditional theorists to the sociological impressionism of someone like Simmel. In the background of most of his writings, although never specified explicitly, Simmel was drawn to thinking about the effects and affects that result from the increasing pace of modern life, with the overall result in the global shift from rural to metropolitan existence.

Inspired by his impressionistic musings, French scholars such as Michel de Certeau's (1984) and Henri Lefebvre's (1991) provided some thoughts on walking in the city which are extensions to the former work on the flâneur – although theirs is about ordinary citizens rather than the exceptionally educated bourgeois who receive pleasure from wandering around cities gazing at but never communicating directly with others. One of the lessons from their studies is that urban movement is hegemonically restricted and controlled. Walkers exist within the built environment that they explore; while some possibilities are denied to them, other possibilities open up. De Certeau calls this 'walking rhetorics' which suggests the idea of creativity for getting around obstacles. Now in the realm of 'buildering' (the climbing of buildings), urban exploration and parkour/free running, such ideas of overcoming the restrictions of urban planning through acrobatics and accelerated movement are part of the core rationale for these practices.

From a different but parallel perspective Synthia Sydnor (2003) has analysed sky-diving within the rubric of the performative, the imaginary and the surreal dreamlike character of a rapid experience of movement and descent. Her construction of free-fall choreography relies on Walter Benjamin's ponderings on the phantasmagorical to consider the 'abstraction of insensible gradations from bodily spaces to environmental ones' (Rinehart and Sydnor 2003, 133). Gilles Deleuze, in his reflections on the categorical spaces of sport through the developing movement of the extreme, also draws on Benjamin to speak about the participant's appropriation of kinetic energy:

> Running, throwing a javelin and so on, effort, resistance, with a starting point, a lever. But nowadays, I see movement defined less and less in relation to a point of leverage. Many of the new sports – surfing, windsurfing, hang-gliding – take the form of entry into an existing wave. There's no longer an origin as starting point, but a sort of putting-into-orbit. The basic thing is how to get taken up in the movement of a big wave, a column of rising air, to 'come between' rather than to be the origin of an effort (1992, 281).

In terms of examining the links between thrills and rapidity, Michael Balint (1959) has offered a psychoanalytically driven approach which reveals the often pessimistically dark association between the dangers, risks and implicit violence associated with acceleration and the typically modern sensual aesthetic experiences it can engender.

This is a discourse which embraces a range of transgressive and rebellious impulses chafing the smooth surface order of institutional modernity. And out of this is formed a narrative of speed which is 'unruly' both in its orientation and in its expression. Subversive and impetuous, conjoining hedonism with a particular sort of existential hedonism, this discourse constantly teeters on the brink of collapse into violence and chaos (Tomlinson 2007, 9).

From such a position, the euphoric landscape in which the accelerated body plays is no longer an enveloping sphere of tracts, expanses and panoramas but rather a beckoning foreground of special sites, niches and locations, each significant for how it technically engages the body in risky play. Indeed, the modern player as sensation seeker encounters the thrillscape as a patchwork of technical possibilities, each to be explored, tested and evaluated with the rules of the game and the singularly trained body in mind. To this attuned and sometimes exceptionally well-trained practitioner, vaguely defined assemblages of natural features transform into distinctly technical spaces and precisely describable arenas that invite exploration, penetration, naming, commentary, repetition and reputation. Whereas the idyllic landscape of the spirit offered the alienated subject the sublimely panoramic envelopment of backgrounds, the ecstatic landscape of the body decisively reverses this symmetry. For the new adventurer, panorama only really provides a setting for foregrounds that, in the game, grounds their body and rivets one's attention.

As a result of such trained investment, hitherto anonymous structures or lengths of cliff and sea become significantly differentiated, complex micro-seascapes of the body, durably fixed in local consciousness through embodied repetition and oral transmission. Moreover, this newly developed landscape becomes further differentiated, as new generations of players move in with different games to colonise intermediate niches. It is as if the opportunistic logic driving the differentiation and hybridisation of extreme activities is similar to the logic that imaginatively dictates the playful colonisation of every marginal niche (Anderson 1991).

Furthermore, from the angle of the sublime and the idyllic, the thrill seeker appears unconscionably invasive, lacking apparent empathy for the bucolic rhythms of the gentler landscape. However, these games do possess their own peculiar environmental sensibility, though not typically in ideological form. In effect, the para-environmentalism of cliff and BASE jumping or kindred activities functions as an un-stated, embodied 'model in action', guided by a practical logic that leads to an inescapable, though implicit, intimacy with natural entities that seem to actively issue a challenge. And indeed, risk recreation seems to unfold right inside the geological folds of the landscape rather than upon it, appearing to belong as much to its physical interior as to the rough textures of its outer surfaces. From this position of intimate interiority, the practitioner of deep and dangerous play is predisposed to accept the invitation of natural features to exchange with, rather than subjugate, them. Playing the game unfolds in both alternate opposition

Figure 7.2   Parkour/free running practice, Brick Lane, London (photo by the author)

to as well as in creative partnership with, the environment in a light-hearted and deadly serious structure of reciprocity. Thus, the extreme landscape provides the extreme protagonist with the goal of the game: the cliff to jump off, the slab to climb, the watery depths in which to dive or the sky to fall through. Likewise, the adventure seeker such as sand dune surfers, iceberg climbers or underwater cave divers add cultural value to the landscape, with minimal physical transformation, by naming, storying, sometimes even protecting it. In this way, deep and dangerous play generates a distinctive hybrid of human and natural agency, dramatically encapsulating, without having to discursively enunciate, the bones of a 'green' relation.

Trans-sport

Another component of acceleration as well as a significant part of the contradictions embedded in surfing culture, if we accept the presence of any significant environmental undertones, is the reliance on motor vehicles. Most adventurer pursuits are activities which in modern times have heavily depended on cars or vans. The first car linked specifically to surfing was a genre known as 'The Woody'. For many these are still the quintessential wave wagons. Built in the 1930s and 40s by companies such as Buick, Chevy, Ford, Morris and Oldsmobile as well as companies that no longer exist such as DeSoto, Hudson, Packard and

Willys-Overland, these ornate cars crafted with wood (typically ash or oak) were originally conceived as intermediary vehicles – meant to pick up and drop off passengers at train depots or stations, hence the American term 'station wagon'. In terms of larger vehicles, vans of many descriptions have been popular, particularly the VW camper. In Cornwall since 1987, an annual event called *Run to the Sun* takes place each summer in Newquay, to which thousands of Volkswagens from around the country and even some from Europe gather for the weekend.

The search for the self in travel is a common theme in both surfing and road narratives. In this sense, the destination is not always as important as the process of getting there – a process that bathes in the freedom from commitment and responsibility. Mobility thus opens to the esoteric. Movement is the means, the development of a kaleidoscopic self-image is the pursuit and a more satisfying self is the destination. As Salter eloquently states 'new paths lead to new images either on the road or in the haven at the end of the junket' (1979, 13).

As with the traditional flâneur, motion is a powerful component made more significant by rapidity and the possibility of exploring wider ranges. Quinney, for one, noted the importance of the immersion of the self into the immediate moment of movement and travel: 'As with all travel – no matter how near or far from home – every moment is a journey of the soul. We spend our lives travelling' (1986, 21). In this sense, the conscious self loses itself in a larger imaginative world, a world where we are intimately grounded to an unhindered space. We travel the world to discover its secrets and in so knowing we become one with the landscape. This phenomenological position implies that the restriction of movement is a form of alienation from the world's mysteries. Such a stance hints at the danger of disembodying ourselves from the landscape, for in so doing we deny ourselves and desacralise nature. Kierkegaard wrote of what it meant for the self to fail to become part of the otherness of the world. He called this condition *The Sickness unto Death* (1849) and claimed that it denied the nature of the ultimate human reality.

Many environmentalists ascribe sickness unto death as an excellent idiom for the current state of the Earth's ecosystems. Among other things, they point the finger of blame at our automobile addiction and infatuation with mobility. The car has indeed had profound impacts upon the quality and character of city and country life around the globe. Without doubt, automobiles have evolved far beyond their utility as transportation devices to become, in many parts of the world, the very symbol of the good life and conspicuous consumption. They are status symbols, objects of fantasy, sources of employment and major forces in the income of many countries (Miller 2001).

Commentaries about the important shift in car use, from family property to personal property, have existed since the birth of this modern technology. The increasing dependency on the car for the fulfilment of daily activities was accurately predicted as a trend that would continue, imposing greater demands on precarious energy supplies as well as solidifying the human landscape with a 'network of institutions that take limitless personal mobility for granted' (Bogart

1977, 15). It is no wonder then that the automobile holds a primary place among those artefacts that have significantly transformed society in the twentieth century. This is so much so, that it is becoming obvious that certain important psychosocial processes lie at the heart of explaining why one's personal vehicle is one of the most significant objects in the age in which we live.

By its ubiquitous presence in western society, the car has shaped the ways in which people can move. It also quickly became a metallic statement of who and what we are. Automobiles and their related concrete networks of roads are readily apparent in our landscapes – standing as monuments to the past, present and future. Even the atmosphere is not safe from their pollution and scrapped vehicles have created a whole new refuse problem. In terms of its relation to surfing, car travel has been intimately connected not only because of the bulky piece of equipment involved and the need to follow conditions dictated by weather patterns but also because of the associations with free roaming and free love. This relationship with hedonism is clearly at the heart of the complex rapport that the surfing lifestyle has had with the need to have access to a vehicle. The performance artist Laurie Anderson has reacted to the automotive industry's despotism in her rendition of a journey of life. The dark glebe is entered and the straight way is lost. The errancy in Anderson is accelerated as her body becomes a motorway: 'I… I am in my body… I am in my body the way… I am in my body the way most people drive… I am in my body the way most people drive their cars.' These lyrics are from the song *Americans on the Move*, in which she goes on to translate a parable of lost direction into a frightful nightscape of rain and ceaseless traffic where you are 'driving through the night to a place you've never been with everything unfamiliar' (quoted in Ezell and O'Keeffe 1994, 232).

The sociologist Eugene Halton (1994) refers to such car fetish symbolism as 'auto eroticism', which places the sports car as America's top symbol of its youth's budding sexuality. Indeed, automobiles embody sex, excitement, and in certain cases liberation, both by the personal privacy that they permit and by the social and financial emancipation that they proclaim. It follows that by incarcerating sexuality, the automobile has the potential of alienating its youthful drivers from the sexuality that comprises them. And so, the elevation of motor vehicles to cultic status conveys malignant control of the machine over individuality. Some authors have even argued that the erotic appeal of the car derives from the combination of such feelings as control, omnipotence and self-enclosed regression. Its inner space is a simulated environment that provides its passenger with a self-propelling womb-like capsule where 'driving can be an onanistic experience in which the driver extends his power manifoldly' (Freund and Martin 1993, 91).

There is another phenomenon that links car travel and surfing – the way in which each can manage to alter our spatial perception. The landscape as seen from a motor vehicle is experienced as a set of visual sequences. Objects appear to move, they alter in colour, shape, size and texture. Compositions form, dissolve and fade whilst perceptions of constancy and motion, sometimes exciting, frightening or simply boring, become increasingly rapid. The connection to the idea of the

Figure 7.3   Car surfing (photo by K. Kary)

accelerated flâneur, explored in the introduction, is quite immediately pertinent here. Additionally, in reducing our field of vision and limiting the use of our other senses, cars often homogenise the experience of landscape.

Speed and constricted space are not the only factors involved in generating a sense of sameness and flatness to the environment. Commercialisation is a culprit as well. Cars have been the target of the visual pollution of words which increasingly affect urban centres and their hinterlands. In many cases, the information on roads becomes so varied and superfluous that it is unreadable. The upshot is a film-like illusion, where mirage and reality are blurred: 'This mode of apprehending the world constitutes the essence of the post-modern experience' (Freund and Martin 1993, 105). There is therefore a liminal component to this surreal form of perception.

Of course the post-modern roadscape is not only shaped by driving experiences. The transient images of television equally mediate experiential encounters with the world. Together they provide much of our spatial information: 'The mutual dependency of the road and television has changed our architecture. The strip has become the Television Road' (Macdonald 1985, 13). This construction of architecture, space and entertainment for the needs of the automobile industry was one of the instigators in the shift from modernity to postmodernity. Sequentially, the architecture of road commerce grew into its own form of communication. In such a virtual landscape, the urban environment, buildings and architecture move from being forms in place to becoming symbols in space.

The geographer Stephen Daniels (1993) has also attempted to sight iconographical roadscape images by creating a category for imaginative geographies in which texts and illustrations generate cultural histories which foster the narrative genre that we have come to know as 'travel writing'. His excessively ocular outlook is limited, however, because ultimately he provides a static way of seeing. It is worth quoting him at some length in order to reveal the inherent restrictions of intensively visualist approaches to landscapes studies:

> I have concentrated on particular landscape images which yield many fields of vision, in their own time and since, in their making and re-making, in their mobilisation by many social interests. Such landscape images achieve the status of national icons ... As itself an exercise in the geographical imagination, this book ... is the product of many journeys ... These descriptions are not just descriptions of places and their national significance but necessarily narrations too. Describing them from the perspective of the late twentieth century has involved re-narrating them, plotting their significance now ... It is not so much a procedure of unmasking images, to disclose their real identity, as of re-visioning images, of showing their many faces from many shifting perspectives (Daniels 1993, 243–245).

The written recollection becomes the medium of choice for communicating what has been visually observed. The use of multiple meanings surrounded by a variety of discourses is what Daniels advances as the eloquence of images. Surely, however, the landscape is equally a lived-in environment. Images provide one type of reality yet every landscape harnesses a wealth of human potential (Bender 1993; Ingold 1993). Roads, streets, avenues and boulevards are not simply links between points or corridors for travellers. Concrete and cobble stones literally consume space. In an average city more space is dedicated to the movement of vehicles than to most other activities. By relying principally on pictorial material, Daniels is able to quickly shift narratives but he does not put into question the observational points upon which he stands. For him, we have historical contexts which explain specific views and vistas but we do not examine how to move between or change certain platforms of power. By examining the landscape from a static position the visual analyst only changes his or her vantage point, without connecting or moving between the shifting perspectives. Constructions of historical contexts can be problematic when one is relying on images generated by the elite. In short, such a methodology helps recreate unequal balances of power.

This is exactly where the geographer J.B. Jackson (1984) would oppose such a praxis by pointing out the absence of any vernacular landscape understanding. In essence his mission was to reveal the traveller's path, a path that is latent with power since it may not be accessible or noticeable to all. Jackson therefore reminds us that the tact of social scientists is suited to revealing the power latent within the layers of the landscape itself. This only becomes possible by relying on actual observations of human mobility. In so doing, we can uncover the patterns to city transport which are not obvious from the layout of the transportation network.

It is this notion of what is noticeable in environmental perception that raises many controversies in the landscape literature. Some authors argue for instance that it is not what we perceive but how we feel about what we perceive that is central in our understanding of human behaviour and what it means to be human. Such a humanistic perspective examines human-environment relationships in terms of embodied ideas. It admits that what we see is greatly influenced by our attention, intention and interest. Further it is grounded in history, where events are always present, ever recurring and fused to terrain; where events are, for all intents and purposes, trans-temporal: renewed and confirmed each time that the words of stories, myths and legends are written or spoken (Ryden 1993). Other scholars, however, continue to strive for objective interpretations of the landscape. They proclaim that noticeability is not a contentious issue since for a phenomenon to be observable we have to be able to either record it, measure it or plot it on a map. This latter positivistic attitude is at the heart of many problematic transport policies. But different views about transportation networks exist. Almost 120 years ago, John Ruskin wrote that some people can be compared to careful travellers who neither stumble on stones nor slip into sloughs but who have from the onset of their journey gone in the wrong direction; others are travellers who, however stumbling and slipping, have their eyes fixed on the true way (Ruskin 1885).

There are many other dimensions in which issues about a change in environmental consciousness could be considered. For instance, in a shrinking world of accessible travel options, international surf tourism is certainly comparable to the production of conventional surfboards in terms of the levels of carbon emissions and overall ecological footprint impact. In the popular surfing magazines there have been a number of articles about carpooling and other alternative modes of transport for surfing, including bikes, the train and the less practical, hitch-hiking. Let us therefore finish with an ethnographic anecdote about this very theme where adventure sport and alternative transport meet.

The Ledge Over the Edge

The scene is the Gunnersbury roundabout in Chiswick, London, on the lay-by to the beginning of the M4 motorway heading west. At about half-nine in the morning, I set out to hitch a lift to Cornwall, my original ethnographic field site. The year was 2003 and it hadn't been long since my student days had ended. To be honest, as a teaching assistant looking for research funding, I was probably less well-off than your average undergraduate 'fresher' who had yet to spend all their student grant or loan on beer. As a result, I was hoping to save a few bob by thumbing a ride.

In not much time at all, less than about 15 minutes (or 170 cars), a vehicle pulled up.

'Where ya headed, mate?' said a shaven-headed man in his early forties whose shoulders looked quite broad indeed and who must have been well over six foot tall. But he did not seem threatening in the least. In fact he seemed to be a rather pleasant fellow, casually dressed in jeans and a T-shirt, with a fairly tidy car – not that an excess of precaution, much less comfort, are the most crucial issues when hitch-hiking. And this is doubly so of course, when one is about to embark on a little pilot study for a project on adventure, risk sport and extreme places.

'As far south-west as you're going, really,' I replied.

'Perfect, hop in, boy, off to the West Country I be going,' he followed, putting on a thick mock accent.

I couldn't believe my luck and this was only the beginning. Within minutes of our conversation it transpired that my new travelling companion was working in west London as a fire-fighter, four days on and four off. He had recently moved into that line of work because of the extended weekend time which it allowed, so he could indulge in his favourite hobby and obsession, surfing. Commenting further, he explained that his sudden and radical shift in career path was a necessary lifestyle change. In the past years his health had been deteriorating and he needed to find a way of supporting what he called an increasing 'surf addiction'.

'As you can see, I'm a pretty heavy bloke … it took me three years of part-time dabbling on the odd weekend of good surf just to stand up on a board … that was really frustrating. But once I nailed it, there was no turning back … so I spent some time thinking about work options that could give me a four-day weekend.'

This was one of those days where I really should have bought a lottery ticket. And things got even better. After a bit over an hour of driving, this chap, let's call him Martin, got a phone call from one of his friends who was already expecting him.

'What's that, mate? Three foot and clean on the north coast … I'm putting my foot on it, be there by three-ish, I've gotta stop at my sister's in Somerset but I'll keep it to one cup of tea, fifteen minutes tops.'

He hung up and explained that it was a little out of the way but he'd promised to bring his sister some DVDs and he wouldn't be able to stop at hers on the way back, did I mind? Oh, and did I mind if that was the only pit stop? 'No time for lunch, I'm afraid,' he continued, 'but you can always borrow a board once we're

Figure 7.4   Paul Shanks on bike (photo by NZ Ministry for the Environment)

there if you fancy.' So yes, it was the kind of day that a field researcher embarking on a fairly new project dreams of.

To top it all off was the contextualising of the surf-addiction lifestyle that resulted from the end of our three-hour drinking session, which followed two hours of surfing. When we said our farewells, he gifted some precious ethnographic snippets.

'Guess it's been a pretty crazy day, huh? Driving all morning at an average speed of over 100 miles an hour, to then hit the cold sea for a while, and the warm beer for a while longer.'

Such sensorial overdrive and distortion is of course a significant justification for risk behaviour put forward by many practitioners of adventurous activities. Moreover, it is frequently this distorted modality of experience that is excessively sought by those participants who engage in extreme or radical practices during moments where they have further altered their states of mind though drug or alcohol usage (Pearson 1979; Lyng 1990; Stranger 1999).

In an elegant and rather rehearsed way, Martin summarised this 'work hard, play harder' ethos by saying, 'But hey, contrary to popular belief, I don't live on the edge, I live on the ledge over the edge.'

Pleased with himself, he chose to elaborate even further, more to his mates than me at this point. If it wasn't obvious by then his final boasting provided a conclusive statement about a lifestyle motto that transpired to be not about a type of romantic 'hippy' dream of escaping the pressures of modern living but was rather about something quite different – leisurely excess: 'Yah, man, we're talking the full combination of sex, drugs 'n' surf the roll, baby! The ledge way over the edge.'

Ervin Goffman's (1967) essay 'Where the action is' becomes relevant at this point. In conceptualising non-spectator, risky sport, he defines action within the very rubric of temporality so important to those interested in social acceleration:

> activities that are consequential, problematic, and undertaken for what is felt to be their own sake ... action seems most pronounced when the four phases of the play – squaring off, determination, disclosure, and settlement – occur over a period of time brief enough to be contained within a continuous stretch of attention and experience. It is here that the individual releases himself to the passing moment, wagering his future estate on what transpires precariously in the seconds to come. At such moments a special affective state is likely to be aroused, emerging transformed into excitement (1967, 185).

This frames the cultural space in which extreme or adventure sports and their associated landscapes are more than simply tolerable but are actually socially vital. In being anomalous, deep and dangerous play is neither game-like, nor is it a non-game. By definition it must encode some level of liminality, of existing at the margins. In this respect, it occupies a special niche, culturally as well as topographically. What is this niche? This becomes a particularly interesting question with the onset of 'the risk society', where it is apparent that such practices have ceased to be exclusively aristocratic and more landscapes have become defined by their presence. Nature and concepts such as the sublime change from spaces that come under our control into spaces where it is impossible to think of an erstwhile wilderness without also thinking of the penetration of this expanse by adventure seekers.

Totalising Events

With the modernisation of traditional sports and the marketing of new ones, sport has dramatically enhanced its potential impacts on the expression of personal and social identities. Sports have themselves been increasingly associated with recognisable styles, fashions and subcultures. The relationship between the body, culture and environment has become a growing area of academic and popular concern. Sport and leisure are an increasingly prominent factor in the formulation of social relations. And anthropologists are all the more prone to notice its significance in affecting the dynamics of their field sites. By taking a look over an extended period of time at the give and take between tourism, mountain travellers and the Sherpa, Ortner (1999) has demonstrated the significance of cultural change in her study of the Himalayas. Andrew Beatty (2005) has also outlined the voyeuristic nature of tourism regarding activities like surfing or the ritual of stone jumping in the Indonesian island of Nias during the early twentieth century. Indeed, in their ironically entitled collection *Tarzan was an Eco-Tourist*, Vivanco and Gordon (2006) remind us of the ubiquitous nature of transnational adventure travel. Since the explorer age of the Victorian era led by such famous writers as Edgar Burroughs, Joseph Conrad, Gordon Cummings, David Livingstone, Jack London, Henry Stanley, Mark Twain and Jules Verne, an ever growing thirst for heroic discovery has spawned the modern imagination of late capitalism.

Alternative sports proliferated once long-distance travel became affordable. People have been turning to these practices in their search for memorable adventures and adrenaline experiences. These activities thus facilitate the fostering of new types of narratives in addition to bolstering new varieties of social solidarities (Le Breton 1991). Activities like paragliding or *hors piste* helicopter skiing may once have been a matter of personal eccentric taste. But with consumer marketing, well-organised clubs and media attention, with several satellite channels dedicated to extreme sports, these pastimes have come to help shape popular culture in a relatively short period of time. From being marginal, exotic and even elitist, they have become mainstream leisure activities.

The daredevil dimensions to these pursuits have been popularised recently by real-life adventure television. The series *Jackass*, initially produced in 2000 by MTV and now distributed as feature films provides a case in point. The premise of this group is to constantly modify things like skateboarding, kayaking or BMX-riding into new bizarre hybrid stunts. They have a strong following among younger audiences mainly because their objective is to perform satirical pranks on each other or on an unsuspecting public.

Among the solitary modern-hero role models are daredevils such as Sébastien Foucan, the instigator of *le parkour* free-running, where practitioners acrobatically weave through urban environments, hopping over barricades, debris and other obstacles. Also there is the 'French spiderman' Alain Robert who, without safety equipment, has climbed over 70 of the world's most iconic structures. Other contemporary examples include the stunt 'magicians' Dorothy Dietrich and David Blaine. By performing bullet catches or caged suspensions for days on end, they attempt to follow in the footsteps of Copperfield, Chung Ling Soo and of course, Houdini.

Many adventure sport activities are either borderline legal or even illegal. This 'alternative' component and its consequent relations with authority is one of the defining characteristics of these pastimes which helps distinguish them from other non-competitive leisure pursuits. BASE jumping is the most common example and there have been recent attempts to ban tombstoning in the UK and waterfall jumping in New Zealand. So alternative sports have not just become a way of pitching the individual against the environment – they are also used subversively, to pitch the self against the State. For instance, in April 2003 Alain Robert scaled la Tour ELF in Paris wearing a 'No War' sign on his back to encourage Chirac to veto the UN resolution authorising use of force by the US against Iraq. Upon his arrest after climbing Shanghai's tallest building, he is reported to have said 'If you obey all the rules, you miss the fun'.

This cultural turn of physical performativity, in societies that have themselves become obsessed with danger and risk (Beck 1992), is interesting because such games come to mean more, signify more, carry more weight than they did in the early colonial period. Adventure sports are indeed becoming more serious while war and political strife become ever more strategic – more game-like, as it were. And so, because they are dangerous, take players to the limit, hazardous sports harbour a certain connection with peacekeeping and violence. For instance, many are used for law enforcement and military training purposes. In an increasingly pacifist context in the 'western world', where most violent conflict is carried out in liminal cultural areas by professionals, citizens are converted into spectators – war itself has become a bloodless spectator sport. Meanwhile dangerous sports amongst the citizenry have become more serious than the play between life and death. This is one reason that their seriousness is being sought (Stebbins 2007). That what they offer in their anomalous character is becoming a social quest to find something significant, a device to signify the newness of social action that is more game-like than it used to be and yet just as serious.

For adventurers, the risk of accident is somehow encompassed by the meaning that controls the consistent continuity of life, even though the accident itself exists outside such continuity. Adventurers achieve a central feeling of life which runs through the adventure's eccentricity and produces new necessities of life in the very width of the span between the externally given possibility of the accident and a certain unifying existential core from which meaning flows. There is thus a constant pendulum that swings back and forth between chance and necessity, between the consistent meaning of the life formed from within and the fragmentary stigmas ascribed from outside (Vanreusel and Renson 1982).

Despite the potential dangers involved in such lifestyles, I have not argued against risk. Nowhere is it suggested that the stakes are too high to participate in the activities described. It must also be noted, however, that I am not promoting risk for its own sake either. Rather, what I've intimated is that there is an urgent need to better understand how humans manage risk in all its colourful diversity, from promiscuous sexual practice, through to fiscal market exchanges as well as attempts to generate models for predicting environmental and technological catastrophes. Such debates and enquiries must now include the alternative sport practices that have helped so many of us develop the personal skills needed to self-reliantly manage risk as well as to overcome fear. These pursuits have emerged rapidly at the heart of counter-cultural currents to the point where they are far from meaningless or marginal to the values of western societies. Studying alternative sports may therefore give us a purchase on understanding some of what is shaping our world today in terms of those forms of leisure and pleasure which are sought through adventure. Such endeavours might even help us rejuvenate the social sciences a little along the way.

This means that the adventurous experience invites interpretation. It even begs for it. But as soon as attempts to provide these are offered, we simultaneously realise the absurdity of trying to capture the fleetingness of such moments. Adventurous experience acknowledges the un-representability of the kinds of emotional situations encountered. These experiences attempt to address those aspects of humanity that are shadowy, half apprehended, on the edge. In other words, beyond the ability of verbal or written representation to describe. They exist to remind us that the sum-total of our encounters with the world do not amount to a straightforward sequence of events. That, however hard we try, life is not a rational or predictable process, even though coherence is sought and can be achieved in hindsight. Such experiences are thus about the density and interwovenness of existence. These are the moments when feeling exceeds perception, when the world of outside sensation prefaces the world of inner thought, when feeling, emotion and the intuitive are un-problematically at the surface of our ontological construction of reality.

Such experiences are oneiric, they carry an up-lifting charge, loaded with significance that cannot be articulated with any exactitude. In this way, they endeavour to remain as resistant to simplification yet as fundamentally ungraspable as any transcendental episode. Indeed the hazardous use of landscape, when linked to positive encounters with danger, allows extreme acts to be interpreted beyond even the notions concerning performance. As events related to the creation and contention of identity and sociality, activities such as surfing, cave diving and cliff-jumping are clearly about performance (Booth 2003; Cater and Cloke 2007). However, the dynamics governing them are far more complex than this. They are also about an intentional search for freedom through danger. Thus, we need to look instead to more comprehensive rationales.

This is not only for political and phenomenological reasons, but also because of the profound cultural meanings embedded in these activities, which are beginning to surface in the domain of sport sociology. There is a deliberate juxtaposition of a double reflexivity in the approach I have described. It is the study, writing and narrating of epic adventures and extreme practices that push high-risk games beyond politics and performance, to the level where they are imaginatively creative existential actions. These forms of deep and dangerous play are therefore enactments of ontological and existential awareness. No longer are they simply seen to be about performing identity or because they are just fun. Now they take on relevance in relation to overcoming life's absurdities. They give meaning and subvert the abstraction of the body while creating an aesthetic for life and landscape.

It is not unusual for sensation seekers to appropriate marginalised landscapes of fear and danger by personifying them with vernacular names and therefore associating them with their own particular causes. This gives special relevance to a site and the issue. By ascribing their own experiences of fear, foreboding and pleasure to such locales, they are projecting onto them a stylised sense of risk and recreation. We have nevertheless been dealing with a different type of 'landscapes of fear' than that postulated by the historical geographer Yi-Fu Tuan in his volume of the same name. Rather, it is one where his concept of 'topophilia', of a deep empathy with the environment, is especially pertinent (1974; 1979). The notion of fear and trembling that I have considered here is therefore part of a sensuous reflexivity. As this book has begun to demonstrate, the ethnographic game can indeed be taken to several extremes. These not only involve imaginary and genuine risks for informants and researchers alike, but equally, an existential challenge to the notion of physical performance, the character of ethnographic research and even the nature of the imagination.

Perjured Ocean

A tsunami approaches, be afraid.
Take your kitten, drive to the hills.
Suspending the reef and
charged with dismissal.
Trust in fear breed through waves
of radio warnings.
It's civil defence, choppers, photographers.
No prints in the sand
but ours stand out.
Running along a dirty beach,
to fetch the most thrilling coffee.

Onlookers line the parade, before waking up.
Chastising the naysayers, friends of danger.
Take a snap of that disinformation.
Is it naughty?
What did you hear?
It's going to be huge, in irony.
When the sea rages you will know.
Today we grant ourselves safe passage.

19.05.2010   P. LAVIOLETTE

References

A

Abrahams, R.D. (1986), 'Ordinary and Extraordinary Experience', in Turner, V.W. and Bruner, E.M. (eds), *The Anthropology of Experience* (Urbana, IL: University of Illinois Press).

Abramson, A. and Fletcher, R. (2007), 'Recreating the Vertical: Rock-climbing as Epic and Deep Eco-play', *Anthropology Today* 23:6, 3–7.

Abramson, A. and Laviolette, P. (2007), 'Cliff-jumping, World-shifting and Value-production: The Genesis and Cultural Transformation of a Dangerous New Game', *Suomen Antropologi: Journal of the Finnish Anthropological Society* 32:2, 5–28.

Ackerman, D. (1999), *Deep Play* (New York: Vintage Books).

Adams, V. (1996), *Tigers of the Snow and Other Virtual Sherpas: An Ethnography of Himalayan Encounters* (Princeton: Princeton University Press).

Anderson, B. (1991), *Imagined Communities: Reflections on the Origin and Spread of Nationalism,* 2nd edition. (London: Verso).

Anderson, S.C. (2002), 'Introduction: The Pleasure of Taking the Waters', in Anderson, S.C. and Tabb, B.H. (eds), *Water, Leisure and Culture: European Historical Perspectives* (Oxford: Berg).

Appadurai, A. (1996), 'Number in the Colonial Imagination', *Modernity at Large: Cultural Dimensions of Globalization* (Minneapolis: University of Minnesota Press).

B

Bachelard, G. ([1938] 1987), [La Psychanalyse du feu] *The Psychoanalysis of Fire* (Trans. by Frye, N.) (Dallas, TX: The Dallas Institute Publications).
—— ([1942] 1983), [L'Eau et les rêves, essai sur l'imagination de la matière] *Water and Dreams: An Essay on the Imagination of Matter* (Trans. by Farrell, E.R.) (Dallas, TX: Pegasus Foundation).
—— ([1943] 1988), [L'Air et les songes, essai sur l'imagination du movement] *Air and Dreams: An Essay on the Imagination of Movement* (Trans. by Farrell, E.R.) (Dallas, TX: The Dallas Institute Publications).
—— ([1947] 1988), [La Têrre et les rêveries de la volonté, essai sur l'imagination de la matière] *Earth and Reveries of Will: An Essay on the Imagination of Matter* (Trans. by Haltman, K.) (Dallas, TX: The Dallas Institute Publications).
Balint, M. (1959), *Thrills and Regression* (New York: IUP).

Barley, N. (1988), *Not a Hazardous Sport* (London: Penguin Books).

Barnes, T.J. and Duncan, J.S. (eds) (1992), *Writing Worlds: Discourse, Text & Metaphor in the Representation of Landscape* (London: Routledge).

Barth, F. (2000), 'Boundaries and Connections', in Cohen, A. (ed.) *Signifying Identities: Anthropological Perspectives on Boundaries and Contested Values* (London: Routledge).

Barthes, R. (1968), *Elements of Semiology* (New York: Hill and Wang).

Baudelaire, C. (1857), *Les Fleurs du Mal* (Paris: Poulet-Malassis et de Broise).

Bauman, Z. (2000), *Liquid Modernity* (Cambridge: Polity Press).

Beal, B. and Weidman, L. (2003), 'Authenticity in the Skateboarding World', in Rinehart, R.E. and Sydnor, S. (eds) *To the Extreme: Alternative Sports, Inside and Out* (Albany: SUNY Press).

Beatty, A. (2005), 'Aid in Faraway Places: The Context of an Earthquake', *Anthropology Today* 21:4, 5–7.

Beck, U. (1992), *Risk Society: Towards a New Modernity* (London: Sage).

Beder, S. (1989), *Toxic Fish and Sewer Surfing: How Deceit and Collusion are Destroying our Great Beaches* (Sydney: Allen and Unwin).

Beine, M., Docquier, F. and Rapoport, H. (2001), 'Brain Drain and Economic Growth: Theory and Evidence', *Journal of Development Economics* 64:1, 275–289.

Bell, C. and Lyall, J. (2001), *The Accelerated Sublime: Landscape Tourism and Identity* (Westport, CT: Praeger).

Bender, B. (ed.) (1993) *Landscape: Politics and Perspectives* (Oxford: Berg).

Bender, B. and Winer, M. (eds) (2001), *Contested Landscapes: Movement, Exile and Place* (Oxford: Berg).

Benjamin, W. (1980) *The Arcades Project* (New York: Picador).

Bentham, J. (1840), *The Theory of Legislation* (ed. Hildreth, R.) (Boston, MA: Weeks, Jordon & Company).

Blanchard, K. (1995), *The Anthropology of Sport* (Westport, CT: Bergin & Garvey).

Blanchard, K. and Cheska, A. (1984), *The Anthropology of Sport: An Introduction* (New York: Bergin & Garvey).

Bogart, L. (1977), 'The Automobile as Social Cohesion', *Society* 14:5, 10–15.

Boissevain, J. (1974), 'Toward a Sociology of Social Anthropology', *Theory and Society* 1:2, 211–230.

Booth, D. (2001), *Australian Beach Cultures: The History of Sun, Sand, and Surf* (London: Cass Publishers).

—— (2003), 'Expression Sessions: Surfing, Style, and Prestige,' in Rinehart R.E. and Sydnor, S. (eds) *To the Extreme: Alternative Sports, Inside and Out* (Albany: SUNY Press).

Borden, I. (1998), 'A Performative Critique of the City – The Urban Practice of Skateboarding, 1958–1998', *Everything Magazine* 2:4, 38–43.

Borden, I., Kerr, J., Pivaro, A. and Rendell, J. (eds) (1996), *Strangely Familiar: Narratives of Architecture in the City* (London: Routledge).

Bourdieu, P. (1977), *Outline of a Theory of Practice* (Cambridge: University Press).

—— (1984) *Distinction*: *A Social Critique of the Judgement of Taste* (Trans. Nice, R.) (Cambridge: University Press).

—— (1988) *Homo Academicus* (Trans. Collier, P.) (Cambridge: Polity Press).

—— (1990), 'Programme for a Sociology of Sport', in *Other Words: Essays Towards a Reflexive Sociology* (Trans. Adamson, M.) (Cambridge: Polity Press).

Brindle, S. (2006) *Brunel – the Man who Built the World* (London: Phoenix).

Brown, R. (2001), *The Art of Suicide* (London: Reaktion Books).

Brun, B. (2007), 'Surfers Stoked on Bio-boards', *Sustainable Industries Magazine* 4:2, 2–3.

Buckley, R., Cater, C. and Godwin, I. (2007), *Adventure Tourism* (Wallingford: CABI Publishers).

Burawoy, M. (ed.) (1991), *Ethnography Unbound: Power and Resistance in the Modern Metropolis* (Berkeley, CA: University of California Press).

Burnett, J. (2005), 'Material culture', in Collins, T., Martin, J. and Vamplew, W. (eds) *Encyclopedia of Traditional British Rural Sports* (London: Routledge).

Busby, G. and Laviolette, P. (2006), 'Narratives in the Net: Fiction and Cornish Tourism', *Cornish Studies* 14, 142–63.

C

Caillois, R. (ed.) (1963), *The Dream Adventure*: *A Literary Anthology* (New York: Orion Press).

—— (1958), *Les Jeux et les Hommes: Le Masque et le Vertige* (Paris: Gallimard).

Camus, A. [1956] (1957), *The Fall* (Trans. by O'Brien, J.) (London: H. Hamilton).

Canetti, E. (1960), *Crowds and Power* (New York: Continuum).

Caplan, P. (ed.) (2000), *Risk Revisited* (London: Pluto Press).

Carter, P. (2004), *Material Thinking: The Theory and Practice of Creative Research* (Carlton, Vic: Melbourne University Press).

Casey, E.S. (1996), 'How to Get from Space to Place in a Fairly Short Stretch of Time: Phenomenological Prolegomena', in Feld, S. and Basso, K.H. (eds) *Senses of Place* (Santa Fe, NM: School of American Research Press).

Castoriadis, C. (1998), *The Imaginary Institution of Society* (Trans. K. Blamey) (Cambridge, MA: MIT Press).

Cater, C. and Cloke, P. (2007), 'Bodies in Action: The Performativity of Adventure Tourism', *Anthropology Today* 23:6, 13–16.

de Certeau, M. (1984), *The Practice of Everyday Life* (Berkeley, CA: University of California Press).

Chagnon, N. (1968), *Yanomamo: The Fierce People* (New York: Holt, Rinehart, Winston).

Childe, V.W. (1980), 'Childe's suicide', *Antiquity* 54:210, 1–3.

Cohen, L. (1963), *The Favorite Game* (New York: Viking).

Coleman, S. and Kohn, T. (eds) (2007) *The Discipline of Leisure: Embodying Cultures of 'Recreation'* (Oxford: Berghahn Publishers).

Combe, W. and Rowlandson, T. (1815), *The English Dance of Death* (London: R. Ackermann).

Conefrey, M. and Jordan, T. (2001), *Mountain Men* (Cambridge, MA: Da Capro Press).

Conland, N. (ed.) (2010), *The 4ᵗʰ Auckland Triennial – Last Ride in a Hot Air Balloon* (Auckland: Auckland Art Gallery Toi o Tāmaki).

Cosgrove, D. and Daniels, S. (eds) (1988), *The Iconography of Landscape: Essays on the Symbolic Representation, Design and Use of Past Environments* (Cambridge: University Press).

Crang, P. (1997), 'Regional Imaginations: An Afterword', in Westland, E. (ed.) *Cornwall: The Cultural Construction of Place* (Penzance: Patten Press).

Crowe, C. (1848), *The Night Side of Nature: Or, Ghosts and Ghost Seers* (London: T.C. Newby).

Csikszentmihalyi, M. (1975), *Beyond Boredom and Anxiety: The Notion of Flow in Work and Play* (San Francisco: Jossey Press).

Csordas, T. (ed.) (1995), *Embodiment and Experience: the Existential Ground of Culture and Self* (Cambridge: University Press).

D

Damasio, A. (1999), *The Feeling of What Happens* (New York: Harcourt Brace).

D'Amicis, F. (2006), 'David Kirke: Sport, nur wenn er extreme ist' [David Kirke: Sport, only when it is extreme], *GALORE Interviews* 21, 10–16.

Daniels, S. (1993), *Fields of Vision: Landscape Imagery and National Identity in England and the United States* (Princeton, NJ: University Press).

Dant, T. (1998), 'Playing with Things: Objects and Subjects in Windsurfing', *Journal of Material Culture* 3:1, 77–95.

Darling, F.F. (1970), *Wilderness and Plenty (BBC Reith Lectures, 1969)* (London: Ballantine Books).

Davenport, G. (1981), *The Geography of the Imagination* (San Francisco, CA: North Point Press).

Day, A. and Lunn, K. (2003), 'British Maritime Heritage: Carried Along by the Currents?' *International Journal of Heritage Studies* 9:4, 289–305.

Deleuze, G. (1992), 'Mediators', in Crary, J. and Kwinter, S. (eds) *Incorporations* (New York: Urzone).

Desjarlais, R. (1994), 'Struggling Along: The Possibilities for Experience Among the Homeless Mentally Ill', *American Anthropologist* 96:4, 886–901.

Dirlik, A. (2001), 'Placed-based Imagination: Globalism and the Politics of Place', in Prazniak, R. and Dirlik, A. (eds) *Places and Politics in an Age of Globalization* (New York: Rowman and Littlefield).

Douglas, M. (1966), *Purity and Danger: An Analysis of Concepts of Pollution and Taboo* (London: Routledge and Keegan Paul).

—— (1992), *Risk and Blame: Essays in Cultural Theory* (London: Routledge).

Douglas, M. & Wildavsky, A. (1982), *Risk and Culture: An Essay on the Selection of Technological and Environmental Dangers* (Berkeley, CA: University of California Press).

Dugaw, D. (2001), *Deep Play: John Gay and the Invention of Modernity*, (Newark DE: University of Delaware Press).

Duncan, J.S. and Ley, D. (eds) (1993), *Place/Culture/Representation* (London: Routledge).

Durand, G. (1960), *Les Structures Anthropologiques de l'Imaginaire: Introduction à l'Archétypologie Générale* (Paris: Dunod).

E

Eco, U. (2007), *Turning Back the Clock: Hot Wars and Media Populism* (Trans. Alastair McEwen) (San Diego, CA: Harcourt Publishers).

Eichberg, H. (2001), *Body Cultures: Essay on Sport, Space and Identity* (Bale, J. and Philo, C., eds) (London: Routledge).

Elias, N. (1982), *The Civilizing Process: State Formation and Civilization* (Trans. Jephcott, E.) (Oxford: Blackwell).

Elias, N. and Dunning, E. (eds) (1986), *Quest for Excitement: Sport and Leisure in the Civilizing Process* (Oxford: Blackwell).

Evans, L. (2003), *Land of Saints: a Cornish Surf Movie*, (Lorien Surf-Film Productions).

Ezell, M. and O'Keeffe, K.O. (1994), *Cultural Artifacts and the Production of Meaning: The Page, the Image, and the Body* (Ann Arbor, MI: University of Michigan Press).

F

Feld, S. and Basso, K.H. (eds) (1996), *Senses of Place* (Santa Fe, NM: School of American Research Press).

Fernandez, J.W. (ed.) (1991), *Beyond Metaphor: The Theory of Tropes in Anthropology* (Palo Alto, CA: Stanford University Press).

Fernandez, J. and Huber, M.T. (eds) (2001), *Irony in Action: Anthropology, Practice, and the Moral Imagination* (Chicago, IL: University of Chicago Press).

Ferrell, D. (2001), 'Climbing Frozen Waterfalls', in Wimmer, D. (ed.) *The Extreme Game: An Extreme Sports Anthology* (Short Hills, NJ: Burford Books).

Finney, B.R. and Houston, J.D. (1966), *Surfing, the Sport of Hawaiian Kings* (Rutland, VT: C.E. Tuttle Co).

Firstbrook, P. (1999), *The Search for Mallory & Irvine* (Chicago, IL: Contemporary Books).

Firth, R.W. (1922), *The Kauri Gum Industry; Some Economic Aspects,* MA thesis. (Auckland: University College).

—— (1930), 'A Dart Match in Tikopia: A Study in the Sociology of Primitive Sport', *Oceania* 1:1, 64–96.

Fiske, J. (1989), *Reading the Popular* (London: Unwin Hyman).

Flint, K. & Morphy, H. (eds) (2000), *Culture, Landscape and the Environment* (Oxford: University Press).

Ford, N. and Brown, D. (2005), *Surfing and Social Theory: Experience, Embodiment and the Narrative of the Dream Glide* (London: Routledge).

Foucault, M. (1977), *Discipline and Punish: The Birth of the Prison* (Trans. by A. Sheridan) (New York: Vintage Books).

Freud, S. (1919), *Totem and Taboo* (London: Penguin).

Freund, P. and Martin, G. (1993), *The Ecology of the Automobile* (Montreal: Black Rose Books).

Frohlick, S. (2003), 'Negotiating the "Global" within the Global Playscape of Mount Everest', *Canadian Review of Sociology and Anthropology* 40:5, 525–542.

—— (2004), ' "Who is Lhakpa Sherpa?" Circulating Subjectivities within the Global/Local Terrain of Himalayan Mountaineering', *Social & Cultural Geography* 5:2, 195–212.

Furedi, F. (1997), *Culture of Fear: Risk Taking and the Morality of Low Expectation* (London: Continuum).

G

Gasteiger, A. (2008), 'Photo requiem, Hillary', *New Zealand Geographic* 90, 53–57.

Geertz, C. (1973), 'Deep Play: Notes on the Balinese Cockfight', *The Interpretation of Cultures* (New York: Basic Books).

Gell, A. (1992), 'The Technology of Enchantment and the Enchantment of Technology', in Coote, J. and Shelton, A. (eds) *Anthropology, Art, and Aesthetics* (Oxford: Clarendon Press).

—— (1996), *Wrapping in Images: Tattooing in Polynesia* (Oxford: University Press).

—— (1998), *Art and Agency: An Anthropological Theory* (Oxford: Clarendon Press).

Gilchrist, H. and Evans, L. (2003), 'Freedom for Kernow/Land of Saints', *Adrenalin Magazine* 16, 90–95.

Goffman, E. (1967), 'Where the Action Is', *Interaction Ritual: Essays on Face-to-Face Behaviour* (New York: Anchor Books).

Göle, N. (1996), *The Forbidden Modern: Civilization and Veiling* (Michigan, MI: University of Michigan Press).

Gonzalas, L. (2003), *Deep Survival: Who Lives, Who Dies, and Why: True Stories of Miraculous Endurance and Sudden Death* (New York: W.W. Norton & Company).

Gregory, D. (1994), *Geographical Imaginations* (Oxford: Blackwell).

Gyimothy, S. (2008), 'Thrillscapes: Wilderness Mediated as Playground', in Knudsen, B.T. and Waade, A.M. (eds) *Re-Investing Authenticity: Tourism, Place and Emotions* (Bristol: Channel View Publications).

H

Hackett, A.J. (2006), *Jump Start*, (Auckland: Random House New Zealand).

Haddon, A.C. (1912), *The Wanderings of Peoples,* 2nd Edition, reprinted with corrections. (Cambridge: University Press).

Halton, E. (1994), 'Communicating Democracy: Or Shine, Perishing Republic', in Riggens, S.H. (ed.) *The Socialness of Things: Essays in the Socio-Semiotics of Objects* (Berlin: Mouton de Gruyter).

Harris, J.C. and Park, R.J. (eds) (1983), *Play, Games and Sports in Cultural Contexts* (Champaign, IL: Human Kinetics Press).

Hawkins, G. (2003), 'Down the Drain: Shit and the Politics of Disturbance', in Hawkins, G. and Muecke, S. (eds) *Culture and Waste: The Creation and Destruction of Value* (Lanham: MD. Rowman and Littlefield Publishers).

Hawkins, G. and Muecke, S. (eds) (2003), *Culture and Waste: The Creation and Destruction of Value* (Lanham: MD: Rowman and Littlefield Publishers).

Heidegger, M. (1988), *Hegel's Phenomenology of Spirit* (Bloomington: Indiana University Press).

Herzog, W. (2009), *Encounters at the End of the World* (Los Angeles, CA: Creative Differences Productions in association with Discovery Channel).

Hewitt, R. (2007), *Treading Water: Rob Hewitt's Survival Story* (Wellington: Huia Publishers).

Heydon, S. (2005), 'Kiwis in Khumbu: Negotiating Landscape and Community at Khunde Hospital', in Ballantyne, T. and Bennett, J.A. (eds) *Landsacpe/Community: Perspectives from New Zealand History* (Dunedin: Otago University Press).

Highmore, B. (2002), *The Everyday Life Reader* (London: Routledge).

Hillary, E. (1975), *Nothing Venture, Nothing Win* (London: Hodder & Stoughton Ltd).

Hirsch, E. and O'Hanlon, M. (eds) (1995), *The Anthropology of Landscape: Perspectives on Place and Space* (Oxford: University Press).

Holman-Jones, S. (2005), 'Autoethnography: Making the Personal Political', in Denzin, N.K. and Lincoln, Y.S. (eds) *Handbook of Qualitative Research* (Thousand Oaks, CA: Sage).

Howes, D. (2003), *Sensual Relations: Engaging the Senses in Culture and Social Theory* (Ann Arbor, MI: University of Michigan Press).

Howitt, A.W. (1904), *The Native Tribes of South-East Australia* (London: Macmillan).

Hubback, J. (1990), *The Sea Has Many Voices* (Henley-on-Thames: Aiden Ellis).

—— (1997), 'Women, Symbolism and the Coast of Cornwall', in Westland, E. (ed.) *Cornwall: The Cultural Construction of Place* (Penzance: Patten Press).

Hudson, S. (ed.) (2003), *Sport and Adventure Tourism* (New York: Haworth Hospitality Press).

Huizinga, J. ([1938] 1956), *Homo Ludens* (Hamburg: Rowohlt Taschenbuch Verlag).

Hunter, J. and Csikszentmihalyi, M. (2000), 'The Phenomenology of Body-Mind: The Contrasting Cases of Flow in Sports and Contemplation', *Anthropology of Consciousness* 11:3/4, 5–25.

Husserl, E. (1931) *Ideas: General Introduction to Pure Phenomenology* (Trans. by Boyce-Gibson, W.R.) (London: George Allen & Unwin Ltd).

—— ([1913] 1973), *Logical Investigations* (Trans. by Findlay, J.N.) (London: Routledge).

I

Ingold, T. (1993), 'The Temporality of Landscape', *World Archaeology* 25:2, 152–174.

—— (2000), *The Perception of the Environment: Essays on Livelihood, Dwelling and Skill* (London: Routledge).

—— (2004), 'Culture on the Ground. The World Perceived Through the Feet', *Journal of Material Culture* 9:3, 315–340.

Ireland, M.J. (1989), *Tourism in Cornwall: An Anthropological Case Study* (PhD dissertation, University of Swansea).

J

Jackson, I. (2006), *Sand Between My Toes: The Story of Lifesaving in New Zealand* (London: Penguin Books).

Jackson, J.B. (1970), *Landscapes: Selected Writings of J.B. Jackson.* (ed. Zube, E.H.) (Massachusetts, MA: University Press).

—— (1984), *Discovering the Vernacular Landscape* (New Haven, CT: Yale University Press).

Jackson, M.D. (1995), *At Home in the World* (Durham, NC: Duke University Press).

—— (ed.) (1996), *Things as They Are: New Directions in Phenomenological Anthropology* (Bloomington, IN: Indiana University Press).

—— (2005), *Existential Anthropology: Events, Exigencies and Effects* (Oxford: Berghahn Publishers).

Janiskee, R.L. (1995), 'Climbing', in Raitz, K.B. (ed.) *The Theater of Sport* (Baltimore: The John Hopkins University Press).

Johnson, M. (1987), 'Toward a Theory of Imagination', in *The Body in the Mind: The Bodily Basis of Meaning, Imagination, and Reason* (Chicago, IL: Chicago University Press).

Jones, T. and Baker, I. (1975), *A Hard-Won Freedom: Alternative Communities in New Zealand* (Auckland: Hodder & Stoughton).

K

Kafka, F. (1915), *Die Verwandlung / Metamorphosis* (Leipzig: Kurt Wolff Verlag).

Kampion, D. & Brown, B. (2003), *A History of Surf Culture* (Los Angeles, CA: Evergreen).

Karl F.R. and Hamalian, L. (eds) (1973), 'Introduction', in *The Existential Imagination* (London: Picador).

Kierkegaard, S. (1843), *Frygt og Bæven: Dialektisk Lyrik* [*Fear and Trembling*] (Copenhagen: Reitzelske Forlag).

—— ([1849] 1941), *The Sickness Unto Death* (Trans. Lowrie, W.) (Princeton: University Press).

Kildea, G. and Leach, J. (1976), *Trobriand Cricket: An Ingenious Response to Colonialism* (Berkeley, CA: Berkeley Media LLC).

Krakauer, J. (1996), *Into the Wild* (New York: Villard).

Kramer, K. (1988), *The Sacred Art of Dying: How the World Religions Understand Death* (Mahwah, NJ: Paulist Press).

L

Lakoff, G. and Johnson, M. (1980), *Metaphors We Live By* (Chicago: University Press).

—— (1999), *Philosophy in the Flesh: The Embodied Mind and its Challenge to Western Thought* (New York: HarperCollins Publishers).

Laporte, D. (2000), *The History of Shit* (Cambridge, MA: MIT Press).

Latour, B. (1999), *Pandora's Hope: Essays on the Reality of Science Studies* (Cambridge, MA. Harvard University Press).

Laviolette, P. (2003a), 'Landscaping Death: Resting Places for Cornish Identity', *Journal of Material Culture* 8:2, 215–240.

—— (2003b), 'Cornwall's Visual Cultures in Perspective', *Cornish Studies* 11, 142–167.

—— (2006a), 'Where Difference Lies: Performative Metaphors of Truth, Deception and Placelessness in the Cornish Peninsula', in Hill, L. and Paris, H. (eds) *Place and Performance* (London: Palgrave Macmillan).

—— (2006b), 'Ships of Relations: Navigating Through Local Cornish Maritime Art', *International Journal of Heritage Studies* 12:1, 69–92.

—— (2006c), 'Green and Extreme: Free-Flowing Through Seascape and Sewer', *Worldviews: Environment, Culture, Religion* 10:2, 178–204.

—— (ed.) (2007) 'Hazardous sport?' *Anthropology Today* 23:6, 1–16.

—— (2009), 'Fearless Trembling: A Leap of Faith into the Devil's Frying Pan', *The Senses & Society* 4:3, 303–322.

Leach, E. (1984), 'Glimpses of the Unmentionable in the History of British Social Anthropology', *Annual Review of Anthropology* 13, 1–23.

—— (1987), 'Tribal Ethnography: Past, Present, Future', *Cambridge Anthropology* 2:2, 1–14.

Le Breton, D. (1991), *Passion du Risque* (Paris Métailié).

—— (1996), 'L'Extrême-ailleurs: Une Anthropologie de l'Aventure', *Autrement* 106, 15–71.

—— (2000), 'Playing Symbolically with Death in Extreme Sports', *Body and Society* 16:1, 1–11.

—— (2004), 'Imaginaires de Fin du Corps', in Vincent, G. (ed.) *Le Corps, le Sensible et le Sens* (Strasbourg : Presses Universitaires).

Lefebvre, H. (1991), *The Production of Space* (Trans. Nicholson-Smith, D.) (Oxford: Blackwell).

Lengkeek, J. (2001), 'Leisure Experience and Imagination: Rethinking Cohen's Modes of Tourist Experience', *International Sociology* 16:2, 173–184.

Lewis, C.S. (1956) 'Chapter 7', in A. Frazer, (ed.) [1971] *Sir Walter Scott 1771–1832: An Edinburgh Keepsake* (Edinburgh: University Press).

Lewis, N. (2001), 'The Climbing Body, Nature and the Experience of Modernity', in Macnaghten, P. and Urry, J. (eds) *Bodies of Nature* (London: Sage).

Livingstone, D. (2003), *Putting Science in its Place: Geographies of Scientific Knowledge* (Chicago, IL: University Press).

Lovelock, J. (1979), *Gaia: A New Look at Life on Earth* (Oxford: University Press).

Low, S. and Lawrence-Zuniga, D. (eds) (2003), *The Anthropology of Space and Place: Locating Culture* (Oxford: Blackwell).

Lowenthal, D. (1985), *The Past is a Foreign Country* (Cambridge: University Press).

Lyng, S. (1990), 'Edgework: A Socio Psychological Analysis of Voluntary Risk Taking', *American Journal of Sociology* 95:4, 851–886.

Lyster, M. (1997), *The Strange Adventures of the Dangerous Sports Club* (London: The Do-Not Press).

M

McDonald, B. (ed.) (2002), *Extreme Landscapes: The Lure of Mountain Spaces* (Washington, DC: National Geographic Society).

McKay, J. (1983), 'In Memorium: John Kent Pearson (1943–1983)', *Australian and New Zealand Journal of Sociology* 19:3, 383–384.

McLean, S. (2003), 'Buried Landscapes of Childhood', in Strathern, A. and Stewart, P.J. (eds) *Landscape, Memory and Identity* (London: Pluto Press).

McNamee, M.J. (ed.) (2007), *Philosophy, Risk and Adventure Sports* (London: Routledge).

MacAloon, J. and Csikszentmihalyi, M. (1983), 'Deep Play and Flow Experience in Rock Climbing', in Harris, J.C. and Park, R.J. (eds) *Play, Games and Sports in Cultural Contexts* (Champaign, IL: Human Kinetics Press).

MacClancy, J. (ed.) (1996), *Sport, Identity and Ethnicity* (Oxford: Berg).

Macdonald, K. (1985), 'The Commercial Strip: From Main Street to Television Road', *Landscape* 28:2, 12–19.

MacFarlane, R. (2003), *Mountains of the Mind: A History of a Fascination* (London: Granta).

—— (2007), *The Wild Places* (London: Granta).

Macnaghten, P. and Urry, J. (eds) (2001), *Bodies of Nature* (London: Sage).

Mainz, V. and Pollock, G. (eds) (2000), *Work and the Image: Visual Representations in Changing Histories (Vol I: Work, Craft and Labour)* (Aldershot: Ashgate).

Marcus, G.E. (1995), 'Ethnography in/of the World System: The Emergence of Multi-Sited Ethnography', *Annual Review of Anthropology* 24, 95–117.

Marshall, H. (1954), *Men Against Everest* (London: Country Life Ltd).

Martin, R.B. (1980), *Tennyson, the Unquiet Heart: A Biography* (Oxford: Clarendon Press).

Matless, D. (1998), *Landscape and Englishness* (London: Reaktion).

Mauss, M. (1934), 'Les Techniques du Corps', *Journal de Psychologie* 32:3–4, 5–23.

Mauss, M. (1992), 'Techniques of the Body', in Crary, J. and Kwinter, S. (eds) *Incorporations* (New York: Zone Books).

Mazzarella, W. (2004), 'Culture, Globalization, Mediation', *Annual Review of Anthropology* 33, 345–67.

Meinig, D.W. (ed.) (1979), *The Interpretation of Ordinary Landscapes* (Oxford: University Press).

Merleau-Ponty, M. (1962), *Phenomenology of Perception* (London: Routledge).

Mill, J.S. (1950), *Mill on Bentham and Coleridge* (London: Chatto & Windus).

Miller, A. (1973), 'On the Road: Hitchhiking on the Highway', *Society* 10:5, 14–21.

Miller, D. (ed.) (2001), *Car Cultures* (Oxford: Berg).

Möller, R.M. (2007), 'Embodiment – Wetsuit 007', *Regina Magazine* 8, 6–11.

Morgan, V. (1981), *The History of the Dangerous Sports Club* (UK: Tralee Productions).

Morphy, H. (1998), *Aboriginal Art* (London: Phaidon Press).

N

Needham, R. (1976), 'Skulls and Causality', *Man* NS 11:1, 71–88.

Norbeck, E. (1974), *The Anthropological Study of Human Play* (Houston, TX: Rice University Press).

O

Okely, J. (1986), *Simone de Beauvoir – a Re-Reading* (London: Virago Press).

—— (1996), *Own or Other Culture* (London: Routledge).

Okely, J. and Callaway, H. (eds) (1992), *Anthropology and Autobiography* (London: Routledge).

Orr, J. (2006), *Panic Diaries: A Genealogy of Panic Disorder* (Durham: Duke University Press).

Ortner, S.B. (1999), *Life and Death on Mt. Everest: Sherpas and Himalayan Mountaineering* (Princeton, NJ: University Press).

P

Palmer, C. (2004), 'Death, Danger and the Selling of Risk in Adventure Sports', in Wheaton, B. (ed.) *Understanding Lifestyle Sport: Consumption, Identity and Difference* (London: Routledge).

Panaho, A. (2008), 'Carving up the Surf', *B-Complete* 1, 60–63.

Pearson, J.K. (1979), *Surfing Subcultures of Australia and New Zealand* (St.Lucia: University of Queensland Press).

Peralta, S. (2004), *Riding Giants* (California: Sony Pictures Classics).

Petit, P. (2003), *To Reach the Clouds: My High-Wire Walk Between the Twin Towers* (London: Faber and Faber).

Polanyi, M. (1966), *The Tacit Dimension* (New York: Doubleday & Co).

Porteous, J.D. (1990), *Landscape of the Mind: Worlds of Sense and Metaphor* (Toronto: University Press).

Pritchard, P. (1997), *Deep Play: A Climber's Odyssey from Llanberis to the Big Wall* (London: Bâton Wicks).

Q

Quinney, R. (1986), 'A Traveller on Country Roads', *Landscape* 29:1, 21–28.

R

Radin, P. (1963), *The Autobiography of a Winnebago Indian: Life, Ways, Acculturation, and the Peyote Cult* (New York: Dover Publications).

Rapport, N. (2003), *I am Dynamite: An Alternative Anthropology of Power* (London: Routledge).

Rapport, N. and Dawson, A. (eds) (1998), *Migrants of Identity: Perceptions of Home in a World of Movements* (Oxford: Berg).

Reed-Danahay, D. (1997), *Autoethnography: Rewriting the Self and the Social* (Oxford: Berg).

Richardson, M. (ed.) (1984), *Place: Experience and Symbol, Geoscience and Man, vol 24* (Baton Rouge, LA: Louisiana State University).

Ricœur, P. (1994), 'Imagination in Discourse and in Action', in Robinson, G. and Rundell J. (eds) *Rethinking Imagination: Culture and Creativity* (London: Routledge).

Ricœur, P. and Valdes, M.J. (eds) (1991), *A Ricœur Reader: Reflection and Imagination* (Toronto: University of Toronto Press).

Rinehart, R.E. and Sydnor, S. (eds) (2003), *To the Extreme: Alternative Sports, Inside and Out* (Albany, NY: SUNY Press).

Robinson, G. and Rundell J. (eds) (1994), *Rethinking Imagination: Culture and Creativity* (London: Routledge).

Rojek, C. (1995), *Decentring Leisure. Rethinking Leisure Theory* (London: Sage).

Rosen, M.J. and Kassoy, B. (2009), *No Dribbling the Squid: Octopush, Shin Kicking, Elephant Polo, and Other Oddball Sports* (Kansas City, MI: Andrews McMeel Publishing).

Rousseau, G.S. (1991), 'Towards a Social Anthropology of the Imagination', in *Enlightenment Crossings: Pre and Post-Modern Discourses, Anthropological* (Manchester: University Press).

Ruskin, J. (1885), *On the Old Road (vol. ii)* (Kent: George Allen).

Ryden, K.C. (1993), *Mapping the Invisible Landscape: Folklore, Writing, and the Sense of Place* (Iowa: University Press).

S

Saler, M. (2004), 'Modernity, Disenchantment and the Ironic Imagination', *Philosophy and Literature* 28:1, 137–149.

Salter, C.L. (1979), 'Thoughts on the Road', *Landscape* 23:3, 11–14.

Sands, R.R. (1999), *Anthropology, Sport and Culture* (New York: Bergin & Garvey).

—— (2002), *Sport Ethnography* (Champaign, IL: Human Kinetics Press).

Sartre, J.P. (1940), *L'Imaginaire* (Paris: Editions Gallimard).

—— (1956), *Being and Nothingness: A Phenomenological Essay on Ontology* (Trans. Barnes, H.E.) (Paris: Gallimard).

Sauer, C.O. (1925), 'The Morphology of Landscape', *University of California Publications in Geography* 2:2, 19–53.

Scott, J.W. (1991), 'The Evidence of Experience', *Critical Inquiry* 17:4, 773–797.

Scott, W. ([1831] 1903), *Tales of my Landlord Fourth Series* (Edinburgh: Cadell). (*Waverley Novels: Castle Dangerous.* The Edinburgh Waverley Volume XLVIII).

Schutz, A. (1970), *Alfred Schutz on Phenomenology and Social Relations* (ed. Wagner, H.R.) (Chicago IL: University Press).

Sennett, R. (1994), *Flesh and Stone: The Body and the City in Western Civilization* (London: Faber and Faber).

Serre, M. (1997), *The Troubadour of Knowledge* (Trans. Faria Glaser, S. and Paulson, W.) (Ann Arbor, MI: University of Michigan Press).

Shanks, M. and Tilley, C. (1987), *Re-Constructing Archaeology* (Cambridge: University Press).

Shaw, P. (2003), *Extreme Ironing* (London: New Holland Publishers Ltd).

Simmel, G. ([1911] 1997), 'The Adventure', in (eds Frisby, D. and Featherstone, M.) *Simmel on Culture* (London: Sage).

Singer, H. (2006), *9/11: The Falling Man* (London: Channel 4 Television Corporation).

Slater, J. (1997), *Last Philosophical Testament, 1943–68 Volume 11* (London: Routledge).

Soja, E. (1996), *Thirdspace: Journeys to Los Angeles and other Real-and-Imagined Places* (Oxford: Blackwell).

Stebbins, R.A. (2001), *New Directions in the Theory and Research of Serious Leisure* (Lewiston, NY: The Edwin Mellen Press).

—— (2007), *Serious Leisure: A Perspective for Our Time* (New Brunswick, NJ: Aldine/Transaction).

Stark, P. (2001), *Last Breath: Cautionary Tales from the Limits of Human Endurance* (London: The Ballantine Publishing Group).

Steel, E. (2006), *The Bridge* (New York: Koch-Lorber Films).

Stewart, C.W. (2003), 'Dreams of Treasure: Temporality, Historicization and the Unconscious', *Anthropological Theory* 3:4, 481–500.

Stoller, P. (1989), *The Taste of Ethnographic Things: The Senses in Anthropology* (Philadelphia: University of Pennsylvania Press).

Stranger, M. (1999), 'The Aesthetics of Risk: A Study of Surfing', *International Review for the Sociology of Sport* 34:3, 265–276.

Sydnor, S. (2003), 'Soaring', in Rinehart, R.E. and Sydnor, S. (eds) (2003), *To the Extreme: Alternative Sports, Inside and Out* (Albany, NY: SUNY Press).

T

Taussig, M. (1997), *The Magic of the State* (London: Routledge).

Taylor, C. (2002), 'Modern Social Imaginaries', *Public Culture* 14:1, 91–124.

Taylor, J. (1994), *A Dream of England: Landscape, Photography, and the Tourist's Imagination* (Manchester: University Press).

Tedlock, B. (ed.) (1987), *Dreaming: Anthropological and Psychological Interpretations* (Cambridge: University Press).

Teilhard, de Chardin, P. (1955), *Le Phénomène Humain* (Paris: Edition du Seuil).

Thomas, M. (2003), 'Vere Gordon Childe and the Abyss of Time', in *The Artificial Horizon: Imagining the Blue Mountains* (Carlton: Melbourne University Press).

Thompson, I.H. (ed.) (2008) *Rethinking Landscape: A Critical Reader* (London: Routledge).

Thoreau, H.D. ([1849] 1993), *Civil Disobedience and Other Essays* (New York: Dover Thrift Editions).

Thornton, P. (1993), 'Cornwall and Changes in the "Tourist Gaze"', *Cornish Studies* 1, 80–96.

Tilley, C. (1994), *A Phenomenology of Landscape: Places, Paths, Monuments* (Oxford: Berg).

—— (2006), 'Objectification', in Tilley et al. (eds) *Handbook of Material Culture* (London: Sage).

Tomlinson, A. (2001), 'Sport, Leisure and Style', in Morley, D. and Robins, K. (eds) *British Cultural Studies: Geography, Nationality and Identity* (Oxford: University Press) (pp. 399–416).

Tomlinson, J. (2007), *The Culture of Speed: The Coming of Immediacy* (London: Sage).

Topp, A. (2009), *Creating Waves: How Surfing Inspires Our Most Creative New Zealanders* (Auckland: Harper Collins).

Tuan, Y-F. (1968), *The Hydrological Cycle and the Wisdom of God* (Toronto: University of Toronto, Dept. of Geography Research Publications).

—— (1974), *Topophilia: A Study of Environmental Perceptions, Attitudes, and Values* (Englewood Cliffs, NJ: Prentice Hall).

—— (1979), *Landscapes of Fear* (New York: Pantheon Books).

Turner, V.W. (1969), *The Ritual Process: Structure and Anti-Structure* (Chicago, IL: Aldine Publishing Company).

—— (1974), *Dramas, Fields and Metaphors*: *Symbolic Action in Human Society* (Ithaca, NY: Cornell University Press).

—— (1983), 'Liminal and Liminoid, in Play, Flow, and Ritual: An Essay in Comparative Symbology', in Harris, J.C. and Park, R.J. (eds) *Play, Games and Sports in Cultural Contexts* (Champaign, IL: Human Kinetics Press).

Turner, V.W. and Bruner, E. (eds) (1986), *The Anthropology of Experience* (Urbana, IL: University of Illinois Press).

Tylor, E.B. (1879), 'Geographical Distribution of Games', *Fortnightly Review* 25, 23–30.

U

Uschmann, O. (2006), 'Wahrer Sportsgeist trägt Frack und Zylinder' [True sportsmanship wears morning dress and top hat], *GALORE interviews* 21, 16.

Ussher, A. (1955), *Journey through Dread: A Study of Kierkegaard, Heidegger and Sartre* (London: Darwen Finlayson Ltd).

V

Vanreusel, B. and Renson, R. (1982), 'The Social Stigma of High-Risk Sport Subcultures', in Dunleavy, A.O., Miracle, A.W., and Rees, C.R. (eds) *Studies in the Sociology of Sport* (Fort Worth, TX: Texas Christian University Press).

Veblen, T. (1899), *The Theory of the Leisure Class* (New York: Macmillan).

Vico, G. ([1708] 1988), *On the Most Ancient Wisdom of the Italians: Unearthed from the Origins of the Latin Language: Including the Disputation with the Giornale De' Letterati D'Italia* (Ithaca, NY: Cornell University Press).

Vivanco, L.A. and Gordon, R.J. (eds) (2006), *Tarzan was an Eco-Tourist... and Other Tales in the Anthropology of Adventure* (Oxford: Berghahn).

W

Wagner, R. (1975), *The Invention of Culture* (Englewood Cliffs, NJ: Prentice Hall).

Weber, M. (1949), *The Methodology of the Social Sciences* (Trans. and ed. Shils, E.A. and Finch, H.A.) (Illinois: The Free Press of Glencoe).

Wheaton, B. (2004), 'Introduction', in Wheaton, B. (ed.) *Understanding Lifestyle Sport: Consumption, Identity and Difference* (London: Routledge).

—— (ed.) (2004), *Understanding Lifestyle Sports: Consumption, Identity, and Difference* (London: Routledge).

Williams, T., Dunlap, E., Johnson, B.D. and Hamid, A. (1992), 'Personal Safety in Dangerous Places', *Journal of Contemporary Ethnography* 21:3, 343–374.

Woolf, V. (1931), *The Waves* (New York: Harvest).

Y

Yarwood, V. (2008), 'Nothing Above Us But the Sky', *New Zealand Geographic* 90, 34–47.

—— (2008), 'Shadow of a Giant', *New Zealand Geographic* 90, 48–52.

Young, M.W. (2004), *Malinowski: Odyssey of an Anthropologist, 1884–1920* (New Haven, CT: Yale University Press).

Young, N. (ed.) (2000), *Surf Rage: A Surfers Guide to Turning Negatives into Positives* (Angourie: Nymboida Press).

Z

Zaloom, C. (2004), 'The Productive Life of Risk', *Cultural Anthropology* 19:3, 365–392.

Zuckerman M. (1994), *Behavioral Expression and Biosocial Basis of Sensation Seeking* (Cambridge: University Press).

Index

Photographs are indicated by page numbers in bold.